Physical

and

Technical Security

An Introduction

Physical and
Technical Security:
An Introduction

Robert Gruber

THOMSON

DELMAR LEARNING ™

Australia • Canada • Mexico • Singapore • Spain • United Kingdom • United States

Physical and Technical Security: An Introduction
Robert Gruber

Vice President, Technology and Trades SBU:
Alar Elken

Editorial Director:
Sandy Clark

Senior Acquisitions Editor:
Stephen Helba

Senior Development Editor:
Michelle Ruelos Cannistraci

Marketing Director:
Dave Garza

Senior Channel Manager:
Dennis Williams

Production Director:
Mary Ellen Black

Senior Production Manager:
Larry Main

Production Editor:
Benj Gleeksman

Art/Design Coordinator:
Francis Hogan

Senior Editorial Assistant:
Dawn Daugherty

Production Services:
TIPS Technical Publishing, Inc.

Library of Congress Cataloging-in-Publication Data

ISBN: 1-4018-5066-9

NOTICE TO THE READER

DEDICATION

This book is dedicated to the United States Marine Corps. They took this lad at the age of eighteen and provided direction. They taught me that anything can be accomplished if you put heart and soul into it. I've believed in that for the last 40-some years, and it has served me well.

CONTENTS

Foreword xiii

Preface xv

CHAPTER 1 **Planning and Defining Physical Security............ 1**

Purpose and Objectives... 1
Planning Physical Security...................................... 2
Levels of Security.. 3
Security Layers.. 10
Planning for Terrorism Threats................................. 11
Reducing the Organization's Exposure to
    Criminal and Terrorist Activities 13
The Concentric Rings Theory 17
The Weak Link Theory... 18
Economy of Force 20
Summary 24
Key Terms.. 25
Discussion Questions 26
Research Questions 27

CHAPTER 2 **Security Electronics.. 29**

Purpose and Objectives... 29
Basic Electronics.. 30
Direct Current 31
Alternating Current.. 36
Summary 53
Key Terms.. 55
Discussion Questions 56
Research Questions 58

CHAPTER 3   **Communications Systems 59**

Purpose and Objectives 59
Speech 60
Wire Line Communications 60
Radio Frequency (RF) 62
Characteristics of Different Frequency Bands........ 63
Data Communications... 68
Spread Spectrum.. 73
Bandwidth 75
Binary 75
Error Checking 78
The OSI Platform.. 79
Summary 80
Key Terms.. 81
Discussion Questions 82
Research Questions 83

CHAPTER 4   **Test Equipment.. 85**

Purpose and Objectives 85
Multimeters 85
Specifications 89
Oscilloscopes 90
Spectrum Analyzer 94
The Time Domain Reflectometer (TDR) 97
Cable Analyzer 102
Non Linear Junction Detector (NLJD) 102
The CPM-700 109
Summary 117
Key Terms.. 119
Discussion Questions 120
Research Questions 121

CHAPTER 5   **Transmission Line Theory 123**

Purpose and Objectives 123
BICSI 124
Networking.. 124
Wire 124
Cable Categories.. 128
Cable Topologies.. 130

Basic Networks 130
Supervision 130
Fiber Optics 131
Wireless 135
Summary 140
Key Terms 141
Questions 142
Research Questions 143

CHAPTER 6   **Video and Optics**............................... **145**

Purpose and Objectives.......................... 145
The Still Camera..................................... 146
Video Tube Technology 154
Charge Coupled Devices (CCDs) 156
Camera Size 157
Video Processing and Storage 159
Summary 168
Key Terms 170
Discussion Questions 170
Research Questions 171

CHAPTER 7   **Alarm Systems**................................. **173**

Purpose and Objectives.......................... 173
A Brief History 174
The Basic Alarm System 175
The Control Unit 175
False Alarms.. 194
Installer Training and Licensing 199
Summary 202
Key Terms 203
Discussion Questions 203
Research Questions 204

CHAPTER 8   **Computers and Security Software** **205**

Purpose and Objectives.......................... 205
Computers for Control 206
Guard Tour Systems 212
ObjectVideo.. 215
Design Software...................................... 217

Summary 224
Key Terms 225
Discussion Questions 226
Research Questions 226

CHAPTER 9 **Low Tech Tools, Small Tools,
and Methods of Use** 227
Purpose and Objectives 227
The Basic Toolkit 228
Running Cable 242
Wireless 243
Summary 244
Key Terms 245
Discussion Questions 245
Research Questions 246

CHAPTER 10 **Locks, Keys, and Access Control** 247
Purpose and Objectives 247
Background 248
Locks and Keys 249
Key Control 251
Automated Key Control 252
Electronic Access Control 253
Component Parts of an Effective
Access Control System 255
Access Control Systems 256
Equipment-Based Systems 258
Secondary Credentials 262
Electric Door Locks 265
Central Control Unit 266
Accessories 269
Multiple Area Authorization 270
Fail-Safe/Fail-Soft 271
Occupant Listing 271
Anti-Passback 272
General Automated Access Control Applications .. 272
Summary 274
Key Terms 275
Discussion Questions 276
Research Questions 276

CHAPTER 11   **Technical Surveillance Countermeasures..... 277**

Purpose and Objectives 277
Who Needs TSCM 278
Methods of Espionage 278
Eavesdropping Methods 279
The Physical Search 283
Inside Walls 285
The Radio Frequency (RF) Phase 286
Telephone Lines 291
The Commercial Environment 299
Finding a Bug or Tap 301
Summary 301
Key Terms 303
Discussion Questions 304
Research Questions 304

CHAPTER 12   **Putting It Together with Risk Analyses
                 and Physical Security Surveys 305**

Purpose and Objectives 305
A GSA View of Security in the Workplace 306
Risk Management 307
The Physical Security Survey 314
Planning and Administration 317
Types of Surveys 320
Summary 321
Key Terms 322
Discussion Questions 322
Research Questions 323

Appendix A   **Common Lock and Key Control Terms 325**

Appendix B   **Answers to Odd Numbered Questions 333**

Appendix C   **Companies and Addresses 353**

                 Index 403

FOREWORD

Finally! A text book that encompasses all the areas of security. Security awareness has become one of the hot topics in the popular consciousness of people in the United States of America and around the world in general. *Physical and Technical Security: An Introduction* is well-written and easy-to-read. Bookstores are filled with "how-to" books on security, and colleges, universities, and corporations have discovered that teaching and learning physical and technical security must be made available to students and employees alike.

As Program Head of the Administration of Justice Program at Northern Virginia Community College (NVCC) Manassas Campus, I have taught courses in all areas of security and believe this text can be used for all areas of security. Indeed, in the face of increasing thoughts of terrorist attacks since the incidents of 9/11, there is a widespread perception of a lack of security in our present day society.

Physical and Technical Security: An Introduction has been designed in a manner that will lend itself to a variety of settings that includes independent study, classrooms, and on-going security training. *Physical and Technical Security: An Introduction* conveys the written information effectively and displays several areas of hands-on material for the new and professional security personnel. The author's writing style is concise and he goes to great lengths to explain complex terms in order to make sure the level of material is appropriate for students. The author's quantity and quality of pedagogical elements, such as the end-of-chapter questions, will prove very useful for instructors and students.

As one reads and studies *Physical and Technical Security: An Introduction,* one should be aware that security is one of the fastest growing industries in the United States if not around the world. Disaster does not occur in isolation. As the author explains, "every organization is exposed to a different level and type of risk depending on its products, services, symbolism, and stakeholders" and "because terrorists choose the mode, time, and place for their attacks, industry and government are forced to address a variety of general security weaknesses and protect around worst-case scenarios in order to maintain a safe work environment."

I have had the opportunity to peruse many texts on security in my capacity as an educator and security professional; however, *Physical and Technical Security: An Introduction* is a text of the future, which would and should be continued in future editions.

Russ Carter
Program Head, Adm. of Justice
Northern Virginia Comm. College

PREFACE

INTRODUCTION

Physical and Technical Security: An Introduction offers an introduction to security from a physical and technical perspective and provides an overview of the various technologies that support the security function in a modern organization. The text provides comprehensive coverage of principal topics such as security electronics, communications systems, test equipment, video and optics, alarm systems, sensors, closed circuit TV, computers and security software, access control, technical security countermeasures and more. Readers will obtain an industry-based perspective and a practitioner's point of view on all phases of physical security, including what works and what does not, through a careful mix of theory and practical application.

Physical and Technical Security: An Introduction is designed to serve the needs of anyone interested in corporate security and safety careers. This book can be used in any introductory security or survey-oriented course. Programs that offer security-related courses include Electronics and Computer Technology, Security Technology, Security Systems and Management, Criminal Justice, and Homeland Security Programs. The topics contained in this text can be used in courses such as physical security, security management, and security systems.

The field of security will continue to grow as a result of the dangers of our modern world. The technology in keeping up with modern threats is becoming more sophisticated and requires knowledgeable, educated practitioners who have a good background in many subject areas.

ORGANIZATION

My hope in writing *Physical and Technical Security: An Introduction* is to give students the desire to study the fascinating field of physical security. Security is a developing area in the electronics field, and the physical security profession is growing by leaps and bounds. Many technicians hired by security contractors and the U.S. government are electronics technicians.

As former Dean of Technology Programs at DeVry University's Arlington, Virginia campus in 2003, I participated in focus groups to discuss educational needs for security engineering technology. This textbook was created as a result of those focus groups and listening to the ideas and recommendations from educators and security personnel from organizations such as the Central Intelligence Agency, Department of Energy, U.S. State Department, and Quanta Systems Corporation, among others. The CIA and U.S. State Department have excellent Security Engineering Officer Programs, and hearing from potential employers of students who would study physical security helped to shape the direction of this textbook.

In addition to gathering industry feedback to develop the text, all of the material has been reviewed by educators at both two- and four-year schools. It is not necessary to follow the chapters in strict order, but the order in which they appear is based on what was formulated from industry and educational feedback.

- Chapter 1 introduces the different levels of security and describes how to plan and design an effective security solution.
- Chapter 2 reviews basic electrical theory.
- Chapter 3 describes the basics of a communication system, such as the different types of communication methods.
- Chapter 4 introduces some of the more important test equipment used in security work.
- Chapter 5 covers the different types of transmission methods, including wire and wireless methods.
- Chapter 6 reviews video and optics, covering topics such as cameras, lenses, and video recorders.
- Chapter 7 presents alarm systems.
- Chapter 8 discusses the operation and uses of computers and security software.

■ Chapter 9 introduces some low-tech equipment. Too often, course developers and writers tend to assume that the students know all about the use of this equipment. If desired, the chapter may be skipped, but it is included for those who would like a review.

■ Chapter 10 explores locks, keys, and access-control devices.

■ Chapter 11 covers technical security countermeasures. It touches on the issue of maintaining information security by countering eavesdropping.

■ Chapter 12 provides a summary of risk analysis and describes how to perform physical security surveys.

FEATURES

Each chapter begins with a clear explanation of the objectives and what will be the learning outcomes. Important terms are placed in italics within the body of the chapter. End-of-chapter questions provide the readers with an assessment of the success of the chapter in achieving the learning outcomes.

Each chapter concludes with a Summary, a list of Key Terms, and Review Questions. The Summary is in a bulleted format to highlight main points for quick review and reinforcement. Two sets of questions provide a way for students to assess their understanding of the material. A set of Discussion Questions represent the important take-away points, and the Research Questions require students to go beyond the classroom to develop their analytical thinking skills.

Other special features include the following:

■ The text places an emphasis on the basics and a general understanding of security systems. For instance, general characteristics, features, functions, and limitations of hardware systems are discussed. Technology may produce more sophisticated equipment, but the operational aspects remain the same. For example, locks can use keys, keypads, or biometrics, but it still boils down to fastening something and making it secure.

■ Theory is mixed with practical application based on the author's experience as technician, engineer, and academic in the security industry, where he has learned what works and what does not work.

■ Student-friendly, conversational writing style allows readers to comprehend technical concepts through clear explanations.

- Chapter 11 explores Technical Surveillance Countermeasures (TSCM). With the abundance of corporate and government espionage, TSCM is a field for which security personnel should have a basic understanding.

- Numerous photos illustrate key components of security systems.

- There are a total of 180 Discussion Questions and 35 Research Questions.

- Numerous appendices provide useful reference material, such as list of resources, organizations, websites, and manufacturers.

- Appendix A includes a list of Common Lock and Key Control Terms.

- Appendix B includes Answers to Odd-Numbered Questions.

- Appendix C includes over fifty pages of companies and addresses that provide security services and equipment. This comprehensive list provides a good starting point to research equipment options for anyone who wants to acquire security equipment.

SUPPLEMENTS

e.resource

A CD is available to instructors and includes an Instructor's Manual, PowerPoint Presentation Slides, an ExamView Testbank, and an Image Library (ISBN: 1-4018-5067-7).

ABOUT THE AUTHOR

Robert (Bob) Gruber holds a Master of Science degree in Information and Telecommunications Systems Management. He is a former United States Marine and has been a Naval Intelligence Specialist and a CIA officer. Bob founded and was president of Robert Douglas Associates LLC, a security consulting firm that specialized in security and access control systems, and counterespionage including technical surveillance countermeasures. Bob was former Dean of Technology programs at DeVry University's Arlington, Virginia campus in 2003. He now continues to teach security and telecommunications at Northern Virginia College. He currently works as a sales engineer with the Security Solutions Group of Master Halco, one of the world's largest perimeter security and fence manufacturers. Bob is a board-certified Physical Security Professional (PSP) and serves on the academic and physical security councils of ASIS International.

ACKNOWLEDGMENTS

Many people contributed to the information in this text, both knowingly and otherwise. My friend Rick Colliver from the Center of Terrorism Preparedness at the University of Findlay contributed much of the content in Chapter 1—thank you Rick! Many unknown government writers provided information from public domain sources; I wish I could thank them individually. My teachers, colleagues, and managers throughout my working lifetime have instilled in me knowledge of physical security.

I owe a very sincere thank you to the following reviewers who gave me their helpful comments and insight.

- Bob Aron, DeVry University, Chicago, IL

- Dan Callahan, University of Denver, Department of Organizational Security and Information Systems Security, Denver, CO

- Rick Colliver, University of Findlay, Center of Terrorism Preparedness, Findlay, OH

- John Kostanoski, State University of New York—Farmingdale, Department of Security Systems, Farmingdale, NY

- John MaGill, DeVry University, Keller Graduate School of Management, McLean, VA

- Barry McManus, Northern Virginia Community College, Administration of Justice Department, Manassas, VA

The good folks at Thomson Delmar Learning promised they would help during each step of the journey. Indeed, they did help, and a huge debt of gratitude goes to my editor, Michelle Ruelos Cannistraci, who kept me on schedule and guided me through the intricacies of authoring, In addition, Dawn Daugherty and Chris Chien were other valuable contacts that provided reviews and suggestions. The rest of the team, including Steve Helba, Francis Hogan, Larry Main, Benjamin Gleeksman, and others, deserve immeasurable gratitude. Robert Kern and Melissa Parker of TIPS Technical Publishing put in countless hours on my drafts and taught me a great deal in the process. Their help and advice was absolutely invaluable.

My gratitude would be incomplete if I didn't thank my two women —my wife Joni and daughter Gina—who had the patience to put up with a guy who spent a year's worth of weekends hunched over a keyboard and neglecting many of the household chores, which they took over for me.

CHAPTER 1

Planning and Defining Physical Security

PURPOSE AND OBJECTIVES

Physical Security has to be planned logically, to protect assets. There is no standard formula for the types of equipment that a company may need in order to achieve overall security. Each situation is unique. A definite road map must be designed to create an effective security solution.

After reading this chapter, you should be aware that:

- Physical security is designed and planned—much like the design and construction of a building. There are usually surveys and then plans are drawn and printed

- The security plan is accomplished at different levels and in *layers* or *concentric rings*

- Plans are developed for certain disasters to protect people, assets, and information

- Overall security can be dependent on the weakest link

PLANNING PHYSICAL SECURITY

Why is it necessary to have a physical security plan? There are many threats to any physical entity, whether it is a corporation, a person, a home, or property. The form of that threat could be a natural disaster such as an earthquake or flood, or any other tragedy that we see daily on TV, or it could be in the form of people wanting what you have, whether it is property or information.

Planning physical security can be simple and straightforward, such as the installation of a burglar alarm system at home. There are several variations possible in a home system, such as inclusion of fire and smoke detectors, or water-level sensors (perhaps in the basement). There is also the choice of whether to make use of service companies that monitor alarm systems via phone lines. If there is an alarm from a break-in, fire, or other monitored function, the service company will receive a dialed-in signal, which will advise them of the type of alarm, and usually instructions as to how they should follow-up. Determining everything needed for a small system is a job that one person can do in a short period of time.

Figure 1–1 Ademco security system components ©Honeywell International, Inc.

At the other end of the spectrum is designing a system for a very large company. As Figure 1–1 shows, there are many options for monitoring, arming, and reporting when it comes to alarm systems. In the case of a large company, the total package produced from a security survey could take reams of paper and hundreds of blueprints and equipment lists.

ASSESSING THE CURRENT SITUATION

There are companies that specialize in performing *security surveys*, and producing a complete package of recommendations. These companies do not sell or install any equipment and they don't recommend any particular brand names. They review existing systems and setup, aid in establishing a budget and assess the threat level. Some of the functions they perform are: providing feasibility studies, designing security consoles, designing the setup of central stations, designing closed-circuit television systems, establishing computer management of the system, designing physical intrusion detection and access control, establishing fire detection and suppression, ensuring code compliance, providing inspection and acceptance, and of course, providing cost estimates. This can take a great deal of time and involve many people, including engineers, fire professionals, architects, accountants, and security professionals.

These security surveys are usually done in phases. After a walk-around and review, establishing guidelines, and operational characteristics, the design phase begins. After design, construction and inspection phases follow. For a large company, like IBM for example, these phases are carried out at multiple locations. This gives you an idea of the amount of time and effort that goes into a physical security survey.

LEVELS OF SECURITY

Before diagnosing which *level of security* is necessary for a particular facility, it is important to consider several things. What type of facility is it? Are we planning for a residence, a business, a government agency, the National Archives? What are the hours of operation and number of personnel involved? Is the facility public or private? Where is the facility located—is it in a good or bad neighborhood? What types of problems may be anticipated? Do we want to protect the facility from threats from the outside, or would the threat come from inside the premises? Would security guards be present? Are there any areas within the premises that need special attention, for instance, an area where cash or valuable goods are kept, or a parking area that should be monitored at night? Keep in mind that every business is unique. A small hobby shop in one shopping mall may have nothing inside except model airplanes and trains, and another just down the street, that looks identical from the outside, may house a million-dollar stamp collection. All of these questions need to be answered to determine the necessary level of security. A new security survey should be performed for each new project, and a list of questions should be answered in each case.

MINIMUM LEVEL SECURITY

The minimum level of security is designed to *impede*. In a small museum, such as a small southern town's Civil War Museum (see Figure 1–2), a minimum level of security is all that is necessary. We have all seen how displays in a museum are set back from the viewing area, usually with a type of "fence" or other barrier, designed to keep the patrons from touching the display. Aisles and walking areas are clearly delineated to keep people on a certain path. Locks and keys are used throughout the building to keep the public out of sensitive areas. The museum is small enough so that employees can "keep an eye" on visitors as they walk through the building.

In a small museum like this, there would typically be a burglar and fire alarm system installed. The system should be such that employees have keys to operate the system, or better yet, the system could be operated by key codes at a push-button panel. A keypad allows special programming for each authorized employee. Days and times of operation can be programmed for each individual, and there is not a problem with lost or duplicated keys.

Despite the increase in efficiency with keypads, most small companies still issue individual keys that operate locks throughout the building. A key-control system is facilitated, usually in the form of a system that maintains two sets of keys, a master and a duplicate, so that the duplicate can be issued and a printed list is maintained, indicating names of personnel and keys issued. As a part of this key system, a cabinet is maintained in which the master keys are stored with corresponding labels attached. The duplicate keys should be stamped with the same identification as the labels on the master set. Only one person should be in charge of the key loan program. If an

Figure 1–2 Low/minimum level security—the Manassas museum.

employee is terminated for cause, the key cylinders for the locks that this employee could operate should be changed.

Outside a minimum-security facility, proper landscaping would provide a clear view of the entrance for patrolling police; windows and doorways should be kept clear of shrubs or bushes. Lighting must be on during evening hours, illuminating windows and doorways. Parking lots and walkways should remain well lit.

LOW LEVEL SECURITY

A low level of security is designed to *impede* and *detect*. The detection portion of this level is what differentiates it from the minimum level, and calls for the addition of new equipment, such as Closed Circuit Television (*CCTV*) and motion detectors. A medium-sized hotel is a good example of a facility that would have this type of security.

In this imaginary hotel all of the minimum-level elements are present, and in addition, the hotel has monitored hallways, upgraded equipment, such as "high-security"-type locks (see

Figure 1–3), and grated windows that face alleyways and reinforced doors. Monitors for CCTV are generally located behind the wall at the reception desk area. Some hotels monitor the inside of elevator cars in addition to the hallways but until recently, most hotels had not installed motion-detecting equipment with their CCTV. However, the price for motion-detecting equipment has dropped to the point where it is now easily included in a system without much additional cost. Most CCTV systems are now actually part of the "network" so that computers can control the cameras and their associated tilt and pan mechanisms, and motion detection can be set up in zones that are easily designed via the computer screen. Motion detectors can be easily set up to replace the bell that used to sit on top of a hotel's reception counter during evening hours. Even analog video recorders are being replaced by high capacity hard drives. The digital nature of a hard drive and computer allows for easy backup, retrieval, and searching functions.

Along with the move up a security level, from minimum to low, the alarm and access control systems will also be higher level. The alarm system will now be set up to arm and disarm "zones" independently. For instance, the business offices may be activated after 6:00 PM, to set door alarms, or motion detectors, but the rest of the hotel will be disarmed (with the exception of the fire alarm, of course). After midnight, perhaps the alarm system will be set to activate motion detection in the hallways to switch automatically to monitor a hallway with activity. The alarm system will be set up with a monitoring company, and since there is money involved with a public business like a hotel, there will be emergency buttons located in certain places for a silent alarm to the monitoring company.

Although most low-level security sites still use lock and key systems, in a hotel, the access control functions would be upgraded to a card-key system in which both employees and hotel guests would use "swipe cards". The alarm and access control systems would be integrated so that exterior doors away from the front of the building would automatically lock after 10:00PM, allowing access only with a card-key, and alarm if someone tried to force them open. The card-keys would be programmed individually for guests, as they check in. Employees such as housekeepers would have master cards, which would be programmed to operate only during certain hours, whereas the same types of master cards used by security guards could be programmed to operate 24/7. Some hotels provide an additional level of security where certain guests can reside on a "club" floor, one where the elevator will only stop if a specially programmed card is used to select the floor.

Figure 1–3   Card reader ©Honeywell International, Inc.

MEDIUM LEVEL SECURITY

A medium security system is set up to *impede, detect,* and *assess.* A location with this type of system, would definitely have an alarm system monitored via phone line and possibly backed up with cellular dialup. There is generally a security perimeter set up that goes beyond the area needing protection. This is often in the form of a fence that is at least eight feet high, with a locking gate or guard facility. The fence is usually topped with barbed wire or some other means of preventing someone from simply climbing over it. Security officers are usually associated with this level of security, although they do not necessarily have to be armed. Shopping malls, large manufacturing facilities, and warehouses usually employ this level of security. The shopping mall wouldn't have the fence, but usually individual stores have some type of shoplifting-prevention monitoring equipment at the entrance and exit. The *assess* portion of this level is what sets it above the minimum level. A means of assessment could be the use of multiple analog video recorders or digital hard drive recorders. A good example of assessing a situation would be in the case of the shopping mall, when inventory in a store is being monitored for detection of shoplifting. If shoplifting takes place, the incident would be recorded for later assessment.

HIGH LEVEL SECURITY

This level is designed to *impede, detect,* and *assess* both *external* and *internal* activity. The outside perimeter (such as the fence described in the medium level) would be fitted with an alarm system that is monitored. CCTV would be used externally and internally, and high-security lighting should be used both inside and outside the facility. Guards may be armed at this level, and they should carry communications equipment such as two-way radios. There should be a formal security plan in place to account for responses to most types of security breaches. At this level there would be a high degree of coordination with law enforcement. This level of security often facilitates the use of *biometric devices* for access control. These types of devices, which will be covered in more detail later in the book, measure certain body attributes (thus, *bio metric*). For example, the retina may be scanned in combination with the use of a card reader, or a thumbprint or handprint may be examined at the access point with a device that compares the reading to records in a computer database.

Good examples of high-level security departments can be found at most large casinos in Las Vegas. These casinos have very elaborate security divisions staffed by highly experienced personnel, most having military or police experience. Other examples include companies that deal with state lotteries, pharmaceutical companies, and contractors dealing with highly classified government projects.

MAXIMUM SECURITY

This level contains everything we have discussed previously, and is designed to *impede, detect, assess* and *neutralize* all unauthorized activity; both external and internal. All security plans contain *layers of security,* but the maximum security level also has built in redundancy. Each level, from the most secure internal area to the outside perimeter, would have several alarm and access-control methods. By the fence devices such as *pressure sensors* may be installed. Some are sensitive enough to detect the slightest disturbance. Security personnel would be highly trained, investigated, and armed with weapons systems more effective than pistols. Internally, *mantrap* technology would be used at various locations throughout the facility (see Figure 1–4). These are entrances or exits where an indi-

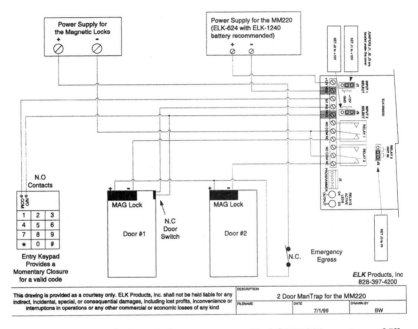

Figure 1–4 Schematic for a 2-door mantrap—Model MM220 courtesy of Elk Products, Inc.

vidual has to go through a door into a small enclosure, wait for the door to close, and then go through a second door to enter or exit. This makes it possible for a security guard to lock both doors when the person is in the enclosure, or for the doors to lock automatically if the person doesn't have proper access-control credentials, thus trapping him. These enclosures would be equipped with reinforced walls and bullet resistant glass.

Examples of maximum-security facilities would be nuclear power plants, the gold repository at Fort Knox, and many prisons. When we talk about security layers in the next section, we will use maximum security as an example.

These are not cookie-cutter designs. Each level, each situation, each location, each company, is unique. In the world of prisons, minimum, medium, and maximum have different meanings than in the world of manufacturing. The parameters of impeding, detecting, and assessing are measured and treated quite differently at a prison, than at a manufacturing facility. A pharmaceutical company that wants to keep its proprietary information private, at the maximum security level, would probably house its research and development facility in a secure, locked and guarded building. In an embassy, under maximum security, a government generally goes beyond that. The Embassy not only has locks, guards, and access-control devices, but also encloses entire floors with lead-lined, grounded, radio frequency-proof walls to keep electromagnetic emissions from escaping—they usually shield each individual computer, monitor and printer under so-called *Tempest* guidelines. Tempest guidelines are government standards and procedures to ensure that electromagnetic emanations won't escape an area where they could be intercepted and listened to. A prison wouldn't need *Tempest*, but would keep inmates under lock and key at all times.

SECURITY LAYERS

As we learned earlier, good security is provided in layers. The first step in designing a security system is to determine *what* must be kept secure, *where* it is located, *when* it should be protected, and *how much* protection is needed. When you answer these questions, you will know where to locate the inner layer. Bear in mind that there may be several inner layers. The next step is to walk from the outside to the inside where the inner layer is. Find all possible paths; walking from the inside out may show alternative routes that wouldn't be noticed when going in the opposite direction. Now think of the facility as an onion; an outer skin, followed by layers and layers until the inner core is reached. More stringent security should be provided at the very inner layer; possibly access-control augmented with biometrics, CCTV coverage with motion detectors for after hours, perhaps even alarm systems. As we move to the outer layers, the security is eased off a bit, and less obvious, layer by layer, until we are in the parking lot where the security consists of good lighting, open landscaping, and CCTV with pan and tilt controls mounted on posts and controlled by a security officer inside the facility.

PLANNING FOR TERRORISM THREATS

According to Donald R. Turnage and William F. Booth, in their book, *Unbreakable Inc. 11 Ways to Ward off the Terrorist Threat,* regarding access control and security systems, "Planning for a terrorist attack is analogous to a homeowner living in a hurricane zone. Understanding the scope of devastation a hurricane can bring, the homeowner plans ahead by adding safety measures that can decrease the odds of the home being totally destroyed. Likewise, corporations must plan and add security measures designed to lessen the odds of becoming a target; and to diminish the effects if and when they are targeted."

Here are 11 ways corporations can address terrorist threats and implement a plan to mitigate them in the course of their everyday work.

1   Examine Operational Measures—An incident management plan is absolutely essential for most corporations

2   Create a Good Security Plan

3   Seek the Advice of a Security Consultant

4   Conduct Employee Background Checks and Know Who is in Your Building

5   Maintain a Clear, Written Security Policy

6   Awareness is Paramount—Employees should remain "Security Conscious"

7   Increase Physical Security Measures

8   Don't Forget the Parking Lots

9   Turn Up the Lights

10   Use *CPTED* Principles—*Crime Prevention Through Environmental Design*

11   Be Aware of Your Building's Surroundings

CHEMICAL AND BIOLOGICAL ATTACK

The Lawrence Berkeley National Laboratory at the University of California Berkeley has released the following advice for building security professionals and first responders to protect facilities from chemical and biological attacks:

Immediate Steps

- Prevent unauthorized access to air intakes and exhausts. The easiest way for a terrorist to quickly contaminate a building with chemical or biological agents is to introduce the agents into the building's ventilation system.

- Secure mechanical or HVAC (heating, ventilation and air conditioning) room doors to prevent unauthorized access. A terrorist with access to a building's HVAC equipment can quickly contaminate the entire building.

- Secure building plans and HVAC plans from unauthorized access. A terrorist can maximize the casualties from an indoor chemical or biological attack if they have knowledge of the building's ventilation system.

- Develop an emergency-response team. Any emergency requires rapid response in a number of areas, such as evacuation assistance and communication with authorities.

- Plan and practice separate emergency response procedures for indoor and outdoor releases of chemical or biological agents. The first response to an outdoor release should include shutting down the building's ventilation system and closing all doors and windows. In contrast, the response to an indoor release should include evacuation.

Long-Term Suggestions

- Ensure building operators can quickly manipulate HVAC systems to respond to different types of attack. Manipulating the HVAC system can help slow the spread of a chemical agent or can rapidly clear it out of a building. Rapid response can save lives.

- Upgrade HVAC filters and seal gaps to prevent air bypass. Particle filters can remove biological agents from the air handling system. However, the tighter the filter, the more air will try to leak around it.

- Establish internal and external safe zones for people to use during a toxic release. By manipulating (and perhaps modifying) the building's HVAC system, safe areas can be created inside the building when there is an outdoor hazardous release. Also, some external areas near a building will be safer than others during an indoor release.

■ Provide separate air exhaust systems for mail rooms and other high-risk locations. Some areas are likely targets for introducing a chemical agent into a building. Isolating the air handling systems from these areas can prevent the harmful agent from spreading throughout the building.

■ "Weatherize" the building by sealing cracks around doors and windows. Gaps around windows and doors, and holes in the building shell, allow conditioned air to escape the building, and outdoor air to enter. For more information from the Lawrence Berkeley National Laboratory, visit *http://www.lbi.gov/.*

REDUCING THE ORGANIZATION'S EXPOSURE TO CRIMINAL AND TERRORIST ACTIVITIES

Contributed by Robert E. Colliver[1]

Every organization is exposed to a different level and type of risk, depending on its products, services, symbolism, and stakeholders. Because terrorists choose the mode, time, and the place for their attack, industry and government are forced to address a variety of general security weaknesses and protect around "worst case scenarios" in order to maintain a safe work environment. If the date, time, and nature of attack were known beforehand, we could simply plan for that event without wasting organizational dollars and effort securing ourselves from an attack we knew would or would not come.

Criminal and terrorist events generally require a level of planning which often includes thorough research of the target combined with a thoughtfully rehearsed and flawlessly timed execution. And without citing Murphy's law, we can demonstrate that the interruption of any of these precursor events can often disrupt the attack itself. Terrorist plans, like protection plans, all have weak links. How do we identify these points? How do we spend our security budget wisely?

---

1. "Rick" Colliver is Director of Global Security with Scotts-Miracle Gro and has spent more than 25 years in corporate security management and law enforcement. Rick remains active as a Reserve Deputy with the Union County Sheriff's Office where he serves as an investigator, hostage negotiator, Emergency Medical Technician and rescue diver. Rick is also an instructor with the University of Findlay's Center for Terrorism Preparedness where he lectures on executive protection, workplace violence, physical security planning, and threat assessment.

There are many different methodologies used by public and private sector organizations to identify segments of the organizational process that are critical and vulnerable. The United States Food and Drug Administration has used a system known as HACCP (Hazard Analysis of Critical Control Points) for many years. Depending on the type of organization in question, the type of methodology employed is not as important as the actual identification of *critical paths*, points that are vital to the success of the organization's processes.

In a manufacturing environment, critical paths might include:

- Materials and ingredients acquisition
- Receiving dock operations
- Processing and assembly flow
- Labeling and packaging
- Finished goods storage
- Order entry and customer classification systems
- Accounts payable and cash application systems
- Internal fraud programs

In other environments, some of the steps would change and others would stay the same. And, in each of these steps a myriad of control points can be found.

Consider what might be critical in a retail operation:

- Onsite vendor relationships
- Ordering and stock rotation
- Warehousing
- Distribution to retail shelves
- Point of sale security

While some control points may seem obscure at first glance, they are obvious, following a failure of the process. Critical control points can also be identified in intentional or accidental disasters, whether they affect large groups of people, or only one. Moreover, by studying what caused certain tragedies to occur, we can see more easily where control points can be leveraged for safety.

Consider what causes "accidents." Generally, things do not just go boom in the night; aircraft do not fall from the sky and ships do not sink without cause. These things happen because of a stream or cascade of minor events that contribute to the final catastrophic event itself. Virtually all intentional and accidental disasters can be evaluated in this way. By evaluating what went wrong, we can better understand how to focus on making certain elements go right.

For example, let us analyze the loss of the RMS Titanic in the North Atlantic on the evening of April 14, 1912. If we begin with the disastrous outcome and work backward, we can reconstruct a fault tree that illustrates critical points along this path where intervention of one kind or another could have saved lives. The primary tools we will use are the words "why" and "how" (see Table 1–1).

Table 1–1 Identifying Critical Points

Control Point	Intervention	Result
Hypothermia of Victims	USCG approved flotation	Lives Saved
	Neoprene suits	Lives Saved
Lifeboat Insufficiency	Add more lifeboats	Lives Saved
Unfilled Lifeboats	Fill and properly launch lifeboats	Lives Saved
Water Intake	Pump water out faster	Lives Saved
Loss of Displacement	Enclose watertight compartment	Lives Saved
Damage to Hull	Use of better metals	Lives Saved
	Plug leaks faster	Lives Saved
Avoid Iceberg	Recognize hazard earlier	Lives Saved
	Slower speed	Lives Saved
	Bigger rudder	Lives Saved

While some of the victims may have actually died of natural causes associated with the stress of the incident itself, some from drowning and some from trauma, most on board the Titanic probably died from hypothermia. When the core temperature of the body drops as a result of exposure to extreme cold, the continued cooling results in an irregular heartbeat that leads to death.

Why were the passengers exposed to cold temperatures? Because they jumped into the water with no protection against the cold temperature. Why did they jump in the water? Because the ship was sinking and there were not enough lifeboats. Why were there not enough lifeboats? Because, maritime regulations in 1912 mandated that the minimum number of lifeboats required on a vessel went by the tonnage of the ship, not by the number of people on board. So, the Titanic merely complied with existing safety regulations. Why were the lifeboats needed? Because the ship hit an iceberg and was sinking. Why did it hit the iceberg? The questions and answers could go on and on.

Hindsight is perfect and almost every effect has a cause. The point is that if any one of these situations had been different, part or all of this disaster might have been avoided. The idea when devising a security strategy is to envision possible flaws or adverse effects that could occur and then take the necessary precautions to avoid them.

UNCERTAINTY

In 1927, Werner Heisenberg (1901–1976) published a paper on "The Uncertainty Principle." The thrust of his paper challenged contemporary thought about the ability to predict the future simply by knowing the present. While not saying, "Everything is uncertain," he did advance theories on "where uncertainty lies." His premise led to speculation about the inability to predict the results of experiments potentially due to the fact that there exist enough variables in the world that no two experiments can ever actually be the same; that a margin of error has to be accepted. We can consider certain key factors in the sinking of the Titanic, but we have to understand that we cannot positively state that any one intervention could have changed the outcome of the event on the evening of April 14. In the end, we must admit that we are never able to duplicate completely an event to a perfect certainty. Therefore, we use history and applicable intelligence to make educated guesses.

The "what-ifing" that comes from analyzing disasters and other critical events in history has resulted in a new field called counterfactual historical analysis; the ability to analyze an incident or process and unplug certain historical or factual elements and plug in a hypothetical event which changes the outcome. This counterfactual analysis can be a valuable tool in providing threat assessments. One popular what-if is the account of Annie Oakley's performance in her husband's Wild West Show. Touring Europe in 1891, there was a part of her act in which she would shoot a cigarette out of her husband's mouth. Having attended several of these shows, the young Crown Prince Wilhelm volunteered to pose for the act. She accepted and succeeded in hitting his cigarette (there is some controversy over whether he had it in his mouth or his hand at the time). Speculation suggests that had she missed and killed the Crown Prince, he never would have become the Kaiser and there would not have been a WWI.

THE CONCENTRIC RINGS THEORY

Known in military circles as "defense in depth," the concentric rings approach assumes that the items or persons being protected are surrounded by several unique circles of protection. For example if the target of your protection is a vault storing vital documents, the inner circle of protection might include the construction of the safe and its door, the secrecy of the combination and perhaps an alarm sensor which detects tampering, opening, and closing.

The next circle of protection might include the locked door on the office where the safe is located and the concrete block construction of the walls. An outer circle would include the building itself; its construction and the access control and surveillance systems. The idea being that an intruder needs to breech several different layers of security in order to successfully compromise the contents of the safe. These layers of protection can include elaborate physical and electronic deterrents but can also be supplemented by psychological barriers. For example, traffic gate arms that raise and lower after a security guard allows entry are generally constructed of lightweight wood. They are intended to serve as a warning device to drivers that they must stop and identify themselves with the officer on duty. They are not "physical" barriers because they are not intended to physically prevent an automobile from entering the property. On the contrary, most are designed to shear off when struck to facilitate replacement and to minimize damage to automobiles. On the other hand, an 8-foot chain link fence with razor wire spooled across the top is an example of a physical barrier. It is intended to "slow down" the unauthorized entry to one's property. Notice that the term, "prevent" was not used. Given the right tools and a suitable period of time in which to operate undetected, a criminal would not have a difficult time penetrating this fence. Therefore, fencing is often supported by closed circuit television (CCTV) surveillance, or the attachment of sensor cables to detect tampering. Again, the idea is that the criminal should have to cross such a significant number of obstacles to gain admission that s/he will consider giving up and attacking somewhere else. Thus, leading to the recognition that any security system, like a chain, is only as good as its weakest link.

THE WEAK LINK THEORY

An organization is protected by many security systems that are unique to its needs. Some of these systems could be electronic as well as procedural (for example, a policy that all personnel must wear identification badges that are also electronic access control cards while on the site). In order to more fully explain the weak-link theory we can examine a simple alarm system.

The earliest alarm systems on record were geese. Shepherds guarding their flocks would sit about complacently until the geese started honking, signaling the approach of predatory animals. Since that time, technology has improved exponentially, but the essence of any alarm system remains the same

- Detect
- Communicate
- Act

No matter how simple or sophisticated, an alarm system must first detect some anomaly, communicate this change to a control switch and then take some action. Detection can be accomplished by magnetic contacts on doors and windows, passive infrared motion detectors, microwave or ultrasonic detectors, or even seismic sensors. This detection signal must then be transmitted over wire, cable, fiber optic, radio frequency (RF), or other medium to a device that is going to ring a bell, sound a siren, turn on a tape recorder or call the police. Sometimes several actions are initiated at once, but the principal remains basically the same.

In the weak-link approach, we need to survey a variety of security systems to determine where each system is likely to fail and determine if that failure represents an acceptable or unacceptable level of risk. If we were evaluating our intrusion alarm system, we would have to consider all perimeter doors, windows and roof hatches as well as critical internal areas that required electronic protection. Beginning with the sensor devices, we would assure ourselves that each is functioning effectively (if it can't detect, then it can't communicate). If found to be functioning within manufacturer specifications, we then look to determine if it is the appropriate type of sensor for the given application (we wouldn't use magnetic contacts on a window that doesn't open). Finally, we would then determine if the sensor device is susceptible to tampering or bypassing without alerting the system further down the line.

Satisfied that the sensor equipment is working effectively, we would continue our inspection with the transmission medium used to communicate signals back to the master control unit. If we are transmitting via twisted pair or coaxial cable, we would need to be assured that cable lengths are less than the maximum distance specified by the manufacturer and all wiring is enclosed in conduit to be more tamper resistant. During this inspection, it would not be uncommon for telecommunications professionals to be asked for support in running a *time-domain reflectometry* (TDR) analysis to determine if there are any breaks, weak points or attachments anywhere in the lines. While used primarily to trouble-shoot telephone lines, a time-domain reflectometer is an instrument that can tell exactly how far away from a given point a line is disrupted, saving hours of walking and testing.

Once we are assured that all signals are being received back in the control room, we can focus our attention on what we want the system to do when signals are received. Critical points at this step deal with the human element. In our sample system discussed here, the first time a human has to be involved is when the signal comes into the station. Do we expect a guard to do something or, will the system take over and automatically redirect CCTV cameras to begin recording the surreptitious entry while at the same time, notifying police and locking down other doors? If the guard is away from the room when the signal comes in, we have identified a "weak link".

If we have installed an impressive array of sensors throughout a large building and have opted to transmit signals back via radio (RF), can the signals get through all of the steel and concrete to be received at the other end? If not, then we have identified a weak link. If the alarm signals come in on the telephone line and the guard is ordering pizza on the same line at the same time the signal comes in...you've got it.

We apply this same philosophy to executive protection programs when reviewing route security for movements of executives from their home to their office. If their house is armored and their office is armored and their car is armored, but the car has to move under the river via a tunnel to get from point "A" to point "B", then the tunnel could be a weak link. Thus, the goal of improving the executive's travel security is to either strengthen the security of the tunnel or look at alternate means of delivering the executive back and forth without passing through the tunnel.

ECONOMY OF FORCE

Some cowboy once remarked, "...never send a boy to do a man's work." On the other hand, you wouldn't ask an organic chemist to rewire your house. A security professional must understand the importance of prescribing appropriate levels of protection to meet the needs of his or her organization. In other words, provide just the right amount of security for just the right price.

The military philosopher, Carl von Clausewitz[2] intended the word "economy" to mean "effectiveness", meaning that extravagant expenditures on unnecessary labor and material can be as detrimental as being under-prepared if a terrorist event occurs.

As a case in point, after taking over as security manager for a Midwestern manufacturing firm, I was walking down a first floor hallway on my way to a meeting with executives in another building. Halfway down the 75-yard hallway, I passed a security guard who was sitting in an uncomfortable chair, engrossed in a paperback book. I surmised that he was on break and since I was running a bit behind schedule, I decided to introduce myself to him at some later time. When I returned about an hour later, the guard was still sitting there working on his book.

I couldn't resist the temptation to ask why he was sitting in the middle of the hallway. He looked up from his book and pointed at a steel door next to him and replied that it was his job to watch people come through that door. Out of curiosity, I opened the door and peered out into a dark courtyard created in the shadow of the two taller buildings on either side of a small driveway. I asked,

---

2. Carl von Clausewitz's military philosophy. *On War*, published by Maria Clausewitz and Dummlers Verlag, Berlin, 1832. Translation by Colonel J.J. Graham published by N. Trubner, London, 1873

"Are there a lot of people that come through here?"

"Nope." He answered.

"Well, who does come and go from here?" I questioned.

"Dunno...a couple of guys from the energy center." He responded, returning his attention to his book.

"Then what's out there that we would need a door here for?" I countered.

"Dunno...you'd have to check with the security manager." He said, obviously annoyed at my persistence.

I nodded and turned to walk away before it hit me, "Hey, I'm the security manager".

When I returned to my desk, I called my boss, who was in charge of Personnel and asked why we had a guard there, how much we were paying him, and how many hours a day was this "post" occupied. He told me that it was because there had been a door there before the new building had been constructed and that after the construction had been completed no one ever thought to close the post. I grimaced,

"And, how long has that been?"

"Two years." Was the reply.

I did some quick mental calculations on the $9.00 an hour billing rate, times the 120 hours a week that the post was covered, times the 104 weeks that the poor guard had been there, struggling with that paperback, and learned that it had cost the company more than $112,000 to secure a door that just wasn't necessary for the conduct of business.

"What idiot spent a hundred thousand dollars to watch a door that should have been blocked off two years ago?" I commented, my blood pressure rising.

After a prolonged silence, my boss replied, "I did."

Since this book is about the process of identifying security weaknesses and prescribing effective protection, and not about wresting your foot from your mouth, you can consult other texts to determine how to politically manage your way through a company's organizational structure. It was a long time before my first promotion.

The moral of the story is that you must effectively manage the balance of risk versus exposure to avoid over or under reaction to security issues. Through training and experience with technical security products and services you can better understand the importance of conducting a thorough and comprehensive vulnerability assessment. Assessment of vulnerabilities, combined with accurate and timely intelligence will be your guide in establishing a sound security program.

There is a three-pronged test for all organizational decisions made in the United States in the 21st century

■ Is it legal?

■ Is it ethical?

■ How will this sound on the Sunday evening news?

Decisions that affect the operation of government entities as well as public companies must be carefully reviewed and applied in a manner that is not only compliant with a host of laws and regulations, but is ethical as well. And just because something is not illegal, doesn't mean that it is ethical. More importantly, decisions must take into account not only the ethics and legality of an issue, but rather how the public will perceive these decisions. Further, as most of us are aware, public perception is driven by the media. The media has two roles: one, as stated on their FCC license, is "to serve the public interest." But, their primary role is to sell advertising. To sell advertising, they must develop a market share; in other words, they have to make a lot of people want to watch their channel or read their pages.

Those of you with a marketing background know that you don't sell share by coming on the television each night and bemoaning, "Nothing much really happened today…but that which happened was pretty much taken care of. All is well." So, as our world advances, in the age of live broadcasts from space and the battlefields, the security planner must approach his/her task not only from a technical perspective but an image perspective as well. Leading us to the importance of adherence to guidelines.

Even before the attacks on September 11, 2001, virtually every department of the United States government was compiling guidelines and regulations to enhance security, not only at government installations, but at industrial locations as well. The FDA and USDA issued guidelines for businesses that process food, The DOT issued guidance for motor carriers, the Coast Guard for ports and vessels and US Customs (now the Bureau of Immigration and Customs

Enforcement) for all importers. These guidance documents are similar to each other in many ways.

The important thing to remember is that if an industry is governed by state or federal regulations, its security plans must first include compliance. Regulations are not generally negotiable. Failure to comply with regulations can lead to:

- Suspension of operations
- Civil and criminal fines
- Jail

Chances are if an organization is regulated, it will also be inspected. Therefore, when conducting vulnerability assessments of its facilities, you should consider using these regulations as a template for your review. After all, they are what the organization will be audited against.

Guidelines, on the other hand, have their own consequences. Guidelines are the government's way of standardizing practices in a "non-official" way, but, more importantly, they are the government's way of saying "I told you so" if something occurs for which you were unprepared or unresponsive. And, as discussed above, failure to meet a guideline will subject the organization to the worst penalty of all; negative press on Sunday evening television.

The other element about performing according to guidelines is that guidelines have a habit of becoming regulations with the stroke of a pen. It will save time and effort if your assessments include government guidelines and recommendations. These templates can be very helpful to those that are inexperienced at conducting vulnerability assessments. The bad news is that just because the government didn't think of something in their template, doesn't mean you are exempt from liability if you overlook something that turns out to be a contributing factor in loss or damage. In lay terms, after the fact you will be judged by:

- What did you know?
- When did you learn it?
- What did you do about it when you learned it?

So, if your assessment uncovers weaknesses and these weaknesses are identified to management (in the form of a report or documented conversation), then the organization is put into the position of being forced to act. For a better understanding of when liability attaches, consult a member of your organization's legal staff.

SUMMARY

- Physical Security has to be planned logically to protect assets. A definite road map has to be designed to accomplish an effective security solution.

- Physical security is designed and planned much like the design and construction of a building itself. The security plan is accomplished at different levels and in *layers* or *concentric rings*.

- Overall security is dependent on the weakest link. In the weak-link approach, we need to survey a security system to determine where that system is likely to fail and determine if that failure represents an acceptable or unacceptable level of risk.

- Planning physical security can be simple and straightforward, such as the installation of a burglar alarm system at home. There are service companies that monitor alarm systems via a phone line.

- The minimum level of security is designed to *impede*. Typically, there would be a burglar and fire alarm system installed. The system should be such that employees have keys to operate the system, or better yet, the system could be operated by key codes at a push button panel. Keys that operate locks throughout the building are issued.

- A low level of security is designed to *impede* and *detect*. The upgraded feature would include "high-security" type locks, reinforced doors, and grated windows that face alleyways. Since we have moved up a security level, from minimum to low, the alarm and access-control systems may also be higher level. Although most low-level security sites would still use lock and key systems, in a hotel, the access control functions would be upgraded to a card-key system where both employees and hotel residents would use "swipe cards". The alarm and access-control systems would be integrated so that exterior doors away from the front of the building would automatically lock after a given time, allow access with a card-key, and alarm if someone tried to force them open.

- A medium security system is set up to *impede, detect,* and *assess*. Security officers are usually associated with this level of security, although they do not have to be armed. Shopping malls, large manufacturing facilities, and warehouses usually employ this level of security.

■ There should be a formal security plan in place to account for responses to most types of security breaches. High-level security could very well facilitate the use of *biometric devices* as part of the access control.

■ All security plans contain a method of using *layers of security,* but the maximum security level also has built in redundancy. A pharmaceutical company that wants to keep its proprietary information private, at the maximum security level, would probably house its research and development facility in a secure, locked and guarded building.

■ Good security is provided in layers. More stringent security should be provided at the very inner layer; possibly access control augmented with biometrics, CCTV coverage with motion detectors for after-hours, perhaps even alarm systems.

■ Craft a good security plan.

■ Seek the advice of a security consultant.

■ Maintain a clear, written security policy.

■ Awareness is paramount—Employees should remain "security conscious".

■ Secure mechanical and HVAC room doors to prevent unauthorized access. Secure building plans and HVAC plans from unauthorized access. A terrorist can maximize the casualties from an indoor chemical or biological attack if they have knowledge of the building's ventilation system.

■ Ensure building operators can quickly manipulate HVAC systems to respond to different types of attack.

■ Particle filters can remove biological agents from the air handling system.

■ Provide separate air exhaust systems for mail rooms and high-risk locations.

■ "Weatherize" the building by sealing cracks around doors and windows.

■ Examining cause and effect and looking at what went wrong in major disasters and critical events in history is a useful tool for developing strategies to prevent reoccurrences of such events.

KEY TERMS

Security Surveys

Level of Security

Biometric Devices

Layers of Security

Pressure Sensors

Mantrap

Tempest

Time-Domain Reflectometry

DISCUSSION QUESTIONS

1   We install security systems to protect us from break-ins and theft. Would security planning also be necessary for natural disasters? Explain.

2   If an alarm takes place, who is usually the first responder in a residential system? In a commercial system?

3   What is a *security survey?*

4   What is the *minimum* level of security designed to do? How about the other levels?

5   Define CCTV.

6   Why are analog video recorders being replaced with digital (hard-disk type) recorders?

7   What is the purpose of a *mantrap?*

8   The United States Food and Drug Administration uses a system known as HACCP. What is that?

9   Who is the person behind *The Uncertainty Principle?*

10   Explain *counterfactual historical analysis.*

11   Is there a difference between the terms, *layers of security* and *concentric rings of security?*

12   What is the earliest alarm system that man is aware of?

13   What do you suppose should be involved in an *Employee Background Check?*

14   What is *HVAC?*

15   What is meant by *weatherizing* a building?

RESEARCH QUESTIONS

1   Some physical security specialists prefer to design concentric circles of protection from the outside-in. They feel it is best to look at the facility as a potential perpetrator would look at it. Others favor designing from the inside out. The military calls this *enclaving*. It has been said that enclaving keeps going in an outward direction until the money runs out. Which method do you prefer? Research these methods and provide reasoning for your preference.

2   A thorough security survey will usually start out with a risk analysis. One type of qualitative risk analysis is called a *FRAP*. What do the letters stand for in this acronym? Briefly describe how a FRAP works.

3   Many times the term, *bullet-proof* glass is used. Why is it preferred to use the term, *bullet-resistant*, instead? Are there degrees of bullet resistance? What about other terminology, such as *fire-proof* vs. *fire-resistant?*

CHAPTER 2

Security Electronics

PURPOSE AND OBJECTIVES

This chapter reviews the electronics used with security systems. Chapter 2 reviews the important electronic principles that a security specialist should know. Some of the principles discussed in this chapter, such as Thevenin's Theorem, are just reviews. If the student needs to learn the theorem in detail, a supplementary electronics or math text is suggested.

The reader should be aware that:

- Electronics are associated with most security functions
- There are devices that must be inserted into, or waved at a sensor at various tour stations, so that an electrical signal can be passed on to measure different parameters
- Alarm systems consist of a control unit that usually contains a combination of types of electronics: contacts, integrated circuits, microprocessors, switches, relays, wires, and so on
- Systems have external loops of some sort—they may be wire loops, or fiber optic, or RF (radio frequency). On the loops are sensors, switches, radio receivers, and optical receivers
- Other types of systems, such as access control or CCTV, use various types of electronics
- These days everything tends to be computerized, and/or attached to a network. Later chapters will discuss test and measurement equipment used extensively in security technology. This equipment measures the various parameters, such as current, voltage, phase, or power that will be discussed in this chapter

BASIC ELECTRONICS

First, a short review of basic electronic theory associated with test and measurement equipment is in order.

Some test and measurement equipment measure power, voltage, resistance, current, or associated attributes, such as phase angle, frequency, velocity of propagation, or changes in these parameters. One should be familiar with the units of measurement for various parameters: *Volts* for voltage (or Electromotive Force—sometimes referred to as EMF), *Amperes* for current, *Ohms* for resistance, and *Watts* for power. Most of the time, we are dealing with relatively low quantities of these units, so we use a fractional measurement such as *milli*amps, *micro*volts, or *milli*watts. Table 2–1 reviews these various units.

Table 2–1 Numerical Units and Prefixes

Multiple	With all the zeros	Prefix	Symbol
10^{12}	1,000,000,000,000	tera	T
10^{9}	1,000,000,000	giga	G
10^{6}	1,000,000	mega	M
10^{3}	1,000	kilo	k
10^{-3}	0.001	milli	m
10^{-6}	0.000,001	micro	μ
10^{-9}	0.000,000,001	nano	n
10^{-12}	0.000,000,000,001	pico	p
10^{-15}	0.000,000,000,000,001	femto	f

Other types of test equipment measure (or take into consideration) parameters such as capacitance, inductance, or impedance. These properties are associated with *alternating current* (AC). In security systems, we work with alternating current and *direct current* (DC). Direct current is produced by batteries or power supplies in which the input is AC.

DIRECT CURRENT

Figure 2–1 is the simplest form of an electrical signal. Direct current is produced by a source that produces a current, which has a consistent non-varying value.

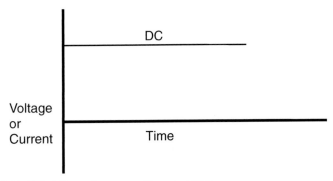

Figure 2–1   DC voltage (or current) versus time.

OHM'S LAW

Ohm's law is a simple equation that is used to calculate voltage, resistance, or current. Given two of the parameters, the third is easily determined. The unit used in power equations is the Watt.

Ohm's Law

$$V = IR \text{ or } I = \frac{V}{R} \text{ or } R = \frac{V}{I} \qquad \textbf{(Eq. 2–1)}$$

where

V = Voltage

I = Current

R = Resistance

P = Power

Ohm's law can be used either for direct current or alternating current. In the case of alternating current, an additional factor is added $E = IR\cos\theta$ to compensate for the phase ($\cos\theta$) of the electrical signal.

RESISTORS

Resistance is an opposition to the flow of current, and is inherent in all devices attached to a circuit. A resistor is a device that is typically made of carbon and is designed to have a specified value. It is very common to work with resistances in circuits and the subsequent current flow. In security work, a circuit could be a grouping of telephones, switches, sensors, light bulbs, or a number of other devices. There are total series resistance circuits, wherein resistances are simply added together, and the current flowing through each resistance is the total circuit current. There are also parallel resistance circuits in which current flow becomes a bit more complicated; they involve *branch currents*. There are also combinations of parallel and series resistances. For *resistors in parallel*, the total resistance is less than that of the lowest individual resistance value. The formula for finding the total resistance of a parallel circuit is

$$R_t = \frac{1}{\dfrac{1}{R_1} + \dfrac{1}{R_2} + \dfrac{1}{R_3} + \dfrac{1}{R_4} + \ldots + \dfrac{1}{R_n}} \qquad \textbf{(Eq. 2–2)}$$

For only two resistors in parallel:

$$R_t = \frac{R1 \times R2}{R1 + R2} \qquad \textbf{(Eq. 2–3)}$$

KIRCHHOFF'S CURRENT LAW

Assume there are three resistors in parallel, 5.0 kohm, 20.0 kohm, and 9.0 kohm (see Figure 2–2).

The same voltage, 125V, is applied to all three resistors. The current in each can be found from Ohm's law:

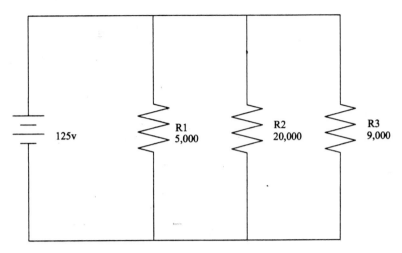

Figure 2–2 Kirchhoff's current law with three resistors.

$$I1 = \frac{V}{R1} = \frac{125}{5000} = 25.0mA$$

$$I2 = \frac{V}{R2} = \frac{125}{20000} = 6.25mA$$

$$I3 = \frac{V}{R3} = \frac{125}{9000} = 13.89mA \qquad \textbf{(Eq. 2–4)}$$

$$I_{TOTAL} = I1 + I2 + I3 = 25 + 6.25 + 13.89 = 45.14mA \qquad \textbf{(Eq. 2–5)}$$

This illustrates Kirchhoff's current law: the current flowing into a branch is equal to the sum of the individual currents leaving the branch. The total resistance of the circuit is

$$R = \frac{V}{I} = \frac{125}{45.14} = 2.77kohms \qquad \textbf{(Eq. 2–6)}$$

This can be verified using Eq. 2–2.

KIRCHHOFF'S VOLTAGE LAW

Ohm's law applies to any part of a circuit as well as to the whole. Although the current is the same in all resistances in Figure 2–3, the total voltage divides between them.

$$I = \frac{V}{R} = \frac{125}{34000} = 3.68\,mA \qquad \textbf{(Eq. 2–7)}$$

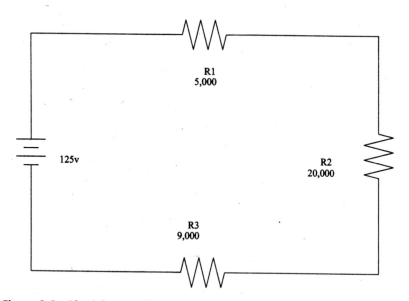

Figure 2–3   Ohm's law applied to part of a circuit as well as the whole.

Voltage drops across each resistor can be determined with Ohm's law:

$$V1 = IR1 = .00368 \times 5000 = 18\,V$$

$$V2 = IR2 = .00368 \times 20000 = 73\,V$$

$$V3 = IR3 = .00368 \times 9000 = 34\,V \qquad \textbf{(Eq. 2–8)}$$

Kirchhoff's voltage law accurately sums up the statement that the sum of the voltages in a closed circuit loop is zero. The battery is a *voltage source*, and each resistor produces a *voltage drop*.

THEVENIN'S THEOREM

Thevenin's theorem is useful for simplifying a circuit. It states that a single voltage source and a series resistor can replace any two terminal networks of resistors and voltage or current sources as in Figure 2–4.

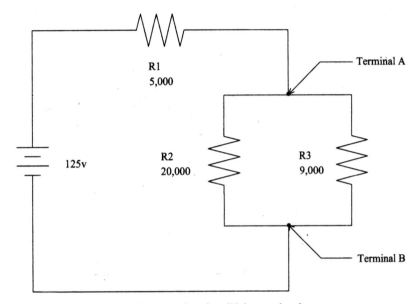

Figure 2–4   Thevenin's theorem for simplifying a circuit.

R1 and R2 form a *voltage divider* with R3 being a load. The current drawn by the load is the voltage across R3, divided by its resistance. The voltage of the Thevenin equivalent battery is the no load circuit voltage across terminals A and B. Without a load, the current through the circuit is

$$I = \frac{V}{R1 + R2} \qquad \text{(Eq. 2–9)}$$

and the voltage between A and B is

$$V_{AB} = I \times R2 \qquad \text{(Eq. 2–10)}$$

By substituting the first equation into the second, we find

$$V_{AB} = \frac{R2}{R1 + R2} \times V = \frac{20000}{25000} \times 125 = 100\,V \qquad \textbf{(Eq. 2-11)}$$

Therefore, when nothing is connected to terminals A and B, V and V_{AB} are equal.

The Thevenin equivalent resistance is the total resistance between A and B. Assume the battery to be an ideal source (with no internal resistance). When viewed from between terminals A and B, R1 and R2 are effectively placed in parallel, and the Thevenin equivalent resistance is then

$$R = \frac{R1 \times R2}{R1 + R2} = \frac{10 \times 10^{7}}{2.5 \times 10^{4}} = 4 \times 10^{3} = 4000\,ohms$$

Once R3 is connected to terminals A and B, the current through R3 will be equal to

$$I3 = \frac{V_{THEV}}{R_{TOTAL}} = \frac{100}{4000 + 9000} = 7.69\,mA \qquad \textbf{(Eq. 2-12)}$$

Why do we care about Thevenin's theorem? Because maximum power transfer takes place between a source and an output device of some type when the impedance of each is the same. If we want maximum power transfer from a security system to, say, a 75 ohm cable, then we can use Thevenin's theory to help design a system that will have an output impedance of 75 ohms.

ALTERNATING CURRENT

Unlike direct current, alternating current varies with time. The AC signal is usually in the form of a sine wave (as seen in Figure 2–5.)

As seen in Figure 2–4, there are several types of measurement that can be made in analyzing an AC value. In terms of voltage, we may measure the average value, the *root mean square (rms)* value, or the peak or *peak to peak* value. All of these measurements are important for design considerations.

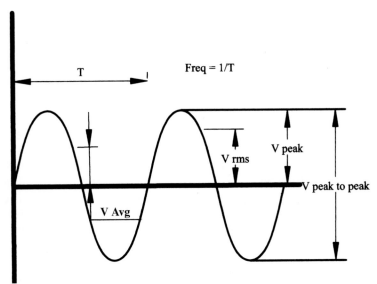

Figure 2–5   Alternating current.

The *frequency* of an electrical signal is important because as it changes, the properties associated with the signal also change. The human ear can usually hear low frequencies: speech, a mosquito's buzzing, and wind blowing through trees. High frequencies can be propelled through the atmosphere for thousands of miles and can bounce off the ionosphere. As frequencies get even higher, they turn into light waves and then into x-rays and beyond. Table 2–2 displays a list of various frequency ranges.

Table 2–2 Frequency Ranges

Regions	Frequency Ranges
Radio Frequencies	3.0×10^{6} Hz to 3.0×10^{11} Hz
Infrared	3.0×10^{11} Hz to 4.3×10^{14} Hz
Visible Light	4.3×10^{14} Hz to 1.0×10^{15} Hz
Ultraviolet	1.0×10^{15} Hz to 6.0×10^{16} Hz
X-rays	6.0×10^{16} Hz to 3.0×10^{19} Hz
Gamma rays	3.0×10^{19} Hz to 5.0×10^{20} Hz
Cosmic rays	5.0×10^{20} Hz to 8.0×10^{21} Hz

We use Ohm's law to calculate voltage, resistance or current in AC circuits just like we do for DC circuits, but we now have to take into consideration the *phase angle* of the signal.

$$V = IR\cos\theta$$

(Eq. 2–13)

DC and AC signals can be combined. An oscilloscope is an instrument that shows oscillations of voltage and current on its screen. On an oscilloscope, the AC would be seen riding on top of the DC signal. At high frequencies, AC signals produce harmonic signals, that is, they will produce lower voltage (attenuated) signals at multiples of the primary frequency. Sometimes, we can use these *harmonic frequencies* to produce different types of waveforms by mixing them together (See Figure 2–6). For instance, if we take the primary

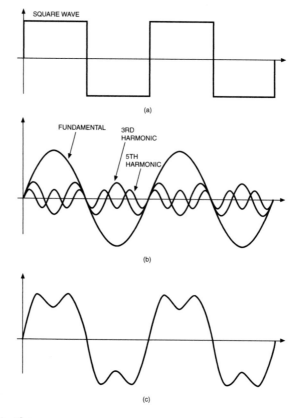

Figure 2–6 The square wave.

frequency and mix it with an infinite number of *odd* harmonics, the resultant waveform would be a square wave. The more odd harmonics (primary frequency of 1, 3, 5 etc., MHz) that are added, the more square the square wave becomes. Square waves are used in digital electronics, and they are formed with harmonics of analog signals. You will see where types of strong harmonics become important when we talk about non-linear junction detectors and finding "bugs" later, when we get into technical surveillance countermeasures.

MODULATION OF SIGNALS

Mixing a low frequency signal, such as a voice signal, with a high frequency, a so-called *carrier frequency* in the *x* MHz frequency range, modulates the carrier. The resultant signal takes on a form that changes at the rate of the voice signal. The carrier could change in frequency (FM or *frequency modulated*), amplitude (AM or *amplitude modulated*), or phase (PM or *phase modulated*). There are many different types of modulation methods. Keep in mind that *light* is made up of electromagnetic radiation at very high frequencies, so it can also be modulated, see Figure 2–7.

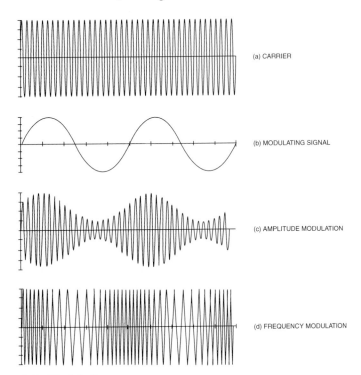

(a) CARRIER

(b) MODULATING SIGNAL

(c) AMPLITUDE MODULATION

(d) FREQUENCY MODULATION

Figure 2–7   Modulation.

REACTANCE

When working with capacitors and inductors (coils), we must not only consider capacitance and inductance, but also the resistance to current flow *reactance*. To calculate inductive reactance, we use the following formula:

$$X_L = 2\pi f L \qquad \text{(Eq. 2-14)}$$

where

X_L is inductive reactance in ohms

f = frequency in Hz

L = inductance in Henries

For capacitive reactance

$$X_c = \frac{1}{2\pi f C} \qquad \text{(Eq. 2-15)}$$

where

X_C is capacitive reactance in ohms

f = frequency in Hz

C = capacitance in Farads

IMPEDANCE

In a DC circuit, the parameter that resists current flow is resistance. In an AC circuit, we may have some other components present, such as capacitors and inductors. These components have properties that will shift the phase angle of the current going through them. The force that impedes the current flow is made up of a reactive component (*reactance*) that is out of phase with the resistive component. The sum of the resistance and the reactance is called *impedance*, signified by the letter Z, and is found by using the formula

$$Z = R + jX \qquad \text{(Eq. 2-16)}$$

where

R = resistive component

X = reactive component

j = square root of –1

To calculate impedance, we use vector addition to add resistance and reactance together. At any given point in time, the resistance will be a certain value, and the reactance will be a certain value, but they will be out of phase with each other. As such, the value of the phase difference will be determined by the instantaneous angles of the sine waves (remember, we're only talking about AC here). So, we end up with something that looks like Figure 2–8.

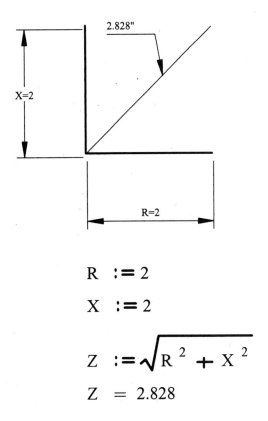

$$R := 2$$

$$X := 2$$

$$Z := \sqrt{R^2 + X^2}$$

$$Z = 2.828$$

Figure 2–8 Calculating impedence.

The formula for magnitude is

$$Z = \sqrt{R^2 + X^2}$$

(Eq. 2–17)

where

Z = impedance
R = resistance
X = reactance $[X_L - X_C]$

To get the resultant phase angle

$$\theta = \tan^{-1}\left(\frac{X}{R}\right)$$

(Eq. 2–18)

Example 2–1

$$Z = 8 + j6$$

$$Z = \sqrt{R^2 + X^2} = \sqrt{8^2 + 6^2} = \sqrt{64 + 36} = \sqrt{100} = 10$$

$$\theta = \tan^{-1}\left(\frac{X}{R}\right) = \tan^{-1}\left(\frac{6}{8}\right) = \tan^{-1}(.75) = 36.87°$$

For our purposes, the mathematics is not as important as realizing that *resistance* is pretty straightforward and easy to work with, whereas *impedance* can be complex and will cause phase shifts in a circuit. Later on, it will be very important to match input and output impedance when working with transmission lines in order to get maximum power transfer.

THE RC TIME CONSTANT

In a circuit where there is capacitance, there is also always some resistance. The resistance may be in the form of a series resistor, some other component, or the wire itself. Capacitors do not instantly charge up. Depending on the amount of resistance in the circuit with the capacitor, there is a definite amount of time for the capacitor to hit 63 percent of full capacity (this is known as a time constant). There is another definite unit of time for the capacitor to charge to 86 percent (another full time constant), then 95 percent, 98 percent, 99 percent, and so on. Theoretically, the capacitor never reaches a *full* charge—it just approaches a full charge. The time constant (in seconds) is denoted by the Greek symbol *tau,* and in a series RC circuit, the formula is

$$\tau = RC \qquad\qquad \textbf{(Eq. 2–19)}$$

where R is in ohms and C is in Farads.

It is important to remember that when hooking up a voltmeter to a circuit that has a capacitor, the needle on the meter will take some time swinging, faster at first, then slower and slower until it finally appears to stop. This is because of the time constant involved in charging up the capacitor. Why is this important to a security engineer? Because some phone taps and other devices are hooked up to a phone line via a capacitor.

DECIBELS

Decibels are used frequently to express electrical quantities. The decibel scale is almost exactly the same as units to measure earthquakes or tornadoes and such. When working with very large quantity differences, and, in the case of power, voltage, logarithms are used with the designated unit of "bel." When talking about gain, loss, or ratios of power output to power input, the differences in normal numbers may be so great in quantity that it is easier to use a logarithmic value. Logarithms are also easier to work with when performing gain and loss calculations, thus we have the decibel. "Log" in the decibel formulas indicates the base ten logarithm.

$$dB = 10\log\frac{P_2}{P_1}$$

$$dB = 20\log\frac{V_2}{V_1} \qquad\qquad \textbf{(Eq. 2–20)}$$

Example 2–2

If an amplifier boosts a signal 50 times and the input is 1 watt, then the output would be 50 watts.

$dB = 10\log\dfrac{50}{1} = 10\log 50 = 10(1.699) = 16.99 dB$. The amplifier has a gain of nearly 17 dB. There are a couple of ratios that should be memorized. One is the value for either doubling or halving power. It does not matter whether it is from 1 to 2 or 500 to 1000; doubling the power is an increase of 3 dB. Halving the power is a decrease of 3 dB (or a factor of –3dB). Another ratio is 4 to 1 (or 1 to 4), which has an increase or decrease of 6 dB.

Table 2–3 demonstrates some common decibel values with power ratios.

Table 2–3 Decibel Values for Power Ratios

dB	Power Ration [P_2/P_1]
–20	10^{-2}
–10	0.1000
–6	0.25
–3	0.50
–1	0.79
0	1.000
1	1.259
3	2
6	4
10	10.00

What makes decibels so handy in electronics work is that gains and losses can be simply calculated by adding or subtracting decibels, respectively, and then as a last calculation, get back to the power gain or loss in watts or voltage in volts, etc. Complicated calculations become simple addition and subtraction problems.

A very common unit of measurement is the *dBm*. This is the logarithmic ratio of some power quantity compared to one milliwatt

$$dBm = 10\log\frac{P}{.001}$$

(Eq. 2–21)

This is a very convenient unit of measurement when working with test and measurement instruments. Even when a piece of equipment is labeled as having a safe amount of input power that the user should not exceed, that unit is expressed in dBm.

NON-LINEAR JUNCTIONS

The study of diodes, transistors, and integrated circuits is well beyond the scope of this book, but a discussion of *non-linear junctions* is necessary in order to understand how some technical surveillance countermeasures test equipment, such as a nonlinear junction detector (NLJD), operates.

First, what is a non-linear junction? To answer that, we will start by discussing a linear response to a phenomenon. If there were a lightbulb in a circuit that contained a variable resistance (like a dimmer switch), and a battery, the circuit could be completed by connecting the battery and this would, in turn, light the bulb. If the dimmer switch was moved back and forth (or round and round depending on the switch), the light would dim and brighten proportionately in response to the movements. This is a linear response.

There are devices in electronics that exhibit a non-linear response. It is this non-linear response that makes a lot of devices work—Many devices require a threshold *input* before they produce an *output,* such as a zener diode. Some devices produce a lot of output with only a small amount of input. Diodes, transistors, and most integrated circuits are non-linear devices, meaning they do not always produce a linear (or straight-line) output for a given input. Non-linear devices are found in virtually every electronic instrument or gadget. Sometimes a non linear response is produced from a signal fed into a non electronic component. For instance, a corroded junction between two pieces of metal can produce a non-linear response when subjected to an RF signal. This can be a problem when working with a non-linear junction detector, which will be discussed in a later chapter.

If a "bug" existed that could be turned on and off at will by a bad guy, it would be very hard to find. Using receivers or spectrum analyzers, the device would have to be on in order to be detected. If we had a device that could detect a non-linear junction, then we could look for anything, on or off, that has diodes or transistors, which most "bugs" do. When we talk about non-linear junction detectors, we will discuss how the instrument works to find these non-linear junctions.

SWITCHES

There are several types of systems that are discussed in this text. One is the basic alarm system. An alarm system is very simple in design, and can be integrated with an access control system. Whether large or small, the basic alarm system usually has a standard set of subsystems: *sensors* and *switches*, a *control unit*, and a type of *alarm*. The sensors and/or switches are configured in various ways to detect movement, temperature change, smoke, water pressure, and so on. The many different types of sensors will be covered in Chapter 7. The magnetic reed switch is a frequently-used type of sensor which merits discussing in this chapter. Door and window contacts typically are made up of two components; a magnet, and a switch, which can be set to normally closed or normally open. When the magnet is brought to close proximity, one side of the switch (a reed) will be pulled either away from or to the other side (depending on whether the switch is configured normally open or closed). This, of course, will change the state of the switch and send a signal down the line (or across the air via RF frequency) to the control panel, which will react accordingly. These switches are very inexpensive and are used in virtually every alarm system that exists. Alarm systems are made up of combinations of circuits. A circuit, by virtue of its name, is a loop. To make a loop with normally closed switches, the switches would be wired in series. When a switch is opened, it would break the normally closed circuit back at the control unit and sound an alarm. Alternatively, to wire a loop with normally open switches, they would be wired in parallel. In that case, if a switch closes, there is a short circuit in the normally open loop, and an alarm sounds. This choice allows us to keep the bad guys guessing, while allowing preference to the designer regarding the use of series, parallel, or combination switches. Television and movies have shown burglars bypassing magnetic switches using small jumper wires, but generally, the easiest way to bypass a magnetic switch (see Figure 2–9) is to place another magnet in the area of the one that will slide away when the door is opened or when the window is lifted. This essentially bypasses the switch so it detects no alarm. the idea is similar to holding something down with your left hand and then substituting your right hand for your left. It is always a good idea to supplement these switches with a secondary sensor, or a special "balanced magnetic" sensor.

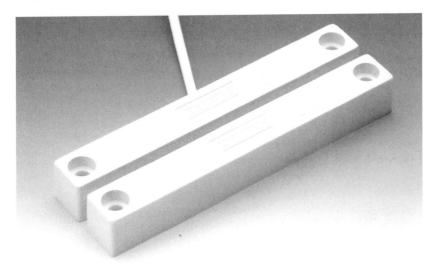

Figure 2–9   Magnetic contacts ©Honeywell International, Inc.

There are many different types of switches used in alarm systems, and their design is only limited by the imagination. Think for a moment of all the different things alarm systems are set up to detect,

- Motion
- Pressure
- Atmospheric Pressure Change
- Touch
- Water
- Wind Movement
- Temperature Change/Rate of Change
- Smoke or Heat

Just looking at these few categories, it is evident that the switches can be mechanical, electronic, virtual, or combinations.

RESONANT CIRCUITS

A circuit that contains both capacitance and inductance will have both inductive and capacitive reactance. This type of circuit is referred to as a tuned circuit. In a tuned circuit, there is a frequency that will cause both inductive and capacitive reactance to be identical, $X_L = X_C$. This is known as the *resonant frequency* of the circuit. The resonant frequency will be very important when we study wireless systems, smart cards, and the transmitters and receivers used with wireless cards.

At the resonant frequency

$$X_L = 2\pi fL = X_c = \frac{1}{2\pi fC} \qquad \textbf{(Eq. 2–22)}$$

where

f = Frequency in Hz

L = Inductance in Henrys

C = Capacitance in Farads

$\pi = 3.1416$

Solving for f, the resonant frequency of any combination of inductance and capacitance is found by the formula

$$f = \frac{1}{2\pi\sqrt{LC}} \qquad \textbf{(Eq. 2–23)}$$

We can modify the formula somewhat to provide for more convenience in working with high frequency (HF) radio

$$f = \frac{10^3}{2\pi\sqrt{LC}} \qquad \textbf{(Eq. 2–24)}$$

where

f = Frequency in megahertz (MHz)

L = Inductance in microHenrys (uH)

C = Capacitance in picoFarads (pF)

$\pi = 3.1416$

Example 2–3

What is the resonant frequency of a circuit having an inductor of 7.0 uH and a capacitor of 40 pF?

$$f = \frac{10^3}{2\pi LC} = \frac{10^3}{6.2832 \times \sqrt{7.0 \times 40}} = \frac{10^3}{105} = 9.5 MHz$$

A handy formula for determining the value of one unknown component (L or C) at resonance is

$$f^2 = \frac{1}{4\pi^2 LC}$$ (Eq. 2–25)

Example 2–4

What value of inductance is needed to make a resonant circuit at 9.5 MHz, if the capacitor is 40 pF?

$$f^2 = \frac{25 \times 10^{-3}}{L \times 40 \times 10^{-12}}$$

$$L = \frac{25 \times 10^{-3}}{f^2 \times 40 \times 10^{-12}}$$

$$L = \frac{625 \times 10^6}{90.25 \times 10^{12}} = 6.9 \times 10^{-6} = 6.9 \mu H$$

The important thing to know about resonance in our study of security devices is that a smart card can be designed so the antenna is resonant at a certain frequency. When the card comes into close proximity of a transmitter transmitting that frequency, the card is activated.

DIGITAL ELECTRONICS

So far, the types of electronic signals that we have been discussing have been *analog*. An analog signal is derived from the word "analogous," meaning "similar to." The output signal would be similar to or analogous to its input. For instance, the electric signal going across telephone lines would be in proportion and similar to the voice of the speaker on one end. An analog signal on an oscilloscope shows a constantly varying signal that rises and falls in synch with the input. Outside of electronics, analog is often called "linear" and is associated with time, temperature, pressure, wind speed, and sound. Think of analog as being the "real world" type of signal. We talk in analog, we hear in analog, and we move in analog. The only problem with analog is that if we are hearing a lot of static along with conversation, we are stuck with the static—we can try to filter it out, but that is difficult and takes a good bit of technology. If we amplify our analog signal, typically we are amplifying the static and other noise right along with the good part of the signal. If we remove the noise before amplification, the amplified signal will be somewhat corrupted from the original. This is where *digital* shines. A digital signal is easy to clean up, and once it is cleaned up, through amplication we can produce a signal that is identical to the original.

Digital differs from analog in that it is not constantly varying. It is in one of only two states. The states can be *on* and *off* (and can actually be a signal that is on or off), or *high* or *low*, or zero or one, or plus five volts or minus five volts, or plus five volts or zero volts. The point is, it is in either a first state or a second state—no other. Microprocessors use only digital technology. Microprocessors are the brains of computers, and computers perform all of their functions by using only on and off, or 1 and 0, or yes and no. These states are associated with Binary logic. When used with Boolean algebra, digital circuitry becomes decision circuitry.

EXAMPLE OF A TRUTH TABLE

In Boolean algebra, algebraic operations of + (addition) and × (multiplication) are replaced by logic operations of OR and AND. With these operations, we can create *truth tables*, which give values of a function for any possible input combination. A Boolean equation, as shown in Figure 2–10, is a shorthand way of writing a truth table.

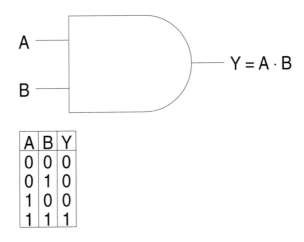

Figure 2–10   Boolean truth table.

BOOLEAN IDENTITIES

Algebra uses certain rules or "identities" such as association, addition, subtraction, multiplication, and division. The following are the Boolean algebra identities. Note that a bar over an entity means NOT. In other words a bar over A means "not" A.

$$A + (B + C) = (A + B) + C \text{ (Associative law for addition)}$$

$$A(BC) = (AB)C \text{ (Associative law for multiplication)}$$

$$\overline{A + B} = \overline{A}\overline{B} \text{ (DeMorgan's theorem for addition)}$$

$$\overline{ABC} = \overline{A} + \overline{B} + \overline{C} \text{ (DeMorgan's theorem for multiplication)}$$

$$A + 0 = A$$

$$A + A = 0$$

$$A + \overline{A} = 1$$

$$A \cdot 0 = 0$$

$$A \cdot 1 = A$$

$$A \cdot A = A$$

$$A \cdot \overline{A} = 0$$

$$A + AB = A$$

$$AB + A\overline{B} = A$$

$$\overline{(\overline{A})} = A$$

$$\overline{(A + B)}\,\overline{(\overline{A} + B)} = 0$$

$$B + A\overline{B} = A + B$$

As you can see, Boolean algebra is different from the algebra that we are used to. These identities are important in logic design and should be memorized by the designer.

Using Boolean algebra and logic design, functions like those that program a chip to perform certain outputs for various inputs can be created.

Example 2–5

IF I leave my car keys in the ignition *AND* open the door, *THEN* ring a bell. *IF* I leave the headlights on *AND* open the door, *THEN* ring a bell.

There are systems available that are combinations of hardware and software, and will allow a person to draw up a logic diagram on a computer screen, using Boolean logic, and then transfer this logic into a programmable chip via special hardware. This makes it very easy to design and build a decision circuit. A person can do this in his living room today, at an initial cost of under a thousand dollars, whereas about ten years ago, the only way these chips could be produced were via a semiconductor manufacturer, at a cost of hundreds of thousands of dollars for the equipment and overhead necessary.

Think of the possibilities for digital electronics in the security field. If a silent alarm is initiated, then a special emergency signal can be sent across phone lines to the sheriff. If smoke is detected, a unique message can be sent to the fire department notifying them where the smoke is coming from. If a window is broken in the middle of the night, then a message can be sent out to a monitoring station. There are hundreds of possibilities, all based on the digital operation of doing something with combinations of ones and zeros.

Since computers work digitally, and high speed networks use digital electronics, access control, alarm systems, and CCTV systems can now be easily interfaced to LANs and WANs. This capability is relatively recent, and because of it the industry has literally exploded with new and innovative technology. Only fifteen years ago, the last employee leaving the office would use a key to turn on the alarm system. Now personnel can use their photo ID keycards (smartcards) to access places, and arm alarm systems, all of which is passed through a computer system that logs the activities, and perhaps even puts the information into a database used for statistical purposes.

SUMMARY

This chapter reviews the electronics used with security systems.

■ One should be familiar with the units of measurement for various parameters; *volts* for voltage (or Electromotive Force—EMF as sometimes referred), *amperes* for current, *ohms* for resistance, *watts* for power. Most of the time, we are dealing with relatively low quantities of these, so we use a fractional measurement such as *milli*amps, or *micro*volts, or *milli*watts.

■ *Ohm's law* is a simple equation, which is used to calculate voltage, resistance, or current. Given two of the parameters, the third is easily determined. Power equations are used to determine power in watts.

■ *Kirchhoff's current law*: The current flowing into a branch is equal to the sum of the individual currents leaving the branch.

- *Kirchhoff's voltage law* accurately sums up the statement that the sum of the voltages in a closed circuit loop is zero.

- *Thevenin's theorem*: a single voltage source and a series resistor can replace any two terminal networks of resistors and voltage or current sources.

- When working with capacitors and inductors (coils), not only is there capacitance and inductance to consider, but also the resistance to current flow, which in this case is referred to as *reactance*.

- *Decibels* are used frequently to express electrical quantities. When talking about gain, loss, or ratios of power output to power input, the differences may be so great in quantity that it is easier to use a logarithmic value. Logarithms are also easier to work with when performing gain and loss calculations, thus we have the *decibel*.

- Switches are very inexpensive and are used in virtually every system that exists. Why do we have a choice of setting a switch to either normally open *or* normally closed? Alarm systems are made up of combinations of circuits. A circuit, by virtue of its name, is a *loop*. To make a loop with normally closed switches, the switches much be wired in *series*. When a switch is opened, it would break the normally closed circuit back at the control unit and sound an alarm. Alternatively, a loop with normally open switches would have them in parallel, then if a switch closes, there would be a short circuit in the normally open loop, and an alarm would sound.

- A circuit that contains both capacitance and inductance will have both inductive and capacitive reactance. This type of circuit is referred to as a *tuned* circuit. In a tuned circuit, there is a frequency that will cause both inductive and capacitive reactance to be identical, $X_L = X_C$. This is referred to as the *resonant frequency* of the circuit.

- Since computers work digitally, and high speed networks use digital electronics, access control, alarm systems, and CCTV systems can now be interfaced to LANs and WANs.

KEY TERMS

Amperes

Ohms

Watts

Alternating Current

Direct Current

Ohm's Law

Resistors in Parallel

Kirchhoff's Current Law

Kirchhoff's Voltage Law

Voltage Source

Voltage Drop

Voltage Divider

Frequency

Harmonic Frequencies

Carrier Frequency

Frequency Modulated

Amplitude Modulated

Phase Modulated

Reactance

Decibels

Dbm

Non-Linear Junctions

Resonant Frequency

Analog

Digital

Truth Tables

DISCUSSION QUESTIONS

1   What are the various units of measurement for the following:

Power, Resistance, Current, Electromotive Force, Inductance, Capacitance, Impedance?

2   Express the following in terms of powers of 10:

Micro, nano, femto, giga, milli, pico, mega, tera, kilo

3   In terms of Ohm's law what are the differences in performing calculations for AC versus DC?

4   What does DC look like on an oscilloscope? AC? What would the waveform look like if we added an AC signal to DC?

5   Without performing any calculation, what could be said about the total resistance in a circuit consisting of two resistors in parallel, where R1 = 20 kohms and R2 = 1 Mohms?

6   Calculate total resistance for the circuit:

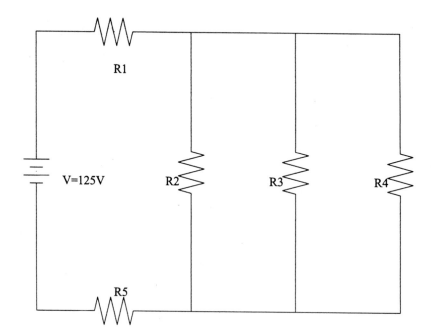

R1 = 100, R2 = 50, R3 = 1 K, R4 = 750, R5 = 1 M

7 If capacitors of value = 50 pF (C1, C2, C3) were put just below each of the parallel resistors, R2, R3, and R4, what would be the total DC resistance of the circuit?

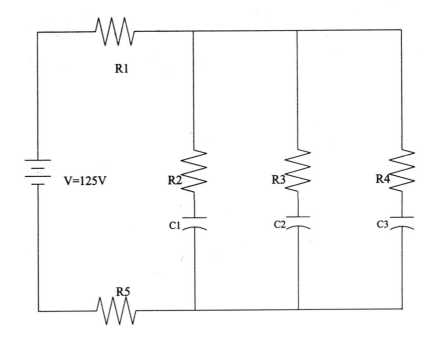

8 Using the circuit from question 7, if frequency f = 12MHz,

What is the total capacitance?

What is the capacitive reactance?

What is the impedance of the circuit?

9 How is a square wave made?

10 What is a *carrier* signal? Explain *modulation*.

11 Why is it easier to calculate gains and losses using *decibels*?

12 Explain how a capacitor charges.

13 What is a 6dB gain?

14 If power input of 1 watt goes through a gain of 30 dB, a loss of 6 dB, and then another loss of 4 dB, what is the power output in watts?

15 Explain dBm. If a spectrum analyzer has a label by the input connector that states, "+15 dBm max", what does that mean?

RESEARCH QUESTIONS

1 The wall outlets of homes use alternating current (AC). Why do we need direct current (DC)? Why is AC not used for all our electrical requirements?

2 What is the origin of the term *Boolean*?

3 Matching output impedance to input impedance is important for maximum power transfer in security devices. Where else is this power transfer important? Without considering *power transfer,* why else would we want a high impedance input?

CHAPTER 3

Communications Systems

PURPOSE AND OBJECTIVES

Communications systems for security are multifaceted. First, the system must communicate with a human. Second, parts of the system must communicate with each other. Third, external entities must be able to communicate with the system.

Communications can be simple, such as a security officer talking to her supervisor. The same security officer may communicate electronically with the system itself, by passing her guard tour wand over an electronic sensor. This action will record that the security officer was at a certain location at a certain time, and was diligently patrolling her stations. The security officer speaking into a 2-way FM radio to another person some distance away is an example of human communication to an electronic source that then communicates that message back to another human.

One may communicate simply by speech, by wire, radio frequency, lightwave, or by a sound other than speech (such as a siren). We will study some of these different methods and learn why and when they are used.

After you have finished this chapter, you should be familiar with:

- Types of communications
- Types of communications methods

- Differences between wire and wireless communications
- Categories of wires
- Categories of wireless technology
- Data communications
- Idea of bandwidth
- Spread spectrum methods
- Binary numbers
- Error checking
- The OSI platform

SPEECH

Duck! This one word contains much meaning; even without a reference to birds. The simplest and most often used form of communication in security is direct voice communication. I use the term direct here, because the voice is transmitted using wire line, radio frequency, and lightwave technologies, among others. Direct voice means voice goes straight from the vocal cords of one person to the ears of another. We use voice related access control in our day-to-day lives. There is a knock on a locked door, a voice from inside asks, "Who is it?" there is a reply, and the door is unlocked and opened. Another example—a car drives up to a security post at a military base. The Military Police officer on duty asks to see a driver's license, and whom the visitor will be seeing. The driver shows a license, responds with details about an appointment on the base, and is subsequently allowed through the gate.

WIRE LINE COMMUNICATIONS

Children have often tried to communicate with a friend using a homemade telephone of sorts, involving two cans, two buttons, and some string. The string runs through a hole in the bottom of the can on either end. Buttons fasten to the ends of the string, so the button will rest against the bottom of the can preventing the string from slipping back out. When the string stretches taught, and the can is brought up to the ear, the bottom of the can vibrates in proportion to the voice talking into the can at the other end. Voila! Basic wire line (string line?) analog communications. Now that we are older, and more sophisticated, we use electricity with our wires in a very similar system to that of the string and can. We do not have to stretch the wire taught anymore, but occasionally, we still bring the receiver to our ears. We use a modulated electric signal to carry a voice across the line, but we still vibrate some kind of material to make sound. Even with some digital data communication such as Morse code (Morse Code is digital in that it facilitates a simple "on" or "off" or "high" and "low" signal), we still result in a vibration. More commonly, with data however, the electric signal feeds directly to some device such as a computer or a sensor, without ever being heard by the human ear.

Data communications is digital in nature, a series of ons and offs, or 1s and 0s. Security systems often use this signal. To what types of security systems am I referring? Intrusion alarm systems, fire alarm systems, access control systems, guard tour systems, these can all use wire from control box to sensor, or from control box to annunciator, or from control box to telephone line. Combinations of digital and analog signals are sent over wire for *CCTV*. The digital portion can be used to control the camera's pan and tilt functions and analog for the picture itself; although, more and more often, even the picture information is being sent digitally.

Depending on the system requirements, many different types of wire are used. If the system only needs basic voice communications, sent via an analog electric signal, then a pair of twisted copper wires, such as the type used for a home telephone will be enough. The wire is twisted to prevent radiation of unwanted electromagnetics that may be induced into other nearby wires. If we want to send a data signal across the wire at a high speed, such as 10 Mbs (that is 10 million bits per second, where each on or off signal is a bit), then we would use a cable that is categorized as either category 3 or 4 cable. The cable in these categories is manufactured and tested to specifications that assure it can transmit efficiently at a certain rate. Cable in categories 5, 5e and 6 is used for higher speeds. Table 3–1 shows some of the different cable categories for Local Area Networks (LANs).

Wired systems are secure as long as they are protected from access by unauthorized people. They can be tapped, meaning a pair of wires can be connected or *bridged*, and information going across the cable can be diverted somewhere else for eavesdropping purposes. Fiber optic cable is much more secure, and wireless is much less secure.

Table 3–1 Categories 5e and up are Designed for Speeds of up to 1000 Mbps

Category	Application/Speed
1	Analog and Voice (UTP) Unshielded Twisted Pair (UTP)
2	Digital Voice, 1Mbps Data (UTP)
3	16Mbps Data (UTP/STP) Shielded Twisted Pair (STP)
4	20 Mbps Data (UTP/STP)
5 5e	100 Mbps Data (UTP/STP) 100 Mbps+ Data (UTP/STP)
6	100 Mbps+ Data (Coax) Coaxial Cable (Coax)
7	100 Mbps+ Data (Fiber optic)

Supplementing any of these methods with encryption makes them more secure.

It is easiest to run the wiring for a security system during construction of the facility. Running cable through an existing structure can be difficult, and sometimes impossible. For example, in the Washington, DC area, many buildings are designated historic sites, which makes it impossible to do any hidden cabling in them.

Keep in mind there will always be some cabling involved with a security system, even if the cabling is limited to a patch panel, or a control box.

RADIO FREQUENCY (RF)

There are times when it is impossible to run wire from point A to point B. There are also times when it is necessary to be mobile without dragging wires along. These are the times when it becomes useful to use radio frequency communications.

There are many different types of radio transmitters and receivers, and they operate on various frequencies depending on needs. Generally speaking, lower radio frequencies provide longer-range communications than the higher frequencies, but the higher frequencies tend to be more stable and reliable over their shorter range (see Table 3–2).

Table 3-2 Ranges for Various Frequency Bands

RF Band	Frequency Range	Coverage
High Frequency (HF)	3–30 MHz	Very long distances (to thousands of miles)
VHF Low Band	25–50 MHz and 72–76 MHz	Moderate distances depending on antenna and other factors. (Typically 5–150 miles)
VHF High Band	150–216 MHz	Short distances—just a bit more than line of sight, typically 2–30 miles depending on antenna and other factors.
UHF	Over 300 MHz	Short distances, typically line of sight. Popular with repeaters.
UHF/Microwave	Approx 800 MHz and up	Up to 3GHz, part of UHF band, but usually referred to as microwave because of the very short wavelength. Limited completely to line of sight
Satellite Band	Over 3 GHz	Line of sight used for short distances or space communications.

CHARACTERISTICS OF DIFFERENT FREQUENCY BANDS

As frequencies rise and fall, they take on different characteristics. Some frequencies will allow radio waves to travel farther than others, some will penetrate the ion layer above the earth, and some penetrate concrete walls better than others do. Radio frequencies have been grouped into different bands, which exhibit similar characteristics.

THE HF BAND

The *High Frequency (HF)* communications band stretches from three to 30 MHz, and is used for long-distance communications. There are two components to an HF radio signal: a ground wave and a sky wave. The ground wave emanates from the antenna, and follows along the surface of the earth. This wave travels anywhere from about a quarter mile to a couple of hundred miles, depending on the composition of the ground, the height and type of antenna, the power output of the transmitter, the efficiency of the system, and a few other factors. The sky wave shoots up at an angle from the antenna, bounces back from the ionosphere[1], hits the earth and bounces up, and so on, and so forth. This bouncing can repeat for thousands of miles (see Figure 3–1).

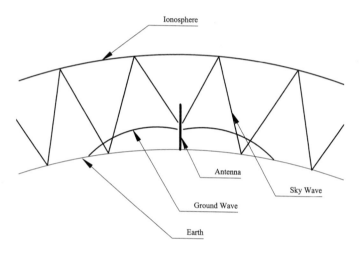

Figure 3–1 Sky wave and ground wave.

In the coverage area where there is both a ground wave and a sky wave, the sky wave may hit the earth in phase with the ground wave, or out of phase with the ground wave. This is what causes fading in and out. Skywaves can cause problems in broadcasting. Spectrum is limited and broadcast stations tend to be local; "skip" would cause all kinds of interference in the band. Why would it create broadcast skip? The higher ionosphere causes a more severe angle of incidence for HF radio waves and allows them to "skip" back down to earth. The lower the HF frequency, the more ground wave there is. Broadcast frequencies that are under the HF band are usually all ground wave (until the ionosphere rises at night), and then we pick up some of that bouncing up and down, so-called broadcast skip. Many of us have heard radio stations from far away at night with a signal that we can't pick up during the day. People who use HF frequencies for

1. The ionosphere is the region of the atmosphere that extends from about 30 miles above the surface of the Earth to about 250 miles. It is named the ionosphere because it consists of several layers of electrically charged gas atoms called ions.

long-range communications pay close attention to propagation charts produced by the government. These charts consider things such as sunspot activity, weather patterns, time of year, time of day, frequency, and other factors in order to predict the effectiveness of communications (see Figure 3–2).

BASE: Canberra- Mideast   Date: 22 June, 2003
IPS Radio and Space Services
Hourly Area Prediction (HAP)

Mhz   2.0   4.0   6.0   8.0   10.0 12.0 14.0 16.0 18.0 22.0 28.0   no suitable freq.

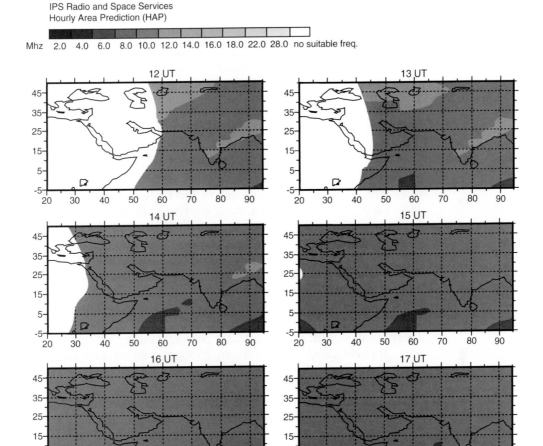

Figure 3–2   Propagation chart for Canberra, Courtesy of IPS Radio and Space Services.

Before satellites, HF communications were used extensively for communications across the oceans or from coast to coast. The mode dropped off with the increasing availability of satellites but has recently had somewhat of a rejuvenation due to the overcrowding of satellites, and the newer, more efficient types of communications equipment that have allowed it to become more reliable. HF is typically static laden, but some of the new digital methods of communicating allow for error checking and retransmission that overcomes the static problem.

VHF COMMUNICATIONS

VHF Communications provides distances that are slightly greater than line of sight. One is led to ask, "Why would anyone use such a limited distance mode of communications?" The answer is that this type of communications is noise free and reliable—not a slave to all the propagation difficulties faced by the HF communicator. VHF (and UHF) frequencies are used for Air/Ground/Air communications, with UHF used mainly by the military. Quite a distance can be covered by using the proper antennas and repeaters. VHF is used extensively by federal, state, and local government agencies. Its area of coverage with the use of repeaters and high antenna locations is ideal for a metropolitan area. After all, there are only a limited amount of frequencies available (this is known as *limited spectrum*). If long distance HF was used by these agencies, you can imagine all the noise and interference that would take place because the various agencies would be "stepping all over" each other. There are two types of VHF, Low Band and High Band. Low band will provide long-distance coverage, about one hundred to one hundred and fifty miles in this case. With the right antenna, a good deal of antenna height, and significant transmitter power, trucking companies, asphalt pavers, and others who are mobile often use Low Band communications. Repeaters are seldom used for Low Band except by the government (usually federal government, or state patrol). High Band is more suitable for security use, and is the preferable mode for local government. Government agencies use repeaters with High Band.

REPEATERS

A repeater is a radio transceiver that receives a signal on one frequency (Frequency A) and retransmits it on another (Frequency B), as seen in Figure 3–3. The repeater is usually located at a high place such as a building roof, or mountaintop. Theoretically, a person talking into a five watt "walkie-talkie" which could normally communicate about

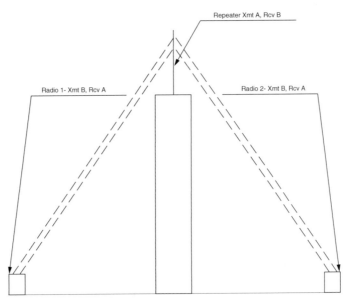

Repeater Xmt A, Rcv B

Radio 1- Xmt B, Rcv A

Radio 2- Xmt B, Rcv A

Figure 3–3   Repeater and radio frequency configurations.

1–2 miles, can go through a repeater and cover as much as 50–60 miles!

Most walkie-talkie types of 2-way FM radios have both repeater frequency and *talk around* frequency modes. A toggle switch will change over the receiver frequency so the two units can talk to one another directly, bypassing the repeater. Changing the frequency allows the users privacy, but more importantly, keeps them from tying up the repeater, as only one person at a time can use it.

There are different types of repeaters. Some just facilitate the basic frequencies and are open to all, while others will only accept traffic from units that also send a subaudible tone authorizing their use. With some repeaters, everyone can hear all conversations; others have a provision for filters, which only allow certain transmissions to be heard—there may be another transmission taking place, which would corrupt or "step on" your transmission if the filter were not present. To prevent transmissions from "stepping on each other," some repeaters now are *trunked*. When the transmit key on the microphone is pressed, it queues up for the next transmission opportunity. A tone tells you when to go ahead and speak. Thus, you are time-sharing.

UHF COMMUNICATIONS

UHF communications are similar to VHF. Distances covered are similar between the High Band portion of VHF and UHF. UHF also uses repeaters, which are used extensively for commercial business. It generally is illegal for a commercial business to use a VHF repeater.

Which mode should be used for voice communications for security work? Government agencies qualify for the use of VHF repeaters. Most commercial businesses must stick with UHF. Also, UHF has a shorter wavelength than VHF. These shorter waves can penetrate and sneak through building structures (steel and concrete) better than their longer wavelength counterparts without creating *multi-path*[2] interference. In a downtown metro area, the highest frequency band available is usually the best choice. On a sprawling suburban campus, lowest possible frequency band is a better choice in order to gain the extra distance. Incidentally, it was mentioned before that HF communications bounce back and forth off of the ionosphere. VHF and UHF communications will go *through* the ionosphere and out into space, so it is useful for communicating with satellites, spaceships, and people walking around on the moon.

So far, we have been talking about 2-way *voice* communications and the information has pertained to the needs of security officers. The next subject will be data communications, where we will see more use of *digital* communications than of *analog*. Remember, analog is a real world mode where the electrical signals are analogous to the voice. Digital brings us to the world of binary operations and a great deal of reliability for data communications.

DATA COMMUNICATIONS

Data communications is generally associated with the equipment part of security. Some examples of things that communicate data digitally are smart cards, access control readers, alarm systems, many CCTV systems especially those with hard disk storage, and bar code readers. Digital communications is much easier to encrypt than

---

2. When a signal bounces off of walls or other barriers, interferences are generated, and the signal reaches its destination at different times. This is called multipath difference. This kind of interference affects RF systems. A subset of multipath is Rayleigh fading. This happens when signals are arriving from different directions and the difference in path length is a multiple of half the wavelength. This can cancel the signal completely, so it is dangerous.

analog, and much easier to clean up if it has been subjected to noise or signal attenuation. Communication in the digital world is very reliable. Although used for analog as well as digital, spread spectrum communications are very often used for transmitting digital data in the security world.

A simple digital data communications device is part of most moderately priced home security systems. The controller or an add-on communicator contains a programmed microprocessor that will send a digital chain of pulses to a phone number. The telephone line is seized by a device called an RJ-31X phone jack, when the security controller dials out. This prevents a thief from simply taking a telephone "off the hook" in the house to prevent an outbound call. The controller sends out a string of data that is interpreted at a monitoring location, and shows the type of alarm, the name and address on the account, and the specific alarm point. All this information is put on a computer screen where the action procedure is also indicated. The action procedure is information about local police, fire, or ambulance telephone numbers, whether the customer should or should not be contacted first, etc. This is very basic digital data communication that can also be sent via cell phone as a backup to the land line method. Incidentally, this type of alarm system will generally send out an alarm code to the monitoring station if the line is cut or damaged, or if any *tamper switch* on the system has been disturbed.

In a commercial environment, data communications between alarm and access control systems, and computers, is set up over the Local Area Network (LAN), or Wide Area Network (WAN). There are various software packages available which are flexible as to the system setup. A security manager, working in concert with a LAN administrator can set up a system similar to the following scenario:

Today is Jane Doe's first day on the job at the XYZ Corporation. After visiting the human resources office, her first task is to have her picture taken at the security desk. The picture is put on her data file. Human resources has already provided security with Jane's personal data, position data, rooms and stations where she has access privileges, and hours (and days) when she may enter the building. The security manager provides Jane with a photo ID card including a built-in *smart chip* which will activate the parking gate, and access control devices throughout the building. She may even be able to credit money to the card and use it like a debit card in XYZ's employee cafeteria. The card will also log her comings and goings so, if it is ever deemed necessary, a rerun of her activities can be produced. Digital data is transmitted every time Jane uses the card, or when she walks past a receiver site. Later, we will talk about how a card can transmit information even when it does not have its own power supply (battery) built in.

In a more sophisticated system, Jane may have to have her iris or retina scanned to allow entry into a certain secure area. Data from this scan could be in the form of many millions of bits of digital information that has to be sent over the LAN and then be compared to information in a database. All this communicating has to happen quickly because there may be fifty more people standing in line behind Jane waiting for their own retinas to be scanned.

An example of a high-density *biometric* system is one in which a camera looks at the eyes of many people and then compares the scans to a huge database, such as in an effort to locate a terrorist in a crowd. In this case, in order to be useful, data must practically fly across the lines, and be formatted in such a way so as to be accessible by super-computers that could perform multiple analyses quickly enough to create an alarm in the event that it does find a known terrorist in that crowd. If this system is not fast enough, the bad guy gets away before anyone knows he is there. This particular system would also most likely be a combination of wires, fiber optics, radios, LANs and WANs.

Demands for higher and higher speed in communication, call for better and better technology. Transmitting over wire lines or via RF means that we must use electrical signals. The problem with electricity is that when we produce a digital one or *on* signal, there is a certain amount of time to get the signal to its *on* value. This time is called *rise time*. There is also *fall time* on the other side of the pulse. Normally electricity is fast. In a vacuum, electricity would travel at the speed of light, but the world is not a vacuum. In the real world electricity actually travels slower than the speed of light, how much slower depends on the *velocity of propagation* factor. This factor changes for different materials. When we transmit at very, very high speeds (billions and billions of bits per second), the rise and fall times of electricity would round out our nice square shaped pulses, and eventually corrupt them to the point of uselessness. Think of a pulse rising instantly and falling instantly—this would produce a square pattern. Injecting rise time and fall time would put a slope on either side (taking away that squareness) In the real world then, how do we get back to the speed of light? How about using light! By using fiber optics, we do just that. Table 3–3 lists some data rates for copper (T1, T2, T3,T4, DS1, DS2, DS3, DS4), DSL, Cable, and fiber (OC) lines.

Table 3–3 Speeds of Transmission for Various OC Categories

Connection	Speed (per second)
ISDN1 / DS-0	64 Kb
ISDN2	128 Kb
Fixed Wireless Upload	256 Kb
G.Lite ADSL Upload	384 Kb
ADSL Upload	768 Kb
G.Lite ADSL Download	1.5 Mb
T1/DS1	1.544 Mb
Fixed Wireless Download	5 Mb
ADSL Download	6.144 Mb
T2/DS2	6.312 Mb
Cable (Up)	10 Mb (approx)
Cable (Down)	27 Mb (approx)
T3/DS3	44.7 Mb
OC1	51.48 Mb
OC3	155.5 Mb
T4/DS4	275 Mb
OC9	466.6 Mb
OC12	622 Mb
OC18	933.12 Mb
OC24	1.244 Gb
OC36	1.866 Gb
OC48	2.5 Gb
OC96	4.976 Gb
OC192	9.952 Gb
OC255	13.271 Gb
OC768	39,813 Gb

It is apparent that the OC (Fiber) modes are much faster than the copper (T/DS) modes or the Cable/DSL modes. It will soon be common to have fiber run all the way into the residence or office from the phone company.

If fiber optic cable is so fast, why isn't it used for all communications? There are other factors to consider—cost, accessibility, mobility. The 802.11 standards, developed by the IEEE[3], provide for efficient data communications for computers and peripheral devices in the increasingly popular wireless method of communication. There are also other standards such as Bluetooth™.

Here is an excerpt from the FCC that covers some interesting information concerning wireless technology:

Federal Communications Commission Spectrum Policy Task Force

Report of the Unlicensed Devices and Experimental Licenses Working Group

.... The growing popularity of computer networking has stimulated a heightened interest in unlicensed technology and one of the fastest growing applications of unlicensed devices is for wireless local area networks (WLANS). Because most businesses and many homes now have multiple computers, users often find it desirable to install local area networks to share resources such as printers, scanners and broadband or dialup Internet connections. Developing a local area network using wireless unlicensed devices can be cost attractive when compared with the costs of wired networks and offers the added benefit of instant portability.

The same *spread spectrum* technology that has been used for cordless telephones and other unlicensed devices has been adapted to meet the surging demand for computer and data networking. Among the more popular of these unlicensed devices are wireless data devices that operate in the 2.4 GHz band in accordance with the *802.11b or "WiFi"* standards and protocols developed by the LAN/MAN Standards Committee (LMSC) of the Institute of Electrical and Electronic Engineers. Unlicensed devices operating under the 802.11b/WiFi protocols can be used to link computers or other digital devices at distances up to about 150 feet and with data rates of up to 11 Mbps. Other IEEE protocols have recently been developed, such as 802.11a which operates at 5 GHz and 802.11g which is an extension of 802.11b, that provides even higher data rates. Another unlicensed wireless networking standard is *Home RF* developed by the HomeRF Working Group. This technology provides data capabilities similar to WiFi but also includes voice capability.

---

3. Institute of Electrical and Electronic Engineers

Federal Communications Commission Spectrum Policy Task Force (Continued)

Unlicensed consumer devices are also being developed to provide very short range (on the order of 10 meters) wireless "personal area" networks (WPANs). "Bluetooth," which uses 2.4 GHz spread spectrum frequency hopping technology, is the dominant WPAN technology at this time. Bluetooth devices are beginning to be included in many devices such as mobile radiotelephones, laptop computers, printers and personal digital assistants (PDAs) and some experts believe that it could become a standard feature in many consumer electronic devices.

Finally, other unlicensed technologies such as power line carrier (PLC) systems that use the electric power lines to transmit data and ultra wideband (UWB) devices are being developed and hold great promise for providing consumers with new data and computer networking capabilities.

The Synergy Research Group recently reported that the wireless LAN market posted its eighth consecutive quarter of double digit growth and that total growth from 2000 has been over 150 percent. It estimates that over 5 million unlicensed wireless LAN devices were shipped in 2001 and predicts that 21 million Americans will be using wireless LAN devices by 2007.

Gartner Research predicts that by 2006 approximately $5.6 billion per year will he spent on Bluetooth technology and more than 560 million Bluetooth enabled devices will be purchased by businesses and consumers. It is estimated that by 2004 over 45 million business laptop computers will use the WiFi standard. Analysts project that by 2007 there will be over 90 million WiFi enabled devices worldwide and over 40 million people roaming in WiFi hotspots....

SPREAD SPECTRUM

Reference has been made to *spread spectrum* technology. In Frequency Hopping Spread Spectrum (FHSS), an information signal, usually a data stream, modulates a radio frequency carrier that is hopped among a number of frequencies in concert with a receiver. For example, if we have frequencies 1,2,3,4,and 5, an algorithm can be produced at both the transmitter and receiver ends for our transmission to hop thusly, in 2 millisecond intervals: 1,4,3,5,2. In Direct Sequence Spread Spectrum (DSSS), the information data stream is combined with a high speed digital spreading code that is used to modulate a radio carrier, producing a radio signal that has a *band-width* covering anywhere from 1 to 100 MHz. In DSSS our signal would simply be spread out over frequencies 1,2,3,4, and 5—no hopping—just spread out, but ideally, we would have to "gather it all together" at the receiver end to get the transmitted signal faithfully reproduced. Both frequency hopping and direct sequence systems are permitted to use output powers of up to one watt in the 802.11 or Bluetooth bands, however, most devices use lower power for various design reasons, such as conserving battery life. Spread spectrum modulation reduces the power density of the transmitted signal at any frequency, thereby reducing the possibility of causing interference to other signals occupying the same spectrum. Similarly, at the receiver end, the power density of interfering signals is minimized, making spread spectrum systems relatively immune to interference from outside sources.

The FCC, in its Docket Nr 99-231 goes on to say,

> ...The Commission's spread spectrum rules have been a tremendous success. A wide variety of devices have been introduced under these rules for business and consumer use including cordless telephones and computer local area networks. Moreover, the past few years have witnessed the development of industry standards, such as IEEE 802.11b, Bluetooth, and Home RF, that promise to greatly expand the number and variety of devices that will operate in the 2.4GHz band. We anticipate the introduction of wireless headsets and computer connections for cellular and PCS phones, wireless computer peripherals such as printers and keyboards, and a host of new wireless Internet appliances that will use this band as well as the other bands that provide for unlicensed operation.

Since the time the spread spectrum rules were first introduced some 15 years ago, the Commission has amended the rules several times to accommodate technology developments and promote new and innovative use of the 915 MHz, 2.4 GHz, and 5.7 GHz bands. Over the years, the data rates achievable by spread spectrum devices have increased from a few kilobits per second to 20 megabits per second, and more. These high data rates were not envisioned when the rules were first drafted. In fact, the original rules were crafted in a manner to highlight the interference immunity characteristics of spread spectrum devices, even at the expense of higher speeds. It appears that our current rules may unnecessarily restrict system designs that could otherwise achieve data rates of more than 20 megabits per second.

BANDWIDTH

Bandwidth is the amount of information that can be sent over a medium in a set amount of time. In the digital world, bandwidth is expressed in bits per second, or sometimes in bytes per second. Regarding analog, bandwidth is expressed in cycles per second. Old radio operators have no problem understanding bandwidth, it is simply the highest frequency used minus the lowest frequency used. For instance, if the center frequency of a transmission was 150 MHz, and the transmission varied 2.5 KHz on either side of the center, the bandwidth would be 5 KHz. The frequency of operation would vary from 149,997,500 Hz up to 150,002,500 Hz. Expressed another way

$$150,002,500 - 149,997,500 = 5,000 \text{ Hz (or 5KHz)}$$

If we were to watch this signal on a spectrum analyzer with the center frequency tuned to 150MHz, we would *see* the signal bouncing between the two frequency limits in the equation. When we get into technical surveillance countermeasures, we will use a spectrum analyzer to look at the RF frequency spectrum. Getting back to bandwidth, looking at the signal on a spectrum analyzer, and seeing all the variations that can take place within the two frequency limits is a good example of analog, or *broadband* signals. When we have a slot of bandwidth available and use it for multiple channels or multiple frequencies facilitating analog, we are using *broadband signal transmission*. Now, if we were to send one signal across the airwaves (or through the wire), and needed a pipeline that would be X cycles per second wide (for instance 5 KHz wide), meaning it could slide X cycles through the pipe in a second, then we are talking *Baseband Transmission Mode*. The entire bandwidth is used for *one signal*, and that signal would be *digital*. The signal (cycles) that were traveling through the pipe would be either on or off at any given time, but would be able to switch on or off at the bandwidth speed.

BINARY

We have mentioned 0s and 1s, or offs and ons, or highs and lows, several times already and said that these states were all useful for digital communications. How? Simply, we can use the binary number system, where there is only the possibility of using a 1 or a 0 in the system. If we were to send signals across a line in groups of seven numbers, and only used 1s or 0s (or high and low electrical signals), then we could be sending the *ASCII* code (Table 3–4).

Table 3–4 ASCII Chart

Binary	Hex	Char	Binary	Hex	Char
0000000	00	NUL	0100000	20	SP
0000001	01	SOH	0100001	21	!
0000010	02	STX	01000010	22	"
0000011	03	ETX	0100011	23	#
0000100	04	EOT	0100100	24	$
0000101	05	ENQ	0100101	25	%
0000110	06	ACK	0100110	26	&
0000111	07	BEL	0100111	27	'
0001000	08	BS	0101000	28	(
0001001	09	HT	0101001	29	)
0001010	0A	LF	0101010	2A	*
0001011	0B	VT	0101011	2B	+
0001100	0C	FF	0101100	2C	,
0001101	0D	CR	0101101	2D	-
0001110	0E	SI	0101111	2F	/
0010000	10	DLE	0110000	30	0
0010001	11	DC1	0110001	31	1
0010010	12	DC2	0110010	32	2
0010011	13	DC3	0110011	33	3
0010100	14	DC4	0110100	34	4
0010101	15	NACK	0110101	35	5
0010110	16	SYN	0110110	36	6
0010111	17	ETB	0110111	37	7
0011000	18	CAN	0111000	38	8
0011001	19	EM	0111001	39	9
0011010	1A	SUB	0111010	3A	:
0011011	1B	ESC	0111011	3B	;
0011100	1C	FS	0111100	3C	<
0011101	1D	GS	0111101	3D	=
0011110	1E	RS	0111110	3E	<
0011111	1F	US	0111111	3F	?

Table 3–4 ASCII Chart (Continued)

Binary	Hex	Char	Binary	Hex	Char
1000000	40	@@	1100000	60	'
1000001	41	A	1100001	61	a
1000010	42	B	1100010	62	b
1000011	43	C	1100011	63	c
1000100	44	D	1100100	64	d
1000101	45	E	1100101	65	e
1000110	46	F	1100110	66	f
1000111	47	G	1100111	67	g
1001000	48	H	1101000	68	h
1001001	49	I	1101001	69	i
1001010	4A	J	1101010	6A	j
1001011	4B	K	1101011	6B	k
1001100	4C	L	1101100	6C	l
1001101	4D	M	1101101	6D	m
1001111	4F	O	1101111	6F	o
1010000	50	P	1110000	70	p
1010001	51	Q	1110001	71	q
1010010	52	R	1110010	72	r
1010011	53	S	1110011	73	s
1010100	54	T	1110100	74	t
1010101	55	U	1110101	75	u
1010110	56	V	1110110	76	v
1010111	57	W	1110111	77	w
1011000	58	X	1111000	78	x
1011001	59	Y	1111001	79	y
1011010	5A	Z	1111010	7A	z
1011011	5B	[	1111011	7B	[
1011100	5C	\	1111100	7C	\
1011101	5D	]	1111101	7D	}
1011110	5E	^	1111110	7E	~
1011111	5F	_	1111111	7F	DEL

Just looking at this code, and knowing how we can send it across electrical lines or airwaves should make it very clear how computers can literally talk to each other. Because this ASCII code uses numbers (binary, but still numbers!), these numbers can be manipulated mathematically in many different ways, using many different types of mathematical algorithms, to *encrypt*, or encode, the information sent. Earlier we mentioned that digital is easy to encrypt; now you can see why.

ERROR CHECKING

When one person says something to another, if the second person does not understand, she can simply say, "What?" and the original message would be repeated. In data communications, one computer cannot say, "What?" to the other (at least not the way we do it), so we must have a way of error checking to make sure the message got to its destination uncorrupted. Again, thank goodness for binary digital signals. Since we are dealing with numbers (ones and zeros), we can produce some mathematical algorithm to check for error detection. The easiest way to do this is to use the *parity check*. In ASCII, we sent seven bits across the wires (or air) to designate a character, letter, or number. We could add one more digit to use as an error-checking bit. For instance, if we had an even number of ones in the seven digits, we may add another one (1) as a parity check. If the number of ones in the seven digit group was odd, then we could add a zero (0). This is a simple method of checking parity, and a good introduction to error checking, but it will not give us a hundred percent assurance that everything was correct. This method was used often in the teletype days, but now with the speed of modern computers and communications systems, there are many other mathematical methods for error checking that are much more reliable (and much more complicated). Some of these methods are; *Block Check Character*, which uses both horizontal and vertical parity bits from blocks of communication, *Cyclic Redundancy Check* (CRC) which is the most common method and uses modulo-2 addition to calculate frame check sequences, CRC Polynomial (which starts to get really complex) and many, many other methods. With some of the complex error checking methods, we can get to well over 99 percent efficiency.

THE OSI PLATFORM

OSI stands for *Open Systems Interface*. This platform spells out certain standards and methods that computers across a network use in order to communicate with each other. Although this platform is usually associated with the subject of networking, it should be recognized that when two or more entities communicate with each other, a *de facto* network has formed.

There are entire books devoted to the OSI platform, but for these purposes all that we need to know is that it is composed of seven layers, and each layer communicates in some way to the matching layer of the system with which we are communicating. If one person speaks only Italian and another only German, they wouldn't understand each other. Similarly, since many computers run on different operating systems, the International Organization for Standardization developed the OSI model to provide for built in "interpreters." Computers certainly do not speak Italian or German to each other, but they do speak Apple or Microsoft, so the OSI model (see Figure 3–4) is a means of providing communications that are common to all the operating systems. A description of each layer follows:

■ Layer 7, the Application Layer, handles semantics. It is not associated with applications such as MS Word, or Quickbooks, or those types of applications.

■ Layer 6, the Presentation Layer, takes care of Syntax. This is where things like cryptography are.

■ Layer 5, the Session Layer, coordinates dialog between the two computers.

■ Layer 4, the Transport Layer, provides for reliability in transferring data.

■ Layer 3, the Network Layer, handles routing and relaying information.

■ Layer 2, the Datalink Layer, is concerned with technology specific transfers.

■ Layer 1, the Physical Layer, addresses the subject of physical connections.

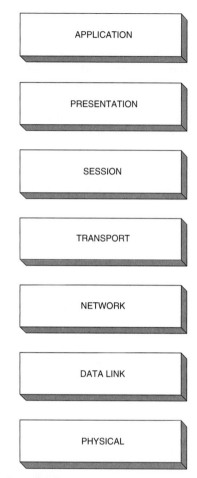

Figure 3–4 OSI platform levels.

SUMMARY

- Communications systems for security are multifaceted.
- The simplest and most frequently used form of communication in security is direct voice communication.
- Basic wire line analog communications is used extensively with security systems. Intrusion alarm systems, fire alarm systems, access control systems, guard tour systems, can all use wire from control box to sensor, or from control box to annunciator, or from control box to telephone line. Combinations of digital and analog signals are sent over wire for CCTV.

- Generally speaking, lower radio frequencies provide longer-range communications than the higher frequencies, but the higher frequencies tend to be more stable and reliable over their shorter range.

- The High Frequency (HF) communications band stretches from 3 to 30 MHz, and is used for long-distance communications.

- There are two types of VHF, Low Band and High Band. Government agencies use repeaters with High Band.

- A repeater is a radio transceiver that receives a signal on one frequency (Frequency A) and retransmits it on another (Frequency B). Most walkie-talkie types of 2-way FM radios have both repeater frequency and *talk around* frequency modes.

- Communication is very reliable in the digital world. Although used for analog as well as digital, spread spectrum communications are often used for transmitting digital data in the security world. A simple digital data communications device is a part of most moderately-priced home security system. In a commercial environment, data communications between alarm and access control systems, and computers, is set up over a Local Area Network (LAN), or Wide Area Network (WAN).

- In Frequency Hopping Spread Spectrum, an information signal, usually a data stream, modulates a radio frequency carrier that is hopped among a number of frequencies.

KEY TERMS

RF

Lightwave

CCTV

Bit

Eavesdropping

Radio Frequency Communications

High Frequency (HF)

Propagation Charts

Repeaters

Limited Spectrum

Talk Around

Velocity of Propagation

Bluetooth

802.11b or "Wifi"

Home RF

Spread Spectrum

Frequency Hopping Systems (FHSS)

Direct Sequence Systems (DSSS)

Bandwidth

Broadband

Baseband

ASCII

Parity Check

Cyclic Redundancy Check (CRC)

Open Systems Interface

DISCUSSION QUESTIONS

1 For security communications, why would all of these scenarios belong?

   Joe sends Shirley an email message.

   Jack, the security officer, waves his guard tour wand at a sensor on the wall.

   John talks to Mike on a 2-way radio.

2 What does CCTV stand for?

3 What is the lowest grade of cabling that could be used for wiring telephones in a home?

4 Why is 300 Hz not an RF frequency?

5 Into which category does 150 MHz fall?

6 The VHF band is subdivided into two categories for communications. What are they called?

7   What is a Propagation Chart?

8   About how far will a Microwave signal travel?

9   What is the minimum number of frequencies that would be used by a repeater? Why?

10   What is *talk-around?*

11   If a courier company were using a repeater, what frequency band would they most likely be using?

12   The Internet is a WAN. What does that mean?

13   What is a *Cafeteria Card?*

14   What does the term *Biometrics* mean?

15   What is the typical bandwidth for an OC3 circuit? To what does OC refer?

RESEARCH QUESTIONS

1   In radio communications, which is more important, the antenna, or the power output of a transmitter? Why?

2   Digital wireless communications is usually thought of as being a new technology. Actually, it predates analog wireless communications. Explain how this can be true.

3   In HF communications, relative to propagation, it is usually believed that as the sun goes down, the frequencies of reliable operation also go down; why is this?

CHAPTER 4

Test Equipment

PURPOSE AND OBJECTIVES

Security work uses many different types of test equipment. The purpose of this chapter is to familiarize the reader with some of the more important instruments that are used on a daily basis. This chapter will cover some of the common features of the different types of test equipment. Keep in mind that different manufacturers offer various options and variations on the equipment that will follow.

After reading this chapter, the student will:

- Recognize the most common pieces of test equipment used in security work
- Be able to determine the proper equipment for a measurement situation
- Be familiar with terminology associated with certain types of instruments
- Recognize limitations as well as advantages of test equipment

MULTIMETERS

The most versatile piece of test equipment in a toolbox is the *digital multimeter* (Figure 4–1). This tester measures resistance (in ohms), voltage (in volts), and current (in amperes), and may have other features depending on its model and make. Some digital multimeters have the ability to measure temperature. Some also include automatic features such as transistor checks, capacitor tests, continuity tests, or diode checkers. Security personnel use this instrument more than any other.

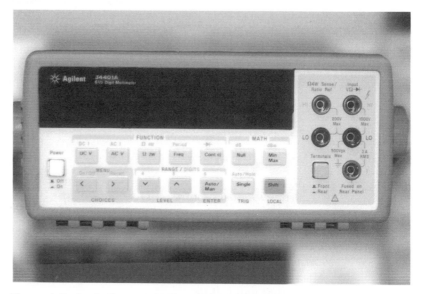

Figure 4–1 An Agilent 6 1/2 digit digital multimeter.

The multimeter started out as a *Vacuum Tube Volt-Ohm-Meter* (VTVOM). It used a high impedance vacuum tube in its circuitry so when the meter was put across a resistor, it would have high relative impedance. High impedance is important so the meter does not affect the resistor that it is measuring. Recall from Chapter 2 that the higher the value of a parallel resistor, the less it affects the resistance across it. Instead of a digital readout, this Volt-Ohm-Meter had a needle on its face. Meters with swinging needles are still used at times because they show the speed and action of a capacitor that is charging or discharging across a resistance. Being able to see a capacitor charging is a valuable property in security electronics because many times a "bug" is capacitively coupled to a phone line or other wire line. Meters with needles are generally referred to as analog meters and those with direct numeric readouts are referred to as digital meters. The Volt-Ohm-Meter also had a low resistance-measuring capability because it was used to measure current in series in a circuit. Series resistances add to the overall resistance, so the meter had to be kept from loading the circuit for current measurements.

Modern multimeters now use solid-state components instead of vacuum tubes, as transistors are more efficient than the vacuum tubes. They exhibit the low or high impedance qualities of the vacuum tube meters but are much lighter and more compact (some will even fit in a shirt pocket!) Now, you no longer have to worry about the vacuum tube wearing out.

Most multimeters have *autoranging*. They will automatically jump to the proper measurement range, whether it is millivolts or volts, for instance. They can also be manually dialed to a range, which bypasses the autoranging.   ·

VOLTMETER

Digital multimeters (Figure 4–2) measure voltage, current, and resistance, among other features; let us first examine the voltmeter portion. Voltage is measured across a resistance, so an ideal voltmeter would have an infinitely high resistance (so as not to load the circuit). This is not possible, but the higher the impedance, the less the voltmeter affects the circuit.

Voltmeters will read both DC and AC. When set for AC, the voltmeters are usually set to read out in *Root Mean Square* (RMS) volts. RMS value is also called effective value because it has the same effect (in terms of power) that a DC voltage has with the same value. Low cost meters read out in average volts. True RMS meters used to be very expensive but have recently decreased in cost. Many meters can show readings in both AC and DC at the same time if both parts are contained in a voltage.

The formula for determining RMS voltage:

$$V_{RMS} = \sqrt{\text{average of } v^2(t)}$$

$$= \sqrt{\frac{1}{T} \int_{t_0}^{t_0 + T} v^2(t)\, dt} \qquad \text{(Eq. 4–1)}$$

where $v(t) = V_{0-p} \sin(2\pi f t)$.

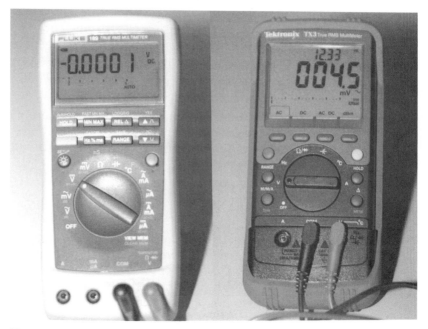

Figure 4–2 Handheld digital multimeters.

AMMETER

Ammeters are used to measure current. An ideal ammeter would sense a current going through it without having any voltage dropped across its terminals. This infers that the meter has no resistance, which, of course, is not possible. If we do keep the resistance low, however, we can get the reading close to exact.

OHMMETER

Ohmmeters measure resistance, which is derived from current and voltage, across two points. The meter supplies its own voltage or current to the device being tested. This allows for measurement of individual components without having them in a circuit. In fact, a circuit measured by an ohmmeter should have all power turned off so it will not affect (or damage) the ohmmeter. Because the ohmmeter measures the resistance between the two probe points, if there are resistances in parallel, the meter will read the total resistance. As far as the meter is concerned, there is only one resistance across the terminals. Figure 4–3 shows an array of various meters.

Figure 4–3   Electronics workbench with multiple stations.

SPECIFICATIONS

Specifications for meters generally are expressed as in Table 4–1

Table 4–1 Sample Multimeter Specifications

DC Volts	Ranges: 0.1, 1, 10, 100, 1000 V Accuracy; +/- (0.005% of reading + 0.0035% of range)
AC Volts	Ranges: 0.1, 1, 10, 750 V Accuracy: +/- (0.06% of reading + 0.03% of range), 10 Hz to 20 KHz
DC Current	Ranges: 0.01, 0.1, 1,0 A Accuracy: +/- (0.1% of reading + 0.01% of range)
Resistance	Ranges: 100, 1 K, 10 K, 100 K, 1 M, 10 M Accuracy: +/- (0.01% of reading + 0.001% of range)

Of course, many other parameters may be listed in a specification table. Meters are generally rated for safety as well as capabilities.

The more digits that a meter reads out, the more accurate the meter will be in security work. Many high impedance "taps" will not show up on a meter that has less than a 4 1/2 digit readout capability because of the high resistance. Meters with less than 4 1/2 digits show very high resistance as being "out of scale" on the meter. Meters become more expensive as the number of digits increase.

Digital multimeters are produced as portable units, with digit capability of generally up to 4 1/2 places, and as bench-top units, with digit capability of up to 6 1/2 digits.

OSCILLOSCOPES

The *oscilloscope* (Figure 4–4) is the second most versatile piece of equipment that a security engineer can use. Unlike the multimeter, which only reads out values, the oscilloscope shows a picture of a signal versus time. The face of an oscilloscope shows an x-y graph, where the x-axis measures time and the y-axis measures amplitude of a signal. The spacing on the grid can be set to a number of values. The oscilloscope allows measurement of many different values including frequency, period, rise time, phase, and abnormalities.

Figure 4–4   An Agilent 100 MHz dual channel oscilloscope.

There are two types of oscilloscopes, digital and analog. The analog oscilloscope has been around the longest, and is found in virtually every electronics shop in the world. More recently, digital scopes have taken over because they show a much better picture. For instance, the analog scope will not accurately show the rise or fall time of a steep square wave, whereas a digital scope will. However, analog scopes still abound and are preferred by technicians for certain applications.

Oscilloscopes are mainly used to perform measurements and show a voltage waveform versus time. Most scopes have a minimum of two channels for input, which makes possible comparisons between different voltage waveforms concurrently. Many scopes have four channel input, and some have a mixed signal capability. A mixed signal oscilloscope usually has two analog inputs and 16 additional digital inputs. Pure logic analyzers, which show relationships of high and low states, can measure 32 channels or more of digital input.

MEASUREMENTS

Certain measurements are made when looking at a waveform, either automatically with the scope or with your eyes and cursors provided on the scope itself. Parameters such as amplitude, frequency, and period are quickly obtained. A great feature of an oscilloscope is that unlike a multimeter, RMS, average, and peak measurements can all be made at just about the same time. By DC coupling the scope, both DC and AC components of the signal can be shown and measured. The operator can immediately ascertain by sight whether there is interference such as noise on a signal, jitter, or other types of glitches. One common measurement on a scope is to inject a signal such as a sine wave at the input to a circuit and put it on the scope's channel one, with the output on channel two. The gain, attenuation, or shift of the wave can then be measured, and the signal can be analyzed by sight to see if there has been any change. Measurements can be made in decibels (dB) as well as direct voltage in the event that the differences are too great for other methods. In addition, the frequency response of a circuit can be analyzed by varying the frequency of the input sine wave and then watching how the response changes at the output.

As mentioned, the scope has an x-y axis on its face with a *graticule*, or grid, throughout. The spacing on the graticule can vary depending on how the operator sets certain switches on the unit. All scopes have a minimum of the following types of controls:

TIMEBASE

This switch controls time between each horizontal grid point. It can be set anywhere from mere nanoseconds all the way up to seconds. This will change the speed of the trace going across the face of the scope. The trace can vary from so fast it looks unmoving down to a crawl where an illuminated dot edges slowly across the face of the display.

VOLTAGE BASE

The voltage base switch changes the value between the vertical spacing on the graticule. The value can range from microvolts to hundreds of volts.

HORIZONTAL AND VERTICAL POSITION SWITCHES

These switches allow the operator to move the traces up and down, or side to side. This is handy for comparing two or more waveforms.

TRIGGERING

Triggering means telling the scope when to start a scan. Without triggering, the waveform would have random start times, which would result in an unstable signal moving across the display. The waveforms are all jumbled together when not triggered properly. Triggering can come from an internal scope mechanism, or from an external source. An external source is handy when doing comparison measurements; for example, an operator may want to check the signals coming from pins on a chip and may want to trigger using an external clock pulse. A properly triggered scope will show a waveform that appears to be stationary on the face of the scope, although the signals are moving rapidly, one on top of another.

INTENSITY

The intensity control simply adjusts brightness of the trace.

AUTOSCALE

Most scopes also have an *Autoscale* button that automatically adjusts the vertical component (voltage), horizontal component (time base), and triggering in order to present the best picture to the operator. Of course, the operator can then switch to manual to make minor adjustments, if necessary.

There are many other types of controls found on the oscilloscope, and the number and capabilities of these controls depend on the cost of the instrument. Many modern scopes have menu buttons across the bottom of the screen, with illuminated menu functions just above the buttons that change from case to case.

BANDWIDTH

Oscilloscopes are rated for their bandwidth. Low priced scopes may have a bandwidth of 20 or 50 MHz, while higher priced scopes have bandwidths of 100 MHz and up, usually in increments of 100 MHz. A 100 MHz scope means the scope will clearly show a 100 MHz waveform. Bandwidth is often confused with *Sample rate* or, the rate at which the samples are taken because the units of measurement are the same.

SAMPLE RATE

This specification is used with digital scopes. Since analog information is changed to digital in these scopes, there is a specified sample rate that takes place. Sampling theory specifies that the sample rate must be greater than at least twice the highest frequency in the signal. To ensure that sampling rate and bandwidth are not confused, bandwidth is specified in megahertz (MHz), and sampling rate is specified in mega samples per second (MSa/sec). Of course, bandwidth and sampling could be specified in GHz or giga samples per second, respectively.

INPUTS

An oscilloscope channel has a high impedance input, as does the multimeter. The purpose is the same: so the circuit being tested is not loaded by the measurement instrument itself.

FUNCTIONS

In a digital scope, the data is in digital form. The scope can produce a number of mathematical functions, such as adding waveforms together, subtracting waveforms from each other, multiplying, integrating, differentiating, and doing FFT (*Fast Fourier Transforms*). Fast Fourier Transforms turn the scope from a time based unit to a frequency based instrument (measuring frequency on the x-axis). In effect, FFTs change the oscilloscope into a *spectrum analyzer*.

CURSORS

Many scopes have horizontal and vertical sets of cursors, which, when set, measure the parameters between them. Parameters such as frequency, period, and voltage can be measured using these cursors. Generally, there is a direct readout of values on the screen.

PROBES

Oscilloscopes come with many different types of probes. There are 1X (one-to-one) probes, 10X (ten-to-one) probes, active probes, differential probes, high voltage probes, and current probes. You can see that an oscilloscope is an extremely versatile instrument. Ten-to-one probes are usually considered the standard probes and are referred to as attenuating probes. They have a resistor and capacitor (in parallel) inside the probe that allows for a much wider bandwidth than a 1X probe. The bandwidth is maximized by adjusting the probe capacitor with its adjusting screw. This alteration is called compensation. The scope itself usually has a square wave output post, and by attaching the probe to this post and then adjusting for a perfectly square wave, the bandwidth is maximized (since a square wave is made up of many harmonics).

SPECTRUM ANALYZER

The spectrum analyzer (Figure 4–5) is a very versatile piece of test equipment that is used extensively in technical surveillance countermeasures. This analyzer is similar to the oscilloscope except that instead of measuring a signal over a time domain, it looks at signals over a frequency domain. The vertical axis is still voltage, but the horizontal axis is frequency rather than time. In the frequency domain, a signal has many frequency components (or spectral lines) that indicate the amount of energy present at each frequency. There are several possible methods to change a time based instrument into a frequency based one, but most modern spectrum analyzers are FFT spectrum analyzers, that is, they facilitate the use of Fast Fourier Transforms electronically to change a time based oscilloscope signal into a frequency based spectrum signal. An analog waveform is sampled and changed from analog to digital, and then the FFT algorithm is used to change the wave from time to frequency domain. The major limitation of FFT is the analog to digital conversion, since the bandwidth of the analyzer is limited to less than half of the sample rate of the analog to digital converter.

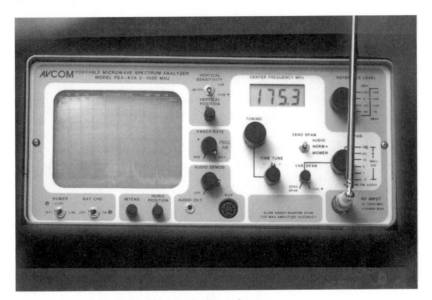

Figure 4–5 Avcom portable spectrum analyzer.

As with radio receivers, the oscilloscope has an Intermediate Frequency (IF) filter. The bandwidth of this IF filter determines the so-called resolution bandwidth of the instrument. Resolution bandwidth determines the narrowest frequency that can be seen on the scope. If there is a bank of filters in the instrument, the narrowest one dominates. Do not confuse the bandwidth of the instrument with the resolution bandwidth. Bandwidth of the instrument refers to the total range that the instrument can measure. For example, the instrument may have the capability to measure from 10 KHz to 3 GHz.

For technical surveillance countermeasures, an engineer would want the best resolution bandwidth possible. There is a method called "snuggling" in which an eavesdropper tunes the bug very close to a stronger signal (such as a radio broadcast signal). If a wide resolution bandwidth were used, the snuggled signal would appear to be a part of the larger signal. With a narrow resolution bandwidth, the two signals are seen to be separate.

LIMITATIONS

Users can control the sweep time of the instrument, along with the frequency range that is swept and the resolution bandwidth. There is a limitation, however, on the rate of sweep depending on the resolution bandwidth chosen by the user. The *sweep rate* in hertz (cycles per second) is not chosen directly by the user but is determined by the frequency rate swept, divided by the sweep time. A formula for the sweep rate of a spectrum analyzer is

$$\text{Sweep Rate} = \frac{BW^2}{k} \qquad \text{(Eq. 4–2)}$$

Where BW is the bandwidth of resolution filter and k is a factor depending on the filter shape (typically 2.)

The limitation comes from the response time of the resolution bandwidth filter. If the spectrum analyzer is swept too quickly, the filter would not have time to respond, and the corresponding measurement would not be accurate. When this takes place, the display tends to have a "smeared" look. Fortunately, in modern instruments, microprocessors choose the fastest accurate sweep time for the user. The user can override this setting if desired.

DYNAMIC RANGE

The dynamic range of a spectrum analyzer refers to the difference between the largest and the smallest signal shown on the scope and measured at the same time. The measurement range differs in that it refers to the difference between the largest and the smallest signal that can be measured (but not at the same time). The smallest signal that can be measured is determined by noise and distortion factors.

INPUTS

Spectrum analyzers are usually equipped with both high impedance and 50 ohm inputs. 50 ohm is considered the higher quality input of the two. As the upper frequency limit is approached, the high impedance input becomes impractical. Some analyzers also have 75-ohm inputs. Low frequency FFT analyzers, such as those found on some oscilloscopes, usually only have high impedance inputs.

MEASUREMENTS

As an oscilloscope shows a picture of the time domain, the spectrum analyzer shows a picture of the frequency domain. Each signal on the covered spectrum shows up as a wave raised to a certain voltage level. This wave may have distortions (harmonic or intermodulation), harmonics, and modulation sidebands, and it can be seen rising and falling in real time. Many spectrum analyzers can also demodulate a signal so that it can be heard through a speaker or headset. This demodulation ability is necessary in technical surveillance countermeasures. The operator sweeps the spectrum and listens to each signal that is detected on the scope.

Intermodulation distortion occurs when two or more signal waves are present at the same time in a circuit that exhibits distortion. When the signals mix, several resultant signals form from addition and subtraction of the two waves. Modulation sidebands can be seen on one or both sides of a signal. These are formed by AM, FM, or PM modulation techniques. The modulation could also be an unwanted by-product of some other operation. Harmonic distortion is quite often present in signals and can be seen readily on the spectrum analyzer. Actually, the spectrum analyzer is much more reliable for measuring harmonic distortion than an oscilloscope.

THE TIME DOMAIN REFLECTOMETER (TDR)

TDRs work using the same principle as radar. On a TDR, an electrical pulse is sent down a cable and any anomaly that the pulse encounters will send back a reflection. If the cause of the reflection increases the resistance, the reflected signal will be in the same direction as the pulse (usually upwards). If the fault decreases resistance, then the reflected signal will be in the opposite direction. Because of this, an open circuit will show up as a reflection almost as strong as the initial pulse, and a short in the circuit will reflect as strongly in the opposite direction. There are many variations in reflections that can tell a great deal about the condition of the cable.

The most useful TDRs for security work are those that show a graphical picture (Figure 4–6), although some TDRs only show a numerical value (Figure 4–7), The numerical value is a distance readout to the first significant fault detected, such as an open or short. These numerical units are useful for determining lengths of cable on a reel, or for finding ends of cable in inaccessible places.

For security work, the graphical TDRs are necessary for finding such things as taps, splices, and branches as well as shorts, opens, and such.

Figure 4–6   Tempo Research's graphical TDR.

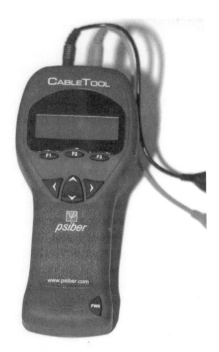

Figure 4–7   Psiber digital TDR.

PULSE WIDTHS

Most TDRs offer a choice of pulse widths. The pulse width allows the pulse to travel along a cable at certain energy levels. The greater the width, the more energy transmitted and the farther the signal can travel. Sometimes, it is necessary to decrease this pulse width because the fault is close to the input side, and the width of the "regular" sized pulse would hide it. When testing a cable, it is a good idea to start with the shortest pulse width available. Pulse widths are measured in units of time. Table 4–2 shows typical range figures for cable that has a Velocity of Propagation of .60 such as twisted pair cable.

Table 4–2 Typical Pulse Widths and Distances

Pulse Width	Typical Range
2 nsec	1500 Ft
100 nsec	3500 Ft
1 usec	13,500 Ft

VELOCITY OF PROPAGATION (VOP)

The TDR can be very accurate, but requires an adjustment for certain electrical parameters before running a test. In a perfect situation, electricity would travel at the speed of light, but since all materials offer some type of resistance to the flow of electrons, the speed of travel has to be adjusted for the type of material in which the electricity is traveling. The Velocity of Propagation (VOP) is a specification of the speed at which a signal travels through a cable, and there is a different factor used for each type of cable material. For instance, VOP for twisted pair cable is .60 (as in Table 4–2). For RG-59, the VOP is .82.

The speed of light in a vacuum is 186,400 miles per second (or 300,000 kilometers per second). This speed is represented by the number 1. All other signals would be slower. Twisted pair cable with a VOP of .60 would allow a signal to travel at 60 percent of the speed of light. TDRs come packaged with a chart showing VOPs for different materials. The proper VOP for cable under test can be set using the adjusting knob on the machine. Of course, VOP can vary with temperature, humidity, age, and other factors. A current VOP can be determined by measuring a known length of the cable to be tested and then adjusting the VOP knob on the instrument to read out the correct length.

Table 4–3 demonstrates some factors packaged with Jovial Test Equipment's "Shortstop" TDR.

Table 4–3 Velocities of Propagation (Courtesy of Jovial Test Equipment)

Wire	VOP (range)	VOP (nominal)	VOP (flat)	VOP (coiled)
12/2 w/G Romex, Coiled or on a spool	53-75	-66-		
12/2 BX, Coiled	63-75	-65-		
14/3 BX, Coiled	63-75	-70-		
12/3 Orange Outdoor Extension Cord	53-60	-59-		
14/3 Orange Outdoor Extension Cord	55-60	-59-		
16/3 Orange Outdoor Extension Cord	55-60	-59-		
8 to 16 Gauge THHN in Conduit	74-84	-77-		
Belden 8737, 2 wire shielded, R/B			-48-	-45-

Table 4–3 Velocities of Propagation (Courtesy of Jovial Test Equipment)

Wire	VOP (range)	VOP (nominal)	VOP (flat)	VOP (coiled)
Belden 8737, 2 wire shielded, R/Shield			-55	-53
Belden 9114, RG-6/U 75 Ohm Coax			-78-	-78-
Belden 8216, RG-174/U			-64-	-64-
RG-58/U 50 Ohm Coax			-63-	-63-
RG-59/U 75 Ohm Coax			-63-	-72-
300 Ohm Black Foam Antenna Wire			-77-	-72-
300 Ohm Brown Antenna Wire			-77-	-67-
16 to 22 Gauge Speaker Wire			-77-	-58-
18 Gauge Twisted Bell Wire			-73-	-69-
Quad Flat Telephone Wire, Red/Green			-62-	-58-
CAT-5, Blue/White pair			-66-	-66-

One reason that a graphical TDR is usually preferred to a decimal readout is that sometimes a cable contains more than one fault. Multiple faults show up not only with damage to a cable, but also with phenomena such as splits, re-splits, and taps. A decimal readout would only show the distance to the first fault. Unless a graphical TDR runs into a complete short or open (or something like a load-coil), the instrument will present a "picture" of the cable.

Using a graphical TDR, if a bridged tap is seen on wires 3 and 4 of a four wire twisted pair; this could be an indication of a problem in technical surveillance countermeasures work. The bridged tap would show up as an initial dip of the signal and then a rise. The distance from the dip to the rise would be the length of the lateral. On a digital readout unit, only the distance figure to the first anomaly (the dip) would be indicated.

When performing measurements with a TDR, it is best to leave open the end of the cable under test. A termination will tend to "soak up" the energy of the pulse. An open end will allow the full strength at the end to reflect back. It is still possible, however, to test a terminated cable, because damage ahead of the termination will be reflected back.

Figure 4–8 shows a TDR waveform.

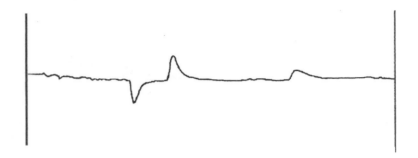

Figure 4–8   TDR waveforms of a bridged tap.

CABLE ANALYZER

Many types of security equipment are now designed to work on the network common to the computer system. Since the type of cabling used will be generally of the categories 5, 5e, or 6, there must be a way of certifying the cable once it has been run, spliced, and furnished with connectors along its path. A device such as the Fluke DSP-4300 Digital Cable Analyzer® provides this certification. This device is used to ensure that the cable installation falls within the standards and specifications of the type of cabling used. The unit comes with a set of universal, compact modules that support many manufacturers' cabling systems.

NON LINEAR JUNCTION DETECTOR (NLJD)

The *non linear junction detector* (Figure 4–9) is a very specialized piece of test equipment that is used to detect electronic devices, whether they are operational or in an "off" state. It analyzes *harmonic* emissions caused by an illuminating signal when it is reflected off a target device.

Semiconductors contain layers of P-Type and N-Type silicon material and the point where they meet is called a Non Linear Junction. This junction also appears when dissimilar metals come into contact with one another, in the form of rust on a fastener, or corrosion on the springs in a piece of furniture.

Figure 4–9   The Orion™ NLJD. (Courtesy of Research Electronics International)

A Non Linear Junction Detector finds potential eavesdropping devices by flooding an area with a microwave RF signal (usually around 880 or 915 MHz). Various harmonic frequencies are then monitored for a reflected signal.

The instrument has an antenna and a control housing. The antenna is mounted on an extendable pole, and nothing more than a microwave waveguide, which both emits and collects the signals (with a duplexer, a device that allows an antenna to be used for both transmission and reception.) The control housing is a multiple channel, highly sensitive receiver tuned to specific second and third harmonic frequencies.

A Non Linear Junction Detector may be used to identify active or inactive transmitters, video cameras, concealed cell phones, microphones, and other types of electronic devices.

Operation involves sweeping the antenna over every surface in the suspicious area. This operation, of course, is only helpful if you are "sweeping" an area that does not have any electronic devices located nearby. The search is typically performed on walls, seats, tables, desks, and other non-electronic "hiding places."

The operator listens for a return signal at an even harmonic. Odd harmonics usually indicate non-threatening junctions between metals, but the even harmonics are produced by the types of junctions found in electronic equipment. Sometimes an even harmonic will be produced by a corroded normal junction. By tapping or "thumping" on the surface being checked, a variation in the headphone frequency will indicate that this is just a corroded joint.

POWER OUTPUT

Obviously, the higher the power output, the more sensitive the instrument is from greater distances. Keep in mind, however, that microwaves can be dangerous at high power levels. The government version of this instrument puts out about two watts, but the commercial variety is usually limited to under a watt.

The Orion's antenna radiates a signal. When this signal encounters an electronic device, the signal is returned at harmonic frequency levels. (If a signal is radiated at 915 MHz, a second harmonic would be found at 1830 MHz, and a third harmonic would be at 2745 MHz.) Other situations can also produce harmonic signals. Two dissimilar metals, joined or touching, and corroded metals both return harmonic signals. We will refer to these as false junctions.

The junctions in electronic devices and those in false junctions are quite different. The junctions in electronic devices are well defined, but those created by false junctions are not as well defined or as clean as a physical junction is. Imagine two perfect cubes joined—this would be a junction found in electronic devices. False junctions are more like two irregularly shaped items touching in places, but not in a smooth, regular pattern.

The following equation describes the electronic characteristics of a basic diode, which is the simplest form of an electronic non linear junction.

$$I = I_s[e^{qV/kT} - 1]$$ (Eq. 4–3)

Where I is the current of the signal, I_s the leakage current, q equals the electron charge, V is the voltage, K equals Boltzman's constant, and T is the temperature.

While more complex semiconductor devices are different from one another, they all produce clean, predictable junction characteristics. For the junctions found in electronic devices, this equation produces a predictable curve. For false junctions, the curve is not this regular. The curve is noisy and unpredictable. False junctions are typically symmetrical; their curve is mirrored for negative values. The current voltage characteristics are illustrated in Figure 4–10.

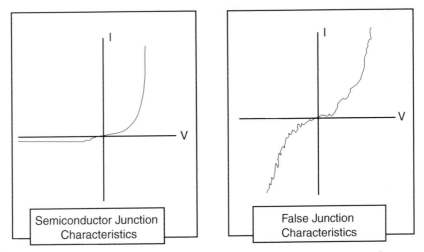

Figure 4–10 Signal curve of junction in electronic device. (Courtesy of Research Electronics International)

This level of regularity in the junction results in differences in the harmonic signals. When the Orion radiates a signal reflected by the junction in electronics, it results in a strong second harmonic signal and a weak third harmonic. A false junction returns a very weak second harmonic and a strong third (see Figure 4–11).

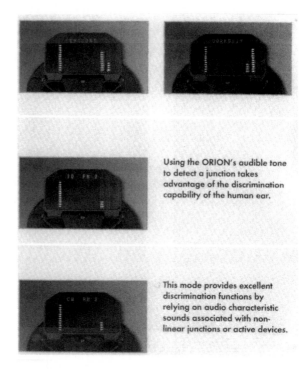

Using the ORION's audible tone to detect a junction takes advantage of the discrimination capability of the human ear.

This mode provides excellent discrimination functions by relying on audio characteristic sounds associated with non-linear junctions or active devices.

Figure 4–11   Orion™ panel (Courtesy of Research Electronics International)

When the signal is returned as a harmonic, the electronic device produces a regular signal pattern.

After evaluating many NLJDs from around the world, it appears that many units do not have good RF isolation between the second and third harmonic receiving functions. This means that a pure semiconductor junction may still appear to have a strong third harmonic and a pure false junction may appear to have a strong second harmonic. Although the unit has the ability to receive both harmonics, it is often very difficult to distinguish between semiconductor and false junctions. If the NLJD has the ability to detect second and third harmonics, it is very important that the two receiving functions are calibrated and do not interfere with each other.

QUIETING EFFECT

Semiconductor junctions produce a receiver quieting effect. Many false junctions do not.

When listening to the demodulated audio of the return harmonic from a semiconductor junction, the noise level decreases significantly approaching the junction. Then, when moving away from the junction, the noise level will increase again just before returning to normal. The audio will reach its lowest level directly over the device and swell on either side of it (see Figure 4–12).

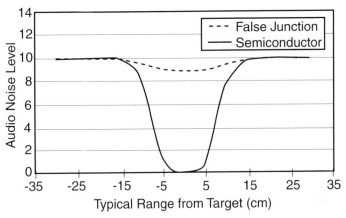

Figure 4–12   Noise curve of an electronic device and false junction. (Courtesy of Research Electronics International)

This is the "quieting effect." When evaluating the demodulated audio, electronic devices actually reduce the noise in their immediate vicinity. For many false junctions the audio noise will not significantly decrease. However, it is possible to detect false junctions that also have some level of quieting; and therefore, using a physical vibration (see below) is highly recommended as well as examining the difference between the harmonic levels for discrimination.

LISTENING FOR PHYSICAL BREAKUP OF A NON LINEAR JUNCTION

If a false junction is detected, a security engineer can easily discriminate between semiconductor junctions and false junctions by listening to the audio and providing a physical vibration to the junction. Pounding on the wall with a fist or a rubber hammer provides an effective physical vibration. A rubber hammer is provided in the Orion toolkit for this purpose. A false junction will break up and a crackling sound will be heard. A true junction will remain silent.

LONG RANGE DETECTION USING AUDIBLE TONES

The Orion has several modes of operation. One mode uses a Continuous Wave transmit signal with a 1 KHz FM modulated tone. With this mode, the operator has access to a tremendous detection range. The detection range allows the operator to hear the FM demodulated tone through the high quality receiver. While the visual bar graph display may only show a very small response, which may be interpreted as noise, the audible tone provides unquestionable detection of a Non Linear Junction. However, the modulated tone mode does not provide any positive discrimination between semiconductor junctions and false junctions.

OTHER USES FOR AUDIO DEMODULATION IN AN NLJD

It is often possible when using an NLJD to not only detect electronics, but also to classify them based on audio demodulation. For example, when detecting some tape recording devices, it is possible to hear the audio from the tape recorder head using the NLJD audio demodulation. Furthermore, if the NLJD provides good audio demodulation, it is often possible to hear the video synchronization pulse when detecting many chip cameras. In addition, by using FM demodulation it is sometimes possible to hear unique, periodic audible sounds resulting from phase-shifts in active electronic devices. It is important to practice using an NLJD so in order to recognize audio sounds peculiar to specific detected devices.

FREQUENCY INTERFERENCE

Most NLJDs are limited to either a single frequency channel or a small frequency range. Because of the increasing number of wireless communication devices and governmental regulations, an NLJD may be operating on a frequency that is being occupied by another transmitter resulting in erratic and unreliable readings. This is a common problem in larger cities of the United States, and to REI's knowledge, the Orion is the only NLJD that is designed to address this problem. The Orion automatically searches for the quietest channels on which to operate in the ambient environment.

RF PROBES

An RF Probe is a type of broadband receiver that is very useful when searching for *near field, transmissions,* or transmissions that are close by, when performing a Technical Surveillance Countermeasures (TSCM) sweep. Because the RF Probe is so versatile in TSCM work, we will dedicate a large section to it. The author has used a Research Electronics International CPM-700 Counter surveillance Probe/ Monitor for many years, and with REI's permission is reprinting some excerpts from the operations manual in order to illustrate the usage of this excellent instrument.

THE CPM-700

This section describes the function of the RF Probe and its use in room sweeps, phone line/RF sweeps, body transmitter detection, and tracking device location.

The RF Probe contains a low noise, extremely broad band amplifier (50 KHz to 3 GHz) which boosts the weak "near field" signals which are emitted from RF transmitters. Signal strength is displayed on the CPM-700 (Figure 4–13) by a bar graph in either high or low sensitivity ranges and is used to indicate the location of an RF device by "honing in" on the highest level.

The RF Probe contains a sensitive amplifier system that is primarily sensitive to amplitude information. Some transmitters may employ an unusual type of modulation, hop frequencies, store information and output it in a burst or have a very narrow bandwidth. These devices may not provide a strong audio signal and therefore the CPM-700 may not give a clear audible output of a known sound source such as a taped music selection, but may only show a reading on the LCD bar graph. Be sure to investigate all suspicious RF levels.

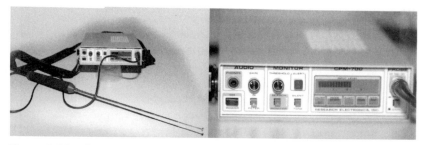

Figure 4–13   The CPM-700 by Research Electronics International.

FREQUENCY

The CPM-700 and its RF Probe combine to create a broadband RF receiver. When covering frequencies from 50 KHz to 3 GHz, it is unnecessary to calculate frequencies and wavelengths. Generally, though RF surveillance devices will transmit on frequencies between 50 and 400 MHz. Lower frequencies require longer antennas, which are usually impractical in a surveillance situation. Frequencies over 300 MHz do not penetrate building structures well because of absorption and reflection.

POWER

Surveillance RF transmitter devices can be divided into four power groups: Micropower, low power, medium power and high power. Transmitting distance is dependent not solely on power but also antenna placement and design, structural environment, ambient noise and the receiver and its antenna. High power bugs generally can broadcast a quarter mile or more using 100 milliwatts or more. Medium power devices use 1 to 100 milliwatts for a coverage distance of 300 feet to a quarter mile. Low power bugs transmit less than 300 feet, using less than 1 milliwatt. A separate breed of transmitters, called "micropower bugs" is designed to be undetectable, using a power of one microwatt or less. These specialized bugs are tiny, with short antennas. The monitor must be very close and very sophisticated. Because of unknowns when planting an RF device, the eavesdropper will usually use more than minimum power to ensure reliability.

PERFORMING A SWEEP

Prior to performing a room sweep, you should devote some thought to how the sweep will proceed. Be sure to concentrate within the "target area." Probe all objects that could contain a hidden surveillance device. You will note as you get close to the "source" of RF energy that the bar graph will continue to rise. (Use Low Gain if "MAX" is displayed.)

NOTE Sometimes a "phantom hot spot" will be found in mid air, which is not the actual source of the RF energy. Verification of an RF signal is necessary to determine if it is an actual surveillance device or a local "friendly" signal. By listening to the headphone audio you can determine if the energy is a local TV video, FM radio or two-way transmission. Hearing your Known Sound Source is positive identification of a surveillance device.

In some areas close to high power commercial transmitters such as TV, AM or FM radio the Low Gain setting should be used because these areas will have more than ten segments displayed in Low Gain. It is normal to see large signal level variations located throughout the sweep area. Often, when the Probe is held near wires or a metal object, the bar graph level will increase, as well as the activity heard through the headphones. This may not be a bug, but rather the metal acting as an antenna extension. Verify by listening for the Known Sound Source.

Small FM wireless microphones are available in today's consumer market. These microphones broadcast on the commercial FM broadcast band. In order to meet FCC regulations, they must be very low power, about two microwatts. This extremely low power makes the microphones very difficult to resolve using the CPM-700. Fortunately, it also makes them useless as bugs due to their short range, which is less than fifty feet under most circumstances. Again, a close physical search will be necessary.

NOTE In a high signal level area, the CPM-700 will be most effective as an inspection tool. In this type of inspection, each object is tested by placing the RF Probe against it, and noting if the level is higher than the normal surrounding levels. Be suspicious of all RF signals.

VIDEO TRANSMITTERS

Surveillance video transmitters will sound the same through the headphones as a "friendly" local TV signal. In many cases, the RF and audio signal levels can be compared by moving to another room. If you notice that a change in light level in the room also changes the tonal quality of the video buzz, pinpoint the area, which will give the strongest reading on the bar graph and search for a transmitter and/or camera.

TELEPHONE SWEEP

Sweep testing a phone for the existence of RF transmitters is performed by measuring the signal strength of the instrument and line when in an "off hook" (in use) condition. Verification of a phone bug is performed by listening for a dial tone through the headphones. You may turn off or lower your Known Sound Source for this sweep since the telephone provides a dial tone and/or messages. If a long recorded message service is available, such as a business report or farm market report, use it as a Known Sound Source to disguise your actions.

RF BODY TRANSMITTERS

The typical "body" type transmitter will have an output level between 50 milliwatts and 5 watts. This type of surveillance device will develop a strong RF signal and is normally detectable within a 25 foot (9 meter) radius.

With the CPM-700 set to the Search Mode, the RF Probe can be used to "physically scan" an individual by checking from head to toe while the user watches the LCD bar graph display. When the sound is turned up, the audio output from the speaker also produces an audio feedback "squeal" as a positive identification.

ROOM MONITORING

The CPM-700 set in the Monitor Mode will detect body type transmitters. The RF Probe can be hidden nearby to sense the RF signal from the transmitter and activate the Alert (Silent or Tone). It is recommended that the probe be placed in the area where the individual sits and operates the transmitter.

TRACKING DEVICES

The CPM-700 will detect and locate RF tracking transmitters that are used to follow vehicles. The typical *Bumper Beeper* (a device attached with a magnet to a bumper, which emanates "beeps" over a radio frequency) will employ a minimum output of 100 milliwatts to more than 5 watts and usually has a pulsed output.

Prior to performing a sweep, the vehicle should be taken to an area that has a low to medium RF environment (maximum of five segments on Low Gain). This will help prevent other signals from causing interference with your readings.

"Beepers" may be powered by the vehicle to which they are attached, or they may contain their own batteries. They can be activated by motion sensors, vehicle circuits, or other methods. The vehicle to be tested should be "conditioned" to simulate actual operation. Automobiles should be started, moved, bounced, or driven to activate any devices that may be sensitive to these inputs.

As with any sweep, a thorough physical search should be performed, especially with the vast number of ways to activate this type of transmitter. Inspect the frame for "add-ons," remove the seats, and check the antenna lead to the radio for other devices in line. You can also measure with a digital voltmeter the vehicle's idle or leakage current drawn from the battery. (All accessories and engine must be off for this test.) Refer to the vehicle's technical manual for the idle current specification.

THE VLF PROBE

The *Very Low Frequency (VLF)* Probe is used to detect and locate very low frequency devices also known as carrier current transmitters. Carrier current transmitters use the AC power lines as a transmission path by placing a carrier signal on the line. (FM wireless intercoms sold through electronics dealers are an example of a carrier current transmitter.) The VLF Probe has been designed to plug into AC outlets and isolate the AC voltage while band passing the 15 kHz to 1 MHz frequencies to the CPM-700. You can also test other wires, cables, or phone lines for the presence of VLF signals by connecting a small jumper lead from each of the input blade terminals of the VLF Probe to the suspect wire pair. Some equipment with switching power supplies, such as computers, copiers, electronic typewriters, etc., may produce VLF signals on the power lines. Selectively turn off these products one at a time to isolate which one is causing the inter-ference. Unless you are sure the interference is from a switching power supply, an inspection of the suspect product is required.

NOTE Dimmer controls and defective fluorescent lamps may cause background hum and buzz due to AC power line harmonics. These can be reduced by removing or replacing the defective fluorescent lamp or by turning dimmer controls on full. Usage of the audio filter will also help reduce low frequency audio hum and buzz. Simply turning off the noisy circuit may also turn off the bug.

Again, a thorough physical search of the target area is necessary to find bugs that may be turned off remotely or operated in a way that generally is not detectable by counter surveillance equipment.

Be sure to examine outlets, wall switches, and lighting fixtures, as well as electrical equipment such as calculators, copy machines radios, etc., for unusual extra wiring or parts.

AUXILIARY INPUT AMPLIFIER

The Auxiliary Input Amplifier is used with a supplied Patch Cord to "listen" to suspicious wiring for the presence of voices or other signals. The balanced input will allow testing of phones and phone lines for modifications as well as after-hour evidence monitoring by using the Monitor Mode and Record Output.

The Aux Input can amplify high or low level signals if the Low or High Gain switch is selected.

PHONE LINE AUDIO TEST

An Auxiliary Input Patch Cord will allow the CPM-700 to test a tele-phone and line for various devices such as infinity, or harmonic bugs, that listen to the room while on hook.

The RF Probe and the VLF Probe can also be used to detect RF or very low RF frequencies present on suspicious telephone wiring.

WIRE/AUDIO VALUATION

During your physical search procedures, you will usually find "unknown" wires and cables. The CPM-700 with its Auxiliary Input Patch Cord allows you to listen to these lines to determine if they are used for legitimate purposes or as a "conductor" for surveillance.

Even if a wire has a legitimate purpose, do not assume it is safe. Background music speakers, intercoms, computers, desktop radios, and audio monitored burglar alarms can all be used for surveillance activities. Normally, a speaker such as a background music speaker cannot be used as a microphone while it is broadcasting sound, but it certainly can be used as such while the music is off. To prevent this, disconnect and remove all unused speakers from the room. Speakers that are in use still need to be secured by wiring them with a switch. Be careful when dealing with an alarm company that monitors the premises by listening on a dedicated line. Even though most companies are reputable, the fact that someone can listen in demands caution. Even if the alarm company disconnects the system during business hours, the microphone and line are still there and can be used by an eavesdropper. The use of switches, like those described above for speakers, can minimize the threat. Depending on the level of security desired, it may be better not to wire a room, such as a conference room, for a monitored audio burglar alarm, which would make it impossible for an eavesdropper to listen in on a dedicated security line.

NOTE Carbon and electret microphones or inline amplifiers may require a DC power supply for operation. Normally, if you conduct a sweep without the eavesdropper's knowledge, or if the eavesdropper has no "remote control" over the power supply, the audio will be present and can be detected. However, if the supply can be shut off, then there will be no audio. Therefore, be sure you verify the intended purpose of all wires discovered. If it appears to be thermostat wiring, make sure it connects the thermostat to the air conditioner and to nothing else. The RF Probe and the VLF Probe should also be used to detect RF and very low RF frequencies present on suspicious wires and cables.

OTHER PROCEDURES

Tempest Approved Equiment

The CPM-700 can be used to compare emissions from Tempest approved equipment. Generally, any Tempest approved product will have very low leakage in comparison to non-Tempest products. Usually, the same concepts of probing apply. Look for RF emissions from equipment, VLF signals on power circuits, and wiring and audio leakages on wires and cables.

Computers and Related Equipment

Today's business offices are host to myriad RF producing equipment. Equipment such as personal computers, facsimile machines, copiers, telex machines, typewriters, and other desktop devices may radiate RF energy. These devices will show some RF levels when probed. They may also emit VLF signals onto the power lines, regardless of any claims made by the FCC.

You must determine whether an eavesdropping device is planted in those machines as well as prevent a sophisticated eavesdropper from gaining information from the machines' legitimate radiation (via the computer monitor or data 1/0 cables).

Older, non-FCC approved equipment may have higher VLF noise. RF inspection will consist of a comparison with other units of the same type and model.

Outside Flooding

If there is an apparent outside RF source flooding your target area, e.g., a signal that shows up mainly in the target area, does not appear in adjacent areas, and originates outside the area, you may suspect RF flooding. This method aims an RF beam at a passive radiator hidden in the room. This radiator uses the absorbed RF energy to transmit back on a harmonic frequency. This type of bug is often planted during construction where it can be buried, since no other external power source is required.

Cable and Closed Circuit TV

Nearly every business or residence today has some type of cable system for TV or FM stereo reception. An eavesdropper can use the cable to reverse feed a signal out of the target area or building. To check for RF, VLF, or audio bugging, disconnect the cable at the point where it enters the building and, using the RF and VLF probes, the Auxiliary Input Patch Cord, and a digital voltmeter (DVM), look for any signal on the building side of the cable. In most cases, there will be no signals or DC voltage present on the cable. Use a DVM to check the incoming line for any DC voltage. Unless your system has a power supply for a preamp (booster), the incoming line DC voltage should be .5 Volts DC or less.

Infrared Link

Infrared (IR) provides a useful transmission medium for surveillance. Its advantages are that it is not detectable by conventional RF detectors, its directional beam, and its extremely small size. Disadvantages include a limitation to line of sight, the need for a visually clear transmission path and the high current consumption that limits battery use. The emitter may be a wide-angle IR diode or a narrow beam laser diode.

Point-to-point surveillance transmission by microwave is not common due to the difficulty of installation and alignment. However, in some cases this disadvantage is outweighed by the advantages: it is reliable and directional and can support many channels of information, including video. Microwave transmission is harder to detect because of its directional beam. The sweep operator must get the CPM Probe in the beam to detect it. A physical search is necessary to uncover the microphone, camera, or transmitter. The transmitter element usually will be outside the building or be beaming through a window. Microwaves do not penetrate structures very well. Inspect the roof and outside walls for any new or unusual black boxes that may hide an antenna. When probing with the CPM-700, shorten the RF Probe antenna to minimize extraneous signals. The RF Probe is able to receive upwards of 3 GHz.

SUMMARY

- Many different types of test equipment are used in security work.

- Digital multimeters measure voltage, current, and resistance, among other features.

- Low cost meters read out in average volts. Ohmmeters measure resistance across two points. Resistance is derived from current and voltage. The meter supplies its own voltage or current to the device under test. The ohmmeter measures the resistance between the two probe points, so remember that if there are resistances in parallel, the meter will read the total resistance.

- Behind the digital multimeter, the oscilloscope is the most versatile piece of equipment that a security engineer can use. Unlike the meter, which only reads out values, the oscilloscope shows a picture of a signal versus time. The face of an oscilloscope shows an x-y graph, where the x-axis measures time and the y-axis measures amplitude of a signal. The spacing on the grid can be set to many different values. Oscilloscopes are mainly used to perform measurements or comparisons between different voltage waveforms concurrently and to show a voltage waveform versus time. Most scopes have a minimum of two channels for input, so comparisons are possible. Many scopes are four channel input, and some have a mixed signal capability. A mixed signal oscilloscope usually has two analog inputs and 16 additional digital inputs. Oscilloscopes come with many different types of probes. There are 1:1 probes, 10:1 probes, active probes, differential probes, high voltage probes, and current probes.

- The spectrum analyzer is a very handy piece of test equipment that is used extensively for technical surveillance countermeasures. This analyzer is similar to the oscilloscope except that instead of measuring a signal over a time domain, it looks at signals over a frequency domain. The vertical axis is still voltage, but the horizontal axis is now frequency.

- TDRs work on the same principle as radar. An electrical pulse is sent down a cable and any anomaly that is encountered will send back a reflection. If the fault tends to increase the resistance, the reflected signal will be in the same direction as the pulse (usually upwards). If the fault decreases resistance, then the reflected signal will be in the opposite direction. Because of this, an open will appear as a reflection almost as strong as the initial pulse, and a short will reflect as strongly in the opposite direction. There are many variations in reflections that can tell a great deal about the condition of the cable.

■ One reason that a graphical TDR is usually preferred to a decimal readout is that a cable may contain more than on fault. Multiple faults show up not only with damage to a cable but also with phenomena such as splits, re-splits, and taps. A decimal readout would only show the distance to the first fault. Unless a graphical TDR runs into a complete short or open (or something like a load-coil), the instrument will present a "picture" of the cable.

■ With a Non Linear Junction Detector, the antenna radiates a signal. When this signal encounters an electronic device, the signal is returned at harmonic frequency levels. Other situations can also produce harmonic signals. The junctions in electronic devices and those in false junctions are quite different. When the signal is returned as a harmonic, the electronic device produces a regular signal pattern. Semiconductor junctions produce a receiver quieting effect, while many false junctions do not.

■ If a false junction is detected, one can easily discriminate between semi-conductor junctions and false junctions by listening to the audio and providing a physical vibration to the junction.

■ An RF Probe is a type of broadband receiver that is very useful for searching for near-field transmissions when performing a technical surveillance countermeasures sweep. The RF Probe often has numerous other functions that are helpful during a TSCM inspection.

KEY TERMS

Digital Multimeter

Vacuum Tube Volt-Ohm-Meter

Autoranging

Oscilloscope

Graticule

Triggering

Autoscale

Sample Rate

Fast Fourier Transforms

Spectrum Analyzer

Sweep Rate

Intermodulation Distortion

TDR

Non-Linear Junction Detector

Harmonic

Near-Field Transmissions

RF Probe

Known Sound Source

Bumper Beeper

VLF Probe

DISCUSSION QUESTIONS

1 Identify some features that can be found on a modern multimeter.

2 Why did the Vacuum Tube Volt-Ohm-Meter use a vacuum tube?

3 With regard to a digital multimeter, what does the term "not wanting to load the circuit" mean?

4 Root Mean Square (RMS) is sometimes referred to by a different name. What is it?

5 To what does a four-channel input on an oscilloscope refer? What is a mixed signal input?

6 Which type of oscilloscope shows a better picture of a square wave: analog or digital? Why?

7 A Fast Fourier Transform is used to change the x-axis from one base to another—name these bases.

8 Why is a TDR sometimes referred to as radar for wire? When would a numeric readout suffice? When is a graphical TDR advantageous?

9 How are pulse widths measured on a TDR? Why would you want to use a larger pulse width?

10 What is VOP, and why is it used?

11 What is the advantage of using a Non Linear Junction Detector?

12   How would a corroded joint be indicated on a NLJD, and how can it be confirmed?

13   What is a near-field transmission? Which instrument should be used to detect near-field transmissions?

14   What does the Infrared (IR) Probe do? Name one difficulty in locating an IR beam. How are microwave transmissions similar to IR transmissions?

15   Can an RF Probe, such as the CPM-700, check electric lines?

RESEARCH QUESTIONS

1   Some RF Probes or broadband receivers use so-called *active antennas*. What is the difference between an active and a passive antenna?

2   We have discussed TEMPEST. What does this acronym stand for?

3   What type of mathematical formula would you use to change the time domain output of an oscilloscope to the frequency domain of the spectrum analyzer?

CHAPTER 5

Transmission Line Theory

PURPOSE AND OBJECTIVES

This chapter will introduce the student to the different types of transmission methods available for alarms, access control systems, CCTV systems, and networks. We will cover not only wire and wireless methods, but also variations of each, such as UHF, 802.11(b), 802.11(g), and 802.11(a) in the wireless world, and coax, fiber, and copper in the wired world.

The chapter touches on the wired and wireless worlds of computer networks as well as alarm systems. With more and more movement toward integration of different types of services into one carrier mode, it is important for the security specialist to be familiar with much more than the simple twisted pair wire or 315 MHz wireless used with alarm and access control systems.

This chapter should prepare the reader to:

■ Become familiar with the BICSI organization

■ Specify different types of transmission media for different applications

■ Know the advantages of wire, wireless, and fiber optic technologies

■ Realize the importance of characteristic impedance

■ Recognize the differences of coaxial cable and twisted pair cable

■ Learn about wireless methods becoming popular due to convergence of data and security systems

BICSI

Headquartered in Tampa, FL, BICSI is a professional, not-for-profit telecommunications association. BICSI publishes the *Telecommunications Distribution Methods Manual* (*TDMM*). The *TDMM* is a valuable resource for those who design telecommunications infrastructure in commercial and multi-dwelling residential buildings. Containing a complete overview of telecommunications distribution, the *TDMM* takes the reader from design through construction, installation, and maintenance. The manual is updated every three years to provide the latest information on techniques, methodologies, codes, and standards. It is the basis for the exam for BICSI's Registered Communications Distribution Designer (RCDD) designation.

NETWORKING

When you hear the term "networking," computers and computer networks often come to mind. Note that although most security and access control systems are connected to a computer network somewhere along the way, they do not have to be, and they may comprise a network of their own. A network is simply a group of devices that communicate with each other, connected by some sort of transmission medium. Alarm systems are made up of controller boxes that communicate with the sensor devices scattered over a property. Access control systems are also made up of devices such as card readers, turnstiles, and biometric devices that communicate over a transmission media to a microprocessor or microcontroller. A very important common denominator among all these systems is the transmission media. In an electronic circuit of any type, the components must be connected. This connection can take the form of wire, electromagnetism, light waves, or other types of media.

WIRE

One familiar type of media is wire. In our homes, wire is used to connect electric outlets, telephones, lights, and more recently cable TV systems, satellite TV systems, and sound systems. One thing that most people do not realize is that each of these networks may require a special type of wire. For our electrical system, the most important considerations are the type of insulation, the current carrying ability of the wire, and aging characteristics (since the wire will be mostly hidden behind walls).

INSULATION

Insulation is the non-conducting material that covers the wire. The characteristics and properties of insulation are certified by agencies such as the Underwriters Laboratories, for the good of the public. Fire resistance, pressure and weathering characteristics, and chemical makeup to ensure non-toxicity are all properties that are carefully tested before the insulation is certified. Of course, the main purpose of the insulating material is to keep the bare wire from touching things such as other wires (creating short circuits), or people (who would be shocked). Some types of insulation are:

- Vinyl, a plastic that may take several forms ranging from very soft to very hard (PVC tubing, for example). Vinyl gets good temperature ratings from well below freezing to above the temperature of boiling water.

- Polyethylene, a substance similar to vinyl, is used mainly for its moisture resistance and outside weather characteristics.

- Teflon, which is expensive but very resistant to heat and wear, is good for code compliance when running cable through duct work.

Table 5–1 contains temperature ranges for various insulators.

Table 5–1 Insulation Temperature Ranges in Degrees Centigrade

Material	Low	High
Chlorosulfonated Polyethylene	–20	90
Ethylene Propylene Rubber (EPDM)	–55	105
Neoprene	–20	60
Polyethylene	–60	80
Polypropylene	–40	105
Rubber	–30	60
Silicone	–80	150
Teflon	–70	200
Vinyl	–20	80

WIRE TYPES

The most basic wire type is lamp cord. This is simply stranded wire covered by a low cost insulation material. The only variations we might see are wire gauge, wire type, and thickness of insulation. The next most basic wire type is building electrical wiring. Since this wire will carry an alternating current with a consistent frequency, the important considerations are wire gauge for current carrying capability and insulation. Building electrical wire is generally solid rather than stranded.

Now we move up to transmission wire, where we will be concerned with characteristics that are meaningless for simple electrical wire, such as *cross talk*, or electromagnetic interference from wire to wire, capacitance, need for shielding to prevent leakage, velocity of propagation, and so forth.

TWISTED PAIR CABLING

In the telephone and security industries, twisted pair cabling is the most common transmission medium. This type of wire, purchased by the box in lengths of thousands of feet (coiled within the box); can be obtained in two, four, six, eight, or more pairs within the outer insulation material. The wire pair, twisted at approximately twenty turns per foot, is between 22 and 26 gauge. The reason for the twist is to prevent cross talk. When electric current passes through a wire, a magnetic field is generated perpendicular to the path of the current. If a second wire is lying next to the current carrying wire, the magnetic field will induce, by inductance, a weak current in the second wire. In the case of a telephone wire, current going through one wire is actually changing at the rate of a sound signal (voice or data) on one end of the circuit. The weak current produced in the near wire would replicate that voice or data current. We have all heard the sound of weak voices over our telephone (in the background). This is cross talk produced by these induced currents. The twist in the wires helps to keep the wires from being parallel to each other at any given point and makes them less susceptible to this electromagnetic inductance, or cross talk. Incidentally, cross talk is usually formed at the connector ends of a wire because this is where a technician will untwist the wire to have a straight end to connect to a screw post or connector. There are standards that specify how much of a straight section of wire is permissible at a connector end in order to prevent cross talk in different categories of wire. Cross talk is also commonly induced in a home when a run of telephone wire is placed right next to a run of electric wire. The 60-cycle AC current in the electric wire will induce a *hum* in the telephone wire.

Electromagnetic interference such as cross talk in voice wires is aggravating, but it can be disastrous in a data line, and that is why we categorize different types of wiring according to stringent characteristics. To prevent interference to the wires within an insulator, wire pairs are sometimes shielded by a copper mesh or metallic foil. A Shielded Twisted Pair is referred to as STP. An Unshielded Twisted Pair is referred to as UTP.

COAXIAL CABLE

Coaxial cable, commonly called coax, is made up of concentric parts including an inner conductor that can be stranded or solid wire (generally copper), surrounded by plastic foam or some other insulating material called a *dielectric*, and an outer conductor of copper or aluminum covered by a strong insulating material. There are many different types of coax cable as shown in Table 5–2.

RG8 and RG58 are used for Ethernet (IP transmission). RG8 is the larger of the two. Seventy-five ohm cable, such as RG59, is used for video. Coaxial cable is popular because it allows for greater bandwidth, better security, less electromagnetic radiation, and longer cable length maximums than twisted pair.

Connectors used with coax are Bayonet Neill-Concelman (BNC) and Twist Neill-Concelman (TNC.)

Table 5–2 Types of Coax Cable

Coax Type	Characteristic Impedance	Gauge of Center Conductor
RG6	75	18 AWG
R8	50	18 AWG
RG11	75	14 AWG
RG58	50	14 AWG
RG59	75	22 AWG
RG62	93	22 AWG

CABLE CATEGORIES

Several different standards organizations influence data cabling. Table 5–3 shows some of those organizations and their subcommittees.

Table 5–3 Cable Standards Organizations

Organization	Subcommittee
EIA/TIA	TR41.8.1
CENELEC	TC 15 WG1
ISO/IEC	ISO/IEC JTC1 SC25 WG3
IEEE	802.3x

BICSI, which we spoke of previously, is one of the predominant standards-influencing organizations. TIA 568A standards are some of the most well known standards because they deal with telecommunications wiring within premises. TIA standards define and specify performance of cabling links even beyond 100 MHz. TIA categorizes cable numerically as shown in Table 5–4.

Table 5–4 Cable Categories

Standard	TIA Category
16 MHz	Category 3
100 MHz	Category 5 (5E to 300MHz)
200 MHz	Category 6
600 MHz	Category 7

Table 5–4 shows the category types of cable required for certain data rates. What happened to Category 4? It was used generally for a type of network (Token ring) which is not used as much as Ethernet and other protocols, and can be covered by Category 5 without significant cost increase. The main difference between cable types is the ability to hold down near end cross talk (NEXT), which will be explained later in this chapter. Table 5–5 shows some numbers for basic link performance produced by Microtest, Inc.

Table 5–5 Basic Link Performance (Courtesy of Fluke/Microtest, Inc)

	Category 3	Category 5	Category 5E	Category 6
Propagation Delay		<548 nS	<548 nS	<548 nS
Delay Skew		<45 nS	<45 nS	<45 nS
Attenuation (dB) @ 1 MHz @10 MHz @100MHz @200MHz	3.2 10.0	2.1 6.3 21.6	2.1 6.3 21.6	2.1 6.2 20.7 30.4
NEXT (dB) @ 1 MHz @10 MHz @100MHz @200MHz	40.1 2.3	60.0 45.5 29.3	64 49 32.3	73.5 57.8 41.9 36.9
PSNEXT (dB) @ 1 MHz @10 MHz @100MHz @200MHz			60 45.5 29.3	71.2 55.5 39.3 34.3
ELFEXT (dB) @ 1 MHz @10 MHz @100MHz @200MHz		57 37 17	61 41 21	65.2 45.2 25.2 19.2
PSELFEXT (dB) @ 1 MHz @10 MHz @100MHz @200MHz		54.4 34.4 14.4	5 38 18	62.2 42.2 22.2 16.2
Return Loss (dB) 1-20 MHz 20-100 MHz 100-200 MHz	N/A	15 15-10log (f/20)	17 17-7log (f/20)	19 19-10log (f/20) 19-10log (f/20)

SOME DEFINITIONS

- NEXT is near end cross talk, the interference measured on a wire next to a signal-carrying wire

- PSNEXT is power sum NEXT, which is actually a calculation derived from a summation of individual NEXT effects on each pair by the other three pairs in a 4-pair cable

- FEXT is far end cross talk, highly influenced by the length of a cable. More often, ELFEXT is the measurement of preference

- ELFEXT is equal level far end cross talk. It is a calculation that subtracts the attenuation factor of the cables

- PSELFEXT is power sum ELFEXT (see PSNEXT above)

CABLE TOPOLOGIES

Typically, when we talk about topology, we are discussing computer networks, but it is important that the security specialist also have a good familiarity with various topologies because he may be involved in providing or working with cabling for systems such as audio, video, cable TV, satellite TV, or telephone.

BASIC NETWORKS

Two basic models encompass most networks in use these days. One is the point-to-point model and the other is a multipoint model. Point-to-point is as it sounds—a cable is wired from one place to another. In a multipoint system, the cable is attached to more than one node. Typically, a bus line or main cable run is tapped into by numerous nodes or stations. The multipoint model is typical of most alarm or access control systems wherein the stations and peripherals are connected in series or in parallel with each other. As in a computer network, an alarm or access control system may be wired in a *hybrid* manner, in which the individual controllers have peripherals that are connected in a multipoint fashion, but these individual, or secondary controllers, can be wired point-to-point to a main control unit.

SUPERVISION

One very important consideration in security systems is the concept of supervision. Not only is it important that the security system work as it should in providing information about a compromised entry or exit point, but the integrity of the system itself must be monitored. In order to ensure that the circuit itself is intact and that no cable has been damaged or disconnected, the circuit is constantly monitored by sending a data pulse down the line and making sure it is returned or reflected back in a timely fashion. In many systems, an *end of line resistor* is fastened between the wire pair at the end of the bus line so that a certain value of reflected signal is returned to the controller. If the reflected signal is attenuated too much (or not enough), then an alarm condition will take place. Why is a certain value of reflectance important? Have you ever seen a movie where the bad guy bridges a wire pair with a splice? This helps to prevent that situation. Remember, we are talking about time *and* attenuation of the returned signal, so the bad guy's splice would have to provide the correct impedance and characteristic to not only attenuate the signal properly, but to provide a delay in the return to make up for the reduced length of the cable (to the newly placed splice). Now, of course, the degree of sophistication in the supervision process is dependent on the type of system, and how much money was spent purchasing it!

FIBER OPTICS

One of the most secure methods of transporting a signal from one point to another is using fiber optics. A fiber optic cable is literally a glass pipe, which carries a light beam. The light will follow the curvature and path of the glass pipe very efficiently, and, using special amplifiers, can be kept at a sufficient strength to travel miles to its receiver point. Some fiber optic cable is made of plastic, but this type of cable is generally used for very short runs. During manufacturing, the fiber optic is formed into a transparent hollow "wire," and is coated by a material that is less suitable for light transmission. This causes the light to be "bounced" away from the walls of the optic as it travels along. The bounced light is incapable of exceeding a critical angle. The cable has a transparent center core, which is covered by cladding and then covered once again by an outer coating. The cladding is manufactured not only to protect the fiber, but also to aid in the reflection process. The outer cover is designed to provide protection against the outside world. When compared to copper, fiber optic cable has a much greater capacity for carrying signals, has no problem with cross talk because it lacks electromagnetics, and offers superb security because the fiber optic is very difficult to tap. Fiber optic cable is surprisingly strong. It stands up against wear and tear very well, and it can be bent and curved almost as much as its copper counterpart can. Fiber can be packaged in many ways: as a single fiber (simplex), a dual zip cord cable (flat packaged), and dual cable (round packaged), as well as in many multiples. There are two types of fiber: *single mode* and *multimode*. The diameter of the fiber determines which type it is. If the diameter is five to ten micrometers, the wire will support only one mode and is referred to as single mode. Light in single mode fiber tends to follow just one path as it bounces along. Single mode fiber is the more expensive of the two and has a cladding of 125 µm. The bandwidth potential of single mode fiber is over 50 MHz. Multimode fiber is further classified as being step-index or graded-index fiber. Step index is multimode glass or plastic with a core diameter of about 100 to 970 µm, and is the most frequently used cable. It is called multimode because the core is wide enough to have light reflect at several different angles as it travels through the fiber. This creates light dispersion and there will be multiple paths as the light travels along. Graded-index fibers have core diameters of from 50 to 85 µm and cladding of 125 µm. Graded-index fibers are used in the telecommunications field where high bandwidth is needed. A standard of 62.5 µm for the core is an industry standard. When discussing fiber optic cable, the nomenclature is expressed by mode and then core and cladding diameters, such as Multimode 62.5/125.

CHARACTERISTICS

When discussing optics we use wavelengths instead of frequency for the rate of transmission. Recall that the formula for wavelength is

$$\lambda = \frac{300}{f} meters \qquad\qquad \textbf{(Eq. 5–1)}$$

where f = frequency in Hertz.

Typical wavelengths of the light carried in fiber optic cable are 850 nm, 1300 nm, 1380 nm, and 1550 nm. The higher the wavelength, the less the attenuation, with 850 nm attenuating at the rate of about 3.6 dB per kilometer, and 1300 nm at 1.15 dB per kilometer.

In the last section, we mentioned dispersion, the spreading of light as it travels through a fiber optic. This limits bandwidth and the ability to carry information. If the bit rate gets too high, pulses can overlap and cause messages to be garbled. The bit rate of the pulses must be kept low enough to prevent distortion. Cable manufacturers specify a *figure of merit* given in MHz per kilometer such as 500 MHz/km. This would translate to:

1500 MHz for 1/4 km

1000 MHz for 1/2 km

500 MHz for 1 km

250 MHz for 2 km

100 MHz for 5 km

CABLE TERMINATIONS

Two critical operations when working with fiber optics are splicing sections of fiber and fastening connectors at the ends. The cores of fiber optics are so small that any mismatch or (or dust) can severely affect light transmission. Fiber has splices because it is usually purchased in lengths no greater than five kilometers, as anything longer than this becomes difficult to pull. However, the cable is useful at much greater lengths, say 20 to 30 km. There are different types of connectors used with fiber optics with names like ST, biconic, SMA, and SDM, although SMA and SDM are increasingly being replaced by ST and SC connectors. Typically, ST is used with multimode, and biconic is used for single-mode. There are many adapter kits on the market to convert one connector type to another.

MULTIPLEXING

Fiber cabling, in addition to its extraordinary capability to carry great bandwidth, can also be multiplexed. A common method is *Wave Division Multiplexing* (WDM). Multiple wavelength systems are commonly referred to as wavelength division multiplexed. In earlier systems, it was common to increase the bandwidth of a 1310 nm link by adding another channel of 1550 nm. Introduction of Erbium Doped Fiber Amplifiers (EDFA), which can amplify all wavelengths at the same time, has moved WDM systems to 1565 nm wavelengths. The most recent WDM systems are now classified as Dense Wavelength Division Multiplexing (DWDM) because the separation of the multiplexed wavelengths has been moved very close together (usually with 100 MHz between channels). If you think of different wavelengths of light as being different *colored* lights, you could think of a multiplexed fiber optic signal as being a rainbow of light traveling through the fiber. Table 5–6 lists some defined wavelength channels used for multiplexing.

Table 5–6 ITU-T Defined WDM Wavelength Channels

Frequency (THz)	Wavelength (nm)
195.6	1532.7
195.5	1533.5
195.4	1534.9
195.3	1535.0
195.2	1535.8
195.1	1536.6
195.0	1537.4
194.9	1538.2
194.8	1539.0
194.7	1539.8
194.6	1540.6
194.5	1541.3
194.4	1542.1
194.3	1542.9
194.2	1543.7
194.1	1544.5
194.0	1545.3
193.9	1546.1
193.8	1546.9
193.7	1547.7
193.6	1548.5
193.5	1549.3
193.4	1550.1
193.3	1550.9

Table 5–6 ITU-T Defined WDM Wavelength Channels (Continued)

Frequency (THz)	Wavelength (nm)
193.2	1551.7
193.1	1552.5
193.0	1553.3
192.9	1554.1
192.8	1554.9
192.7	1555.7
192.6	1556.6
192.5	1557.4
192.4	1558.2
192.3	1559.0
192.2	1559.8

WIRELESS

Original wireless transmissions took place in the noisy HF frequency band from 3 to 30 MHz and were digital in the form of Morse Code telegraphy or radio teletype (RTTY). The dots and dashes of Morse Code were easy to determine because they came across slowly, typically between 10 and 30 words per minute (based on a five-letter word), and were picked up by the human ear, which could differentiate the noise from the actual signal. As the need for faster data transmission speeds increased, the frequencies of operation got higher and higher because the higher the frequency, the quieter the signal. Since the human ear was no longer the intended receiver of the signal, it became necessary to get the best possible signal-to-noise ratio. Unfortunately, the range of wireless communications decreases with an increase in frequency until range becomes pretty much line-of-sight. We have now reached the point where the rate of data being sent over wireless systems is in the millions of bits per second, and with satellites handling long-distance communications, line-of-site is sufficient and we can travel right up into the higher GHz ranges.

In the security business, distance is not a big concern because distances from security sensor to control unit usually are not great, and signals can be amplified with the use of repeaters. A definite concern with wireless communication is communications security. We do not want our signals to be jammed or spoofed. Fortunately, cryptographic methods are available, and we do have the ability to send our signals via spread spectrum transmission.

FREQUENCY BANDS

In the wireless world, several frequency bands have been defined. These bands have been grouped into frequencies that exhibit similar characteristics. The HF band is categorized as between 3 and 30 MHz. Properties of this band are that it is useful for long distance world-wide communications. It has two components: a ground wave and a sky (or skip) wave. The ground wave stretches out at a certain distance depending on the type of antenna, the terrain, and the power output of the transmitter; typically, the range is between 10 and 100 miles. The sky wave skips along from earth to ionosphere, with its distance and number of skips dependent on the time of day, the season, sunspot activity, and other factors that affect the iono-sphere. From 30 to 300 MHz, we have the VHF band, which is much quieter than the HF band, but does not have the long distance char-acteristics of HF because there is very little, if any, skip produced. These radio waves will usually penetrate the ionosphere and go straight up into space. This band provides for distance that is slightly greater than line of sight. The VHF band is favored by public service and government agencies because repeaters can be located on high structures to provide good metropolitan coverage, and a quiet radio speaker when there is no one talking. The next frequency band, from 300 to 3000 MHz (or 300MHz to 3 GHz), is classified as UHF, with the higher frequencies in the band referred to as "microwave". These frequencies will definitely penetrate the layers of ions around Earth and go into space, and are actually used for space communications. We have talked to people on the moon using these frequencies! The lower frequency portion of this band is used by commercial enter-prises, which also utilize repeaters. Delivery trucks and radio-dispatched cabs use these frequencies. The 800 and 900 MHz parts of the band contain the cellular phone frequencies and some cord-less phone varieties. Getting into the GHz frequencies has recently brought about new uses for data communications. Below we examine some of the so-called 802.11 activity.

802.11 Standards and Frequencies

The Institute of Electrical and Electronic Engineers (IEEE) has produced 802.11 standards, which specify parameters for frequency bands and modes used for data and some other types of communications. The best known 802.11 subtypes are 802.11(a), 802.11(b), and 802.11(g).

802.11(b)

802.11(b), sometimes referred to as "Wi-Fi", is probably best known, and the most common type as of this publication. 802.11(b) operates in the 2.4 GHz band, does not require licensing by the FCC, and carries data at 5–11 Mbps (Megabits per second) using Direct Sequence Spread Spectrum (DSSS) and Frequency Division Multiplexing (FDM). There is a trade-off between range and throughput. Your equipment should auto-sense signal strength and slow the transmission rate if the signal gets weak. It should back down from 11 Mbps to 5.5, 2, or even 1 Mbps. Remember that, although 1 Mbps may sound low, many businesses have a T1 telephone line as their connection to the Internet. As a T1 only moves data at 1.544 Mbps, this should not be a problem. The top speed is 11 Mbps, but that is only over the air. Access points typically have 10baseT Ethernet connections, so the theoretical maximum to the wire is still only 10 Mbps. Ethernet cards currently on the market have only one transceiver in them. That means half-duplex communications only (you can talk or listen with a transceiver, but not both.) This means that while the cards are specified for 11 Mbps, the speed will most certainly vary.

802.11(a)

The 802.11(a) standard operates in the 5 GHz frequency range. The Federal Communications Commission has allocated 300 MHz of spectrum for unlicensed operation in the 5 GHz band, 200 MHz of which is at 5.15 GHz to 5.35 GHz, with the other 100 MHz at 5.725

GHz to 5.825 GHz. The spectrum is split into three working areas. The first 100 MHz in the lower section is restricted to a maximum power output of 50 mW (milliwatts). The second 100 MHz has a more generous 250 mW power budget, while the top 100 MHz is tabbed for the outdoors, with a 1-watt power output. In contrast, 802.11(b) cards can radiate as much as 1 watt in the United States. However, most modern cards use only a fraction (30 mW) of the available power output. Although segmented, the total bandwidth available for IEEE 802.11(a) applications is almost four times that of the 2.4 GHz band at 300 MHz. The 802.11(b) spectrum is troubled by use of wireless phones, microwave ovens and other technologies, such as Bluetooth. In contrast, 802.11(a) is relatively free of interference. Moving to the 5 GHz band from 2.4 GHz will lead to shorter distance communications with the same power and transmission scheme. The 802.11(a) technology overcomes some of the distance loss by increasing the output to the maximum 50 mW; however, power alone is not enough to maintain 802.11(b) distances in an 802.11(a) world. A new technology called Coded Orthogonal Frequency Division Multiplexing (COFDM) was developed specifically for indoor wireless use and offers performance superior to that of spread-spectrum solutions. COFDM works by breaking one high-speed data carrier into several lower-speed sub carriers, which are then transmitted in parallel. Each high-speed carrier is 20 MHz wide and is broken up into 52 sub channels, each about 300 KHz wide. COFDM uses 48 of these sub channels for data, while the remaining four are used for error correction. COFDM delivers higher data rates and a high degree of multipath reflection protection, thanks to its error correction. Each sub channel in the COFDM implementation is around 300 KHz wide. At the low end, Binary Phase Shift Keying (BPSK) is used to encode 125 Kbps of data per channel, resulting in a 6 Mbps data rate. Using Quadrature Phase Shift Keying (QPSK), we can double the amount of data encoded to 250 Kbps per channel, producing a 12 Mbps data rate. Using 16-level Quadrature Amplitude Modulation (QAM) encoding 4 bits per Hertz, we can achieve a data rate of 24 Mbps. The 802.11(a) standard specifies that all 802.11(a) compliant products must support these data rates.

802.11(g)

For 802.11(b) compatibility, 802.11(g) incorporates 802.11(b)'s Complementary Code Keying (CCK) to achieve bit transfer rates of 5.5 and 11 Mbps in the 2.4 GHz band. In addition, 802.11(g) has

802.11(a)'s Orthogonal Frequency Division Multiplexing (OFDM) for 54 Mbps speeds but in the 2.4 GHz range. 802.11(g) can also handle optional modes to achieve throughput ranges in the 22 Mbps range. These are Intersil's CCK-OFDM mode with a maximum throughput of 33 Mbps and Texas Instrument's Packet Binary Convolutional Coding (PBCC-22), with a throughput range of 6–54 Mbps. Both 802.11(a) and 802.11(g) are said to offer up to 55 Mbps speed. In practice, 802.11(a) delivers about 20 Mbps. That may not sound like much unless you know that 802.11(b)'s prated 11 Mbps speed is generally 4 Mbps in practice. Early versions of 802.11(g) chipsets have real-world speeds in the 6 Mbps range. It is also clear from FCC tests that 802.11(g) has the same, or slightly better range than 802.11(b), 2.4 GHz, a common frequency with many appliances has to put up with a lot of noise interference. This can result in lower throughput, which in turn can reduce its range. 802.11(a)'s 5 GHz, on the other hand, has much less interference to deal with and its part of the spectrum appears, from FCC regulations, likely to stay free of most other devices. 802.11(g) can handle only three channels at once.

Bluetooth

Bluetooth is used for both voice and data and is considered for security applications because of its inherent security. The name Bluetooth comes from tenth century Danish history. Harald Blatand, whose name the English translated to Harold Bluetooth, was a king of Denmark. He unified his country as Bluetooth's developers are hoping for unification of portable electronic products to a uniform wireless protocol. Bluetooth is a spread spectrum method of communications that uses frequency hopping spread spectrum (FHSS) as opposed to the direct sequence spread spectrum (DSSS) of the other communications methods we have discussed. Bluetooth utilizes a "channel-hopping" scheme that transmits data over 79 channels at 1600 hops per second. This frequency of hopping makes Bluetooth a very secure method of transmission. It also protects the transmissions from interference from things such as microwave ovens and cordless phones, which may corrupt other modes. Bluetooth can also utilize additional cryptography to make it even more secure. One popular encryption method utilizes 128-bit encryption, which is considered very strong.

SUMMARY

- Wire is a commonly used, familiar medium. In our homes, wire is used to connect electric outlets, telephones, lights, and more recently cable TV systems, satellite TV systems, and sound systems. For electrical systems, the most important considerations are the type of insulation, the current carrying ability of the wire, and aging characteristics (since the wire will be mostly hidden behind walls).

- Insulation is the non-conducting material that covers the wire.

- Lamp cord is the most basic wire type. It is simply stranded wire covered by a low cost insulation material.

- Next in line is building electrical wiring. Since this wire type will carry an alternating current with a consistent frequency, the important considerations are wire gauge for current carrying capability and insulation. Building electrical wire is generally solid rather than stranded.

- In the telephone and security industries, twisted pair cabling is the most frequently used transmission medium. The wire pair, twisted at approximately 20 turns per foot, is between 22 and 26 gauge. The reason for the twist is to prevent cross talk or electromagnetic interference from wire to wire.

- If a second wire is lying next to the current carrying wire, the magnetic field will induce a weak current in the second wire. In the case of a telephone wire, current going through one wire is actually changing a signal (voice or data) on one end of the circuit, at the rate of sound. The weak current produced in the near wire would replicate that voice or data current.

- Standards specify how much of a straight section of wire is permissible at a connector end in order to prevent cross talk in different categories of wire. The 60-cycle AC current in the electric wire will induce a hum in the telephone wire. Electromagnetic interference such as cross talk in voice wires is aggravating and can be disastrous in a data line, which is why we categorize different types of wiring according to stringent characteristics. To prevent interference to the wires within an insulator, wire pairs are sometimes shielded by a copper mesh or metallic foil.

- Coaxial cable is popular because it allows for greater bandwidth, better security, less electromagnetic radiation, and longer cable length maximums than twisted pair.

- Connectors used with coax cable are BNC and TNC.

- TIA standards define and specify performance of cabling links even beyond 100 MHz. TIA categorizes cable numerically.

- A fiber optic cable is literally a glass or plastic pipe that carries a light beam. Plastic cable is generally used for very short runs. During manufacturing, the fiber optic is formed into a transparent hollow "wire," and is coated by a material that is less suitable for light transmission. Fiber optic cable is surprisingly strong. Fiber can be packaged in many ways, as a single fiber (simplex), a dual zip cord cable (flat packaged), dual cable (round packaged), or in multiples. There are two types of fiber: single mode and multimode. The diameter of the fiber determines which type it is. The bandwidth potential of single mode fiber is over 50 MHz. Multimode fiber is further classified as step-index or graded-index fiber. When discussing fiber optic cable, the nomenclature is expressed by mode and then core and cladding diameters, such as multimode 62.5/125.

- When discussing optics we use wavelengths instead of frequency for the rate of transmission. Typical wavelengths of the light carried in fiber optic cable are 850 nm, 1300 nm, 1380 nm, and 1550 nm.

- Fiber cabling, in addition to its extraordinary capability to carry great bandwidth, can also be multiplexed. Multiple wavelength systems are commonly referred to as wavelength division multiplexed. One could think of a multiplexed fiber optic signal as a rainbow of light traveling through the fiber.

- The Institute of Electrical and Electronic Engineers (IEEE) has produced 802.11 standards, which specify parameters for frequency bands and modes used for data and some other types of communications.

- Bluetooth is a spread spectrum method of communications that uses frequency hopping spread spectrum (FHSS) as opposed to the direct sequence spread spectrum (DSSS) of the other communications methods we have discussed. This frequency of hopping makes Bluetooth a very secure method of transmission.

KEY TERMS

BICSI

RCDD

STP

UTP

Dielectric

BNC

TNC

Near End Cross Talk

End of Line Resistor

Single Mode

Multimode Fiber

WDM

DWDM

Skip

DSSS

COFDM

BPSK

QPSK

QAM

QUESTIONS

1 How often is BICSI's *Telecommunications Distribution Methods Manual* (TDMM) updated?

2 How does one become a Registered Communications Distribution Designer (RCDD)?

3 Name three different methods of connecting components in an access control system to form a network.

4 What are some of the properties of an insulator that would be tested by the Underwriter Laboratories?

5 Which type of insulation would one find on cabling that is running through duct work?

6 Define cross talk. Describe a wire method for preventing cross talk. Where would cross talk be a more serious problem, data or voice? Why?

7 What is the difference between UTP and STP?

8 Define the term "Supervision" as it applies to alarm systems. Why is an *End of Line Resistor* used?

9 What is the difference between multimode and single mode fiber? Which is more expensive, and why?

10 What is the relationship between WDM and FDM? What is DWDM?

11 Why is it frequently necessary to splice fiber cable?

12 Give some typical ranges (in miles) for the following: HF, VHF, UHF, and GHz Communications.

13 What is the frequency band for HF communications?

14 In terms of type of transmission, what makes Bluetooth different than 802.11?

15 What size wire is generally used in the telephone and security industry at a customer location? Why is it twisted?

RESEARCH QUESTIONS

1 Now that most security hardware is networked, the cabling discussed in this chapter is attached to the equipment via an NIC. What is an NIC? Associate the NIC with the OSI platform.

2 Why are we unable to use twisted pair wire for networking? Why is it so important to use expensive category 5 or 6 or better cable?

3 Fiber optic cable is often used with perimeter security by attaching it to the fence fabric. How do you think a fiber optic could register fence vibration?

CHAPTER 6

Video and Optics

PURPOSE AND OBJECTIVES

The use of video is very important in the security business. In this chapter, you will learn about cameras, lenses, recording devices, and other peripherals associated with surveillance. These days video is much more than just cameras and video recorders. With the proliferous use of computers and networks, video has to have the ability to become part of a network along with access control systems, alarm systems, and database servers. Subjects covered in this chapter include the following:

- Still cameras

- Lenses

- Digital cameras

- Video cameras

- Video recorders

- Digital Video Recorders (DVRs)

- Recognition Systems and Databases

THE STILL CAMERA

In its simplest form, the still camera is a lightproof box with a film plane in the rear and a lens in the front. The optical system of the lens is configured so that when the lens is opened to allow the entry of light, an image of the landscape in front of the lens will be focused and projected onto the film plane (see Figure 6–1).

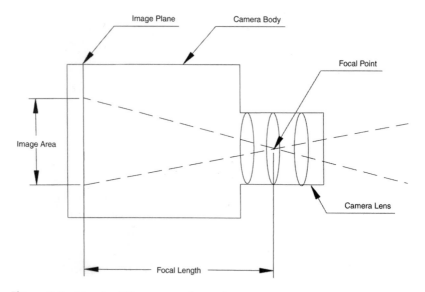

Figure 6–1 Simple still camera schematic.

We are starting with a simple still camera, because we can look at each of these three components individually and then relate each of them directly to more sophisticated camera systems including digital and video.

THE LENS

A camera lens can be very simple; it can be identical to a magnifying glass. A camera actually can go without a lens. One of the first cameras made was called a *pinhole camera* because it actually just had a small hole, which allowed light (and an image) to enter the camera body and be projected onto the film plane. Of course, a pinhole camera offers terrible fidelity of the image. Many types of lenses exist now, some of moderate quality carrying a moderate price tag, and some with superior quality demanding a likewise superior price. How do these lenses work? If parallel rays of light pass through a convex lens (shaped like the inside of a bowl,) they converge to a single point on the optical axis. This point of convergence is the focal point of the lens. The focal length of a fixed-focal-length lens is indicated by the distance from the center of the lens to the focal point. A lens has two focal points, one on the object side, called the primary focal point, and one on the image side, called the secondary focal point. When the term "focal point" is used alone, it means the secondary focal point.

The lenses used on cameras are compound lenses, consisting of several individual lenses combined to correct *aberrations*, or defects, in the image-forming ability of a lens or optical system. Violet light will be focused closer to the lens and red light will be focused farther away. If we place a card at the location of the violet focus, we will see colored shadows or halos around it with red on the outside. If we place a card farther away, at the location of the red focus, we will see colored shadows or halos around the central red dot with violet on the outside. This problem with image formation is called *chromatic aberration*. We can correct for chromatic aberration by replacing a simple, single-element lens with a lens made of two or more pieces of glass that have different dispersion characteristics. However, they function as a single lens located at an imaginary point called the "principal point."

The focal length is the basic factor used to calculate the image position and magnification of a lens. The focal length of a lens is important as a factor describing the angle of view of the lens. The focal length and principal point of a zoom lens are changed by zooming, so as you zoom, you change the angle of view of the lens. A short focal length gives a wide angle of view, and a long focal length gives a narrow angle of view, which causes the image to be magnified. The price of these lenses varies greatly and is dependent on the quality of what is commonly referred to as the "glass," the body construction, features such as auto focus, image stabilization, and the light capturing ability known as the lowest *f*-stop of the lens.

The *f*-stop capability of a lens is important because it determines the lowest light level at which the lens will operate efficiently. The *f* in *f*-stop comes from the Italian word *finestra*, meaning "window." A lower *f*-stop number causes a larger diaphragm opening in the lens, which allows light to enter. The iris ring of most lenses is marked with a series of *f*-numbers with various ratios from 1:1.4, to 1:22. The brightness of the image is inversely proportional to the square of the *f*-number. Each time the ring is turned one number up the *f*-scale, the brightness is decreased by half. As the iris ring is turned down one number, the brightness is increased by two. There are some important things to remember about *f*-stops. The most important in the security world is that as you decrease the *f*-stop number (open the lens up more); a smaller portion of the view is in focus. As the *f*-stop number increases (opening of the lens decreases,) the depth of field becomes greater, meaning more of the picture is in focus. On a "normal" lens, meaning one that replicates the way the human eyeball sees the world, an *f*-stop of *f*16 would have just about everything in focus. A normal lens differs with different film formats. For example, on a 35mm camera a normal lens is considered to be a 50mm lens (remember, that means the distance from the lens' focal point to the film plane is 50mm). The "normal" lens has about the same angle of view as the human eye.

Taking depth of field into consideration is important. A security engineer may work into her design a camera that looks down a long hallway, where the light is somewhat dim. By choosing a lens with a low *f*-stop to capture as much light as possible, the designer may be narrowing the depth of field to the point where only a five-foot long slice of a 100-foot long hallway would be in focus. So, how in the world do we get a whole 100-foot long hallway with dim light into focus? Well, enter some new factors. If we start with a normal lens and move to a longer, or *telephoto*, lens we find that the depth of field for any given *f*-stop gets even narrower, but if we move in the other direction to a short, or *wide-angle*, lens, we find that the depth of field gets much wider for any given *f*-stop. A designer will have to take into consideration many factors in order to optimize any certain situation. Telephoto lenses will give a good image at the end of that long hallway, much better than a wide-angle lens, but will have a narrow depth of field, and can only be focused on a narrow area. Wide angle will give us good focus along the whole hallway, but the image at the end of the hall will be relatively small, and perhaps unrecognizable. Perhaps somewhere in the middle area, closer to a normal lens, but slightly telephoto, would be best for our hallway if we could work on increasing the light?

There are many considerations when determining lens size for a given situation. If we had a camera permanently fixed in a spot where it was aimed toward a window, we would have to consider the effect of sunlight during different times of day. There are lenses called "auto-iris" in which the diaphragm operates automatically depending on light conditions. These lenses are more typically found with closed circuit video cameras than with still cameras, although many banks still use mounted still cameras with specialty lenses, because they produce better images than video cameras. These still cameras in banks are set up to fire shots at regular intervals when an alarm situation is triggered.

Another important consideration with the lens is the *shutter speed*. This is the speed at which the shutter opens and closes. It ranges from "B" or "bulb" where the shutter opens on the first press of the trigger, and closes on a second press, all the way up to speeds greater than 1/4000th of a second.

Origin of the term "Bulb"

"Bulb" came from the time when film was so slow that it took a great deal of light to produce an image. A photographer used a lens that was always open, and the film plane was covered by a sliding board. He would slide the board out, and then a high intensity bulb (or charge of gunpowder) was set off to provide enough light to expose the film. Then the photographer would slide the board back over the film plane.

Now we have a third factor that can be used in our bag of tricks for getting the best picture in a certain situation. Thus far we have:

- *f*-stops that can control light input and depth of field
- Length of lens, which can be used to focus at varying distances with varying focusing abilities
- Shutter speed, which may be used in conjunction with *f*-stop, to control the amount of light that will strike and influence the film

Using different combinations of *f*-stop, lens length, and shutter speed, allows for different depth of field requirements, different light situations, and certainly the ability with high speed shutter operation to "freeze" worldly happenings. A fourth option, "film speed," gives us even more latitude to create the best picture in various situations. Different film types have numbers assigned by ISO, the international standards setting organization. A low number such as ISO 25 means the film is very *slow* and needs considerable amounts of light to produce an image. A "high speed" or high ISO film, such as

ISO 400, requires less light. With slow speed film, the grain is finer and can produce great resolution and ability for enlargement. High-speed films are lumpier, producing less resolution. Now film speed is our fourth factor, which can be used in combination with *f*-stop, shutter speed, and length of lens. This fourth factor is external to the lens, but works so closely with lens combinations that it is worth mentioning at this point. Later, when we talk about video and digital imaging, even though we will not be using film any more, we will still be able to use a *speed* factor associated with the recording media. Finally, it should be noted that some cameras are known as view-finder cameras. These cameras allow you to aim the camera through a separate window that is synchronized with the lens. These cameras typically have fixed lenses, and are on the inexpensive side. Single lens reflex cameras, are those that allow the photographer to view and aim the camera directly through the lens, thanks to a mirror configuration inside the camera. These cameras generally allow for interchangeable lenses and are on the expensive side. Figure 6–2 shows some lenses used in Closed Circuit Television.

Figure 6–2   CCTV lense selection ©Honeywell International, Inc.

The Lens Terminology box lists some terms that you may come across when discussing lenses.

Lens Terminology

Aberration: A defect in the image forming capability of a lens or optical system.

Achromatic: Free of aberrations relating to color or wavelength.

Aperture: An opening in an optical system that limits the amount of light passing through the system.

Astigmatism: A lens aberration that causes off-axis light bundles to focus to an elliptical, rather than circular, spot.

Bandwidth: The range of wavelengths over which an optical system is designed to function.

Chromatic: Having to do with color, or wavelength.

Coma: An off-axis lens aberration resulting from a variation of lens focal lengths as a function of aperture zone or annulus.

Complex Lens: A lens assembly consisting of several compound lenses.

Compound Lens: A lens assembly consisting of a number of simple lens elements.

Concave: A solid curved surface similar in shape to the inside of a bowl.

Concentric: Curved lines or surfaces having a common center of curvature.

Condenser Lens: A lens assembly designed to collect energy from a light source.

Conjugates: A pair of points that are invariably related to each other, such as the object and image points for a lens system.

Convex: A solid curved surface similar to the top of a mushroom.

Distortion: An off-axis lens aberration that changes the geometric shape of the image due to a variation of focal length as a function of field angle.

Doublet: A lens assembly made up of two simple lens elements.

Effective Focal Length: A series of parallel rays entering a positive lens will be bent toward the optical axis and brought to a focus, "focal point." If the entering and exiting rays are extended to their intersection points, these points form the lens' "principal plane." The intersection of the principal plane with the optical axis is the "principal point" of the lens. The "Effective Focal Length" (EFL) of the lens is the distance from the principal point to the focal point.

Lens Terminology (Continued)

Field of View: The portion of an extended object that is imaged onto the detector of an optical system.

Iris: An adjustable opening that limits the amount of light passing through an optical system.

Lateral Color: An off-axis lens aberration resulting from a variation in lens focal length as a function of wavelength.

Lens: An optical component that converges or diverges an incident wavefront.

Light: Electro-magnetic radiation with wavelengths in the spectral bandwidth perceived by the human eye (ca. 400–700 nm).

Magnification: The ratio of image to object size in an optical system; magnification may be real (linear) or apparent (angular).

Monochromatic: Having a single wavelength or color.

Nanometer (nm): The average wavelength of white light is about 550 nanometers.

Objective Lens: That lens in an optical system initially responsible for collecting light from the source or object and forming an image of it.

Polychromatic: Having many wavelengths.

Power: In an optical sense, the reciprocal of the focal length of a lens is equal to its power.

Resolution: The ability to distinguish fine detail or resolve information within an image.

Speed: The speed of a lens is a measure of its light gathering ability, which affects the image brightness; also referred to as f-number. Lens Speed or f/# = f/D, where f = Focal length of lens and D = Lens aperture diameter.

Stop: An aperture within an optical system that limits the amount of light transmitted and/or imaged.

Stray Light: Light passing through an optical system to the image plane that is unrelated to the primary image; stray light results in a loss of contrast and resolution.

If you understand lens theory with still camera technology, you will have no trouble transitioning to video cameras or digital cameras. Main differences in lenses from still cameras to video or digital cameras are the same as from still camera to still camera, that is, the focal length of the lens will have different relationships to different media types and sizes, and the type of mounting of the lens to the camera body differs among equipment, but the basics remain the same.

MEDIA

Thus far, we have been discussing film. Let us continue with film briefly. In still photography, the image is brought into the camera via the lens, which is designed to focus the image onto the film plane. The film plane differs in size depending on the type and size of film for which the camera is designed. Most of us are familiar with 35mm film. 35mm is a small format film that actually has a frame size of 24mm × 36mm. Medium formats are 120mm, 6cm × 6cm, and 6cm × 7cm. Then there are large format films such as 4in × 5in, 8in × 10in, and even up to 30in × 40in for large track (yes, like railroad tracks) mounted cameras. Earlier, we discussed film *speeds*, which are determined by their sensitivity to light. Slow speed films produce fine-grained, high-resolution images, but require more light than the faster, grainier films. When light strikes film, it causes a photosensitive reaction on silver halide crystals, which are painted onto the film backing. Chemical processing will cause the silver salts to turn dark in the places where light struck, the more light exposed on the film, the darker the silver salts become after processing. The image produced on the film is actually a *negative* image, thus processed film is referred to as a negative. From the negative, a positive print is formed. Fast films have less surface area on the silver halide salts, so they become exposed faster. Slow films have more (smaller) grains of silver halide which have more total surface area, so they take longer to expose, but because of the increased number of silver salt particles (and the fact that they are smaller), the produced image will exhibit finer resolution. Black and white films just have one layer of emulsion for light to effect. One type of black and white film is called *panchromatic*, meaning that it is affected by "all" colors. Color films have several layers of emulsion. At least one for red, one for blue, and one for green, and perhaps even more filter and buffer layers, and each of these layers has to be exposed by separate wavelengths of light.

Why have we been talking about film when we should really be more interested in digital and video photography? Because it is easier to explain first how light interacts with silver halides on a film base and then go into more complex concepts than it is to get straight into light causing an electronic action.

VIDEO TUBE TECHNOLOGY

In order to get a moving image, video tubes were produced as part of the camera, replacing the film plane in a still camera. These tubes would react to a scanning beam made up of light and dark images that came in through the lens. The first camera tubes were invented in the 1920s and were called Iconoscopes. A later version was called the *vidicon tube*. Up until the *CCD chip* became popular in the 1980s, the vidicon tube was the standard way to convert an image to an electronic signal. The vidicon tube was a vacuum tube with a photosensitive screen inside that your image was focused onto. An electron beam scanned this screen (usually made of a phosphorus coating) and converted any part of the screen that was illuminated to an electrical signal one point (called a pixel) at a time. This point-by-point image was then reassembled by the TV tube (cathode ray tube, CRT) that performed the reverse operation by scanning the front of the CRT with an electron beam that lit up one pixel at a time to match the transmitted picture. The United States set up a committee called the National Television System Committee (NTSC) whose job it was to set standards that all video signals must follow so TV sets, cameras and TV transmissions would be compatible with each other. They picked specifications already developed by Radio Corporation of America (RCA).

NTSC Standards

NTSC calls for a frame rate of 30 frames per second, meaning that is the number of pictures the video camera takes every second. The video signal is 1 volt in amplitude peak to peak. It also has a 75 ohm impedance. Standards such as the horizontal and vertical sync signals, color burst frequencies and several other technical specifications are specified by the NTSC as well.

The original cameras were only black and white. Color cameras were developed later, so the committee (NTSC) had to meet again in 1953 to establish the NTSC standard for color. Color video was accomplished using three vidicon tubes with red, green and blue filters in front of them. The color CRT likewise had a red, green, and blue electron gun that recreated the image sent electronically by the vidicon tube. In the 1990s Texas Instruments improved on the vidicon principle and developed the Tivicon tube. The system consisted of a self-contained closed circuit television camera equipped with a Tivicon tube and an array of six 200-milliwatt GaAs (gallium arsenide) emitters powered by a small portable DC supply. This equipment provided good high contrast images at distances of up to 75 feet with an f/1.4 25mm lens. The approximate illuminator cone angle was 23 degrees. Tests run on the system gave good pictures at 250 feet with a larger illuminator and a telephoto lens. For distances greater than this, gallium arsenide illumination from the camera site became very bulky and expensive. In many applications, the illuminator could be placed closer to the subject than the camera for better brightness and economy. Due to the long lifetime and power consumption of the emitters, it was possible to place a complete active surveillance system in remote or inaccessible places without fear of frequent maintenance. Coupled with infrared film cameras, the system was used to spot subjects for permanent recording with invisible radiation. The versatility of the Tivicon and the emitters allowed their use in an unlimited variety of television surveillance systems. The Tivicon was capable of 900 TV line resolution, enough for document reading or monitoring control panels. Because the photosensitive material in the Tivicon was silicon rather than a fragile film, it was able to operate at temperatures of −40° to +150°F for long periods without damage or degradation of image quality. In addition, it was not susceptible to damage by very high light levels, nor did it bloom if it looked into intense points of light. The Tivicon also had lower lag or smear than normal vidicons so that it was used in *pan* and *tilt* applications without loss of information. The most important feature from a surveillance standpoint was the Tivicon's increased sensitivity and near infrared response. Tivicon was not only compatible with present-used light sources like tungsten and mercury but it also worked extremely well with both xenon arcs and gallium arsenide solid-state infrared sources. Since the Tivicon required no high voltage or special operating conditions, most standard vidicon cameras accepted it without modification. It was available in both commercial and military versions. The Texas Instruments one-inch Tivicon solid-state image pickup tube uniquely combined semiconductor integrated circuit techniques with electron tube technology. By combining a wafer of silicon containing 2.4 million photodiodes (620,000/cm^2) with a standard one-inch diameter vidicon electron optic structure, an image pickup tube was produced which had entirely new properties and provided many benefits to the television image tube industry. The spectral response of the Tivicon image tube was unmatched by any other image tube available at the time. The Tivicon image tube, when viewed externally, appeared identical to a one-inch vidicon tube except for the metallic appearance of the silicon array behind the tube's faceplate. The electron optics used and voltages normally applied to a Tivicon image tube were those also applied to vidicon tube. The only electrical differences between a vidicon tube and Tivicon image tube were target voltage range and a higher signal current.

CHARGE COUPLED DEVICES (CCDS)

Most video cameras now use CCDs instead of vacuum tubes. The CCD chip used in video cameras (Figure 6–3) is more desirable than film in many ways. The CCD has a higher dynamic range, meaning it can distinguish between subtler changes in color than film can. The typical CCD can see the difference between up to a million different shades of gray. It is more sensitive than film in a wider range of the visible and invisible spectra of light. The typical CCD is sensitive into the near infrared up to 10000 Angstroms. CCDs have no memory like the phosphorus vidicon tubes had. This is because after one image is integrated, the pixels are completely reset before the next image begins to affect them. With CCDs, there is no streaking or burning-in such as with vidicons. Figure 6–4 shows a cross-section of an MOS capacitor and the charge transfer in a three-phase CCD array.

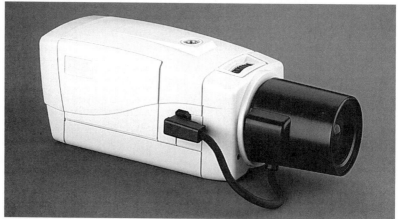

Figure 6–3   An Ademco Systems CCTV camera ©Honeywell International, Inc.

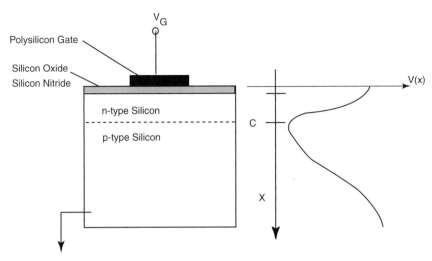

Figure 6–4   Charge transfer in a three-phase array.

CAMERA SIZE

We have discussed how still cameras use film, and how video cameras have evolved from tubes to CCDs. The next thing to consider is the physical size of the camera. Most of us are familiar with still cameras and how their size can vary from pocket-sized up to the larger studio portrait cameras, but think of how the size of video cameras has changed in just the last few years. TV studio cameras still tend to be quite large because of all the attachments that are necessary. Security related cameras, however, have really been subject to drastic changes. The cameras that used to use tubes were typically about a foot long, by about three inches wide, and four or five inches high. These large cameras were mounted such that they were highly visible, either in enclosures outside main buildings or by themselves, inside. The high visibility, incidentally, was not always detrimental. Many "dummy" cameras were sold, having just the body and no insides. The sight of a "camera" on the wall is often enough to discourage miscreants, whether there is really a recording device inside or not. There are situations, however, that call for disguised cameras. Disguising large cameras was a difficult task. With the advent of CCD technology, complete cameras can be manufactured on a circuit board that is only about one inch square, with a tiny lens that protrudes only about 1/8 to 1/4 inch from the board. These tiny cameras are excellent quality and can be mounted in clocks, lamps, overhead sprinklers, and exit signs; virtually anywhere you can imagine putting them (see Figure 6–5). The cameras require low voltage and can transmit images over inexpensive cable or even via wireless transmission.

Miniature camera mounted inside the cabinet to look out the "O" in the SONY label.

Figure 6–5   Hidden miniature CCTV camera inside a working tabletop radio.

TRANSMITTING THE CAMERA'S SIGNAL

With the older tube cameras, it was necessary to use coaxial cable to transmit the video signal to a monitor, or a video recorder. Until recently, there were not many wireless systems available for commercial use because of the necessity of transmitting a broadband (about 6 MHz) signal that required an antenna many times larger than the camera itself. Systems available now can transmit video information just as computers transmit data; via IP (Internet Protocol). These systems call for the use of an IP-compatible cable such as Category 5 cable with RJ45 connectors. Although the necessity is gone, there are still many cameras available today that use coax if desired. Since transmission can be via IP, wireless devices of the 802.11 type (or Bluetooth) can be used. Video can now be a part of the overall Information Technology system.

PAN, TILT, AND ZOOM (PTZ)

Cameras used with a security system are a combination of fixed devices, and Pan, Tilt, and Zoom cameras (PTZ). pan, tilt, and zoom is just what it sounds like; it allows the operator to pan the camera from side to side, tilt it up and down, or zoom the lens in and out. Just a few years ago, a pan and tilt mechanism was a camera mounted mechanism that had a separate power supply, and separate cabling. Imagine all the wires that had to run from the camera location to the control center. With cameras now using IP for transmission, video data can be multiplexed with control data for pan, zoom and tilt, and the whole thing can be controlled from a very nicely-designed Microsoft Windows interface which not only shows the video, but also has the controls for pan and tilt built into the graphical user interface (GUI). The old way of controlling pan and tilt was with a joystick device usually attached to the security manager's console. An added feature of the new system is the ability to control telephoto lenses and other features such as the camera's iris, for adjusting to changing light conditions. Of course, fixed cameras are still an integral part of the system. Generally, fixed cameras are attached to dedicated video recorders, and the pan and tilt units can be used for "searching" with a special recorder. Fixed cameras are left alone, so that evidentiary video can be produced with no time gaps, if necessary. Another great advantage to using a system with IP transmission is that it is possible to control the video remotely, even via the Internet. With no need for a dedicated telephone line, an operator could sit at a control location thousands of miles away, viewing the image, and control pan, zoom, and tilt. Figure 6–6 illustrates pan and tilt capabilities.

VIDEO PROCESSING AND STORAGE

Once we have video from the camera, it must be "transported" to some destination. It has to be available for display on a monitor and it should be stored for future reference.

For many years, it has been relatively easy to accomplish the above. Cameras mounted at various locations are connected to a video recorder either directly via coax cable, or with a connector matrix box of some sort in between. For a small system with four cameras or less, most video recorders provide direct connections, and the recorder itself will record four separate tracks which can be played back sequentially or simultaneously. For larger systems, the cameras are connected to a box that has the ability to multiplex the signals for the recorder (see Figure 6–7).

Figure 6–6 Pan, tilt, and zoom mechanism (inside dome) ©Honeywell International, Inc.

Figure 6–7 Multiplexer ©Honeywell International, Inc.

A SMALL SYSTEM

Typically, up to four cameras may be connected directly to the Video Cassette Recorder (VCR). Figure 6–8 shows an example of a small video system. The recorder itself is a time-lapse recorder that can be set up in many different ways. For instance, most time-lapse recorders have the following provisions:

- Four Video Inputs

- Four Alarm Inputs

- Quad, Full Screen and Sequential Switching Modes

- 256 Level Gray Scale (or color)

- Real Time Refresh Rate (60 fields per second)

- Interlace or Non-Interlace in Full Screen or Enlarge Mode

- Two to One Enlarge

- Freeze Functions Available

- Video Loss Alarm Output

- On-screen Camera Titling

- Auxiliary In/Out

- Remote Panel Option

Figure 6–8   Ademco video components ©Honeywell International, Inc.

The recorder can be set up to record and play at: 2, 12, 24, 48, 72, 120, 168, 240, 360, 480, 600, 720, or 960 hour speeds (see Figure 6–9). This means that you can record for up to 40 days at the 960 hour speed on one video cassette! Of course, you would only be recording one frame every 8 seconds. A thief may escape the picture completely in 8 seconds. Table 6–1 lists the relationship of record time to pictures per second and seconds per picture.

Recording at the 72 to 120 hour speed is generally sufficient for good coverage without missing much action. It is recommended that special "heavy duty" tapes be used with these machines so that the tapes will not shed coating material on the recording heads, but

Figure 6–9 Video time-lapse tape recorder ©Honeywell International, Inc.

Table 6–1 Recording Times For a Time Lapse Recorder

RECORD TIME (HOURS)	RECORD/PLAYBACK PICTURES/SEC	RECORD/PLAYBACK SEC/PICTURE
2	60	.016
12	10	.10
24	5	.20
48	2.5	.40
72	1.7	.58
120	1.0	1.0
168	.70	1.2
240	.50	2.0
360	.30	3.33
480	.25	4.0
600	.20	5.0
720	.16	6.25
960	.12	8.0

most users still use regular two hour video cassette tapes with good results. There are thousands of these types of systems in use today, especially in small grocery shops where the camera(s) monitor the registers, and perhaps some of the aisles.

DIGITAL VIDEO RECORDERS

Before discussing medium and large video systems, it would be a good idea to talk about digital video recorders (Figure 6–10). These types of recorders are gaining popularity rapidly with both small and large users because they are now accompanied by very reasonable price tags. These recorders are actually the same type of hard drive found in computers. Video signals can be analog or digital. If they start out as an analog signal, there is usually a conversion to digital somewhere along the line. You will see that in large, and even some medium sized systems, the signals from cameras are transported

Figure 6–10   Selection of Digital Video Recorders ©Honeywell International, Inc.

digitally regardless of the initial mode. A digital video recorder opens the door to an amazing number of new things that can be done with the system. Since we are working with a hard drive, it can easily be attached to a computer system running software that integrates the video right into the access control and alarm systems. Motion detection can be set up via software, zones can be turned on and off at will using a GUI, pan and tilt systems can be operated at the computer console. A custom map can graphically represent the entire system. Search and recover operations can be accomplished with VCR-like software controls, or by using a query language like those used in many database programs. Printouts of video sequences are copied to tape (using a standard video recorder), to a CD, or to another small portable hard drive or memory chip. A great feature of digital video recorders is that software can be run on the recorder itself, since it is actually a hard drive. Video control software can reside on the drive, which will allow for automatic frame rate adjustment (according to a preset schedule) or resolution adjustment. Motion detection can be established by designating a zone on the monitor itself. The system will monitor pixel level disturbances, and the level of these disturbances can be set to allow for wind or small animal interference. By establishing a zone for motion detection, a field around a fence could be monitored where movement inside the fence would be ignored. With the software integration of alarm systems and video, an alarm can activate the pan and tilt system of a camera to steer to the alarm area immediately and start running the video recording at real time. Controlling video and access control points with software could allow a person to be tracked within the premises. The tracking could be accomplished with the use of access card readers, biometrics, or using motion detection (as well as combinations of the three). The system could also look for anyone who is loitering in an area. Keep in mind that a motion detection function can be set up to alarm if motion suddenly stops and does not start again within a set time period. This "loitering" capability is very important because it is not just restricted to monitoring people, it can also watch for vehicles that have stopped and remained motionless for certain periods of time. When we talk about large systems, it will be apparent that a security officer may have 30 or 40 monitors active at the same time on one console. With software control, it is possible to provide some sort of alarm to get the security officer to immediately look at a certain monitor, which is in a predetermined condition.

Here are features found on most DVRs:

- Allowance for remote viewing of live and recorded images
- Internal motion detection capability
- Continuous recording, even during search and playback
- No need for tapes, although CD/R capability frequently built-in
- Easy downloading
- Auto reboot in event of power failure
- Hard drive sizes up to Terabyte ranges
- Internal modem and/or network card
- Variable resolution settings
- Alarms/Trigger inputs
- *NTSC* or *PAL* format
- Multiple camera input built in (usually up to 16)

MEDIUM AND LARGE SYSTEMS

CCTV and media storage for medium and large systems are almost always a part of an entire access control, alarm, and networked security system. Medium sized systems can have hundreds of CCTV cameras mounted throughout the facility, with mixes of coaxial cable runs and video running over IP on the network (LAN) itself. The video signals will eventually get through several devices, which will digitize and multiplex the signals so that they can be processed via software at the control console. At the console, the video will be monitored and stored on combinations of VCRs and DVRs. In the large systems, there will be hundreds of cameras from several facilities, which could be hundreds or even thousands of miles apart. In a large system, there are several operating consoles, which segment video, alarm, and access control responsibilities, but maintain the ability to communicate video data over IP to one another other.

Here are some of the components of a large surveillance system:

Cameras

- Color as well as black and white
- High resolution
- Low light level
- Compensation for backlight
- Image intensification
- Covert
- Digital or analog

Switches

- Matrix switches
- Multiplexers
- Bridging
- Manual or auto operation
- Manual or auto sequencing
- Looping or terminating
- Alarms
- Branch controllers

Monitors

- Color or monochrome
- Rack mount
- Desktop
- High or low resolution

Recorders

- Digital
- Multiple sites
- Image enhancing
- Alarm searches
- Internet based
- Networked (LAN/WAN)
- Time-lapse
- VHS
- S-VHS
- Search functions
- Time-date searches
- Real-time recorders
- Event recorders

Media Transmission

- Dedicated phone line
- Microwave
- Fiber Optic
- RF (Including 802.11)

Management

- PC management
- Remote digital or VCR programming
- Dial up phone line access
- Internet-based monitoring and control

It would not be unusual in a medium or large system to have up to 255 separate digital recorders (see Figure 6–11) with up to 16 cameras each, using just one IP address on the network. There are drop-down menus available on the software for simultaneous viewing of multiple cameras. Anyone with proper authorization could connect through the network and view activity. As a matter of fact, multiple users could watch the same events simultaneously. Just as in a network, there are levels of access available. The system is Windows-based for comfort level in software operation.

Figure 6–11   A bank of Digital Video Recorders ©Honeywell International, Inc.

SUMMARY

- Video is much more than just cameras and video recorders.

- The optical system of the lens is configured so that when the lens is opened to allow the entry of light, an image of the terrain in front of the lens will be focused and projected onto the film plane.

- If parallel rays of light pass through a convex lens, they converge to a single point on the optical axis. This point is the focal point of the lens. The focal length of a fixed focal length lens is indicated by the distance from the center of the lens to the focal point/plain. A lens has two focal points, one on the object side, called the primary focal point, and one on the image side, called the secondary focal point. The lenses used on cameras are compound lenses, consisting of several individual lenses combined to correct "aberrations".

■ The focal length of a lens is important as a factor describing the angle of view of the lens.

■ Lenses for still cameras generally vary greatly in cost all the way up to thousands of dollars.

■ The *f*-stop capability of a lens is important because it determines the lowest light level at which the lens will operate efficiently. The lower the number, the greater the diaphragm opening in the lens that allows light to enter.

■ On a 35mm camera, a normal lens is considered to be a 50mm lens (remember, that means the distance from the lens' focal point to the film plane is 50mm).

■ In an "auto-iris" lens, the diaphragm operates automatically, based on changing light conditions. These lenses are more typically used with closed circuit video cameras than with still cameras, although many banks still use mounted still cameras with specialty lenses, because they produce better images than video cameras.

■ In still photography, the image is brought into the camera via the lens, which is designed to focus the image onto the film plane. The film plane differs in size depending on the type and size of film for which the camera is designed. We discussed film speeds, which are determined by their sensitivity to light. Slow speed films produce fine-grained, high-resolution images, but require more light than the faster, grainier films. The image produced on the film is actually a negative image, thus processed film is referred to as a negative. Color films have several layers of emulsion.

■ With early video cameras, in order to get a moving image, video tubes were part of the camera, replacing the film plane in a still camera. These tubes reacted to a scanning beam made up of light and dark images that came in through the lens. The original cameras were only black and white.

■ Most video cameras now use CCDs instead of vacuum tubes. The CCD chip used in video cameras is more desirable than film in many ways.

■ With the older tube type cameras, it was necessary to use coaxial cable to transmit the video signal to a monitor, or a video recorder. Systems now available can transmit video information just as computers transmit data, via IP (Internet Protocol).

■ Cameras used with a security system are a combination of fixed devices, and pan and tilt cameras. An added feature of the new system is the ability to control telephoto lenses and other features such as the camera's iris, for adjustment to changing light conditions. Of course, fixed cameras are still an integral part of the system.

- For larger systems, the cameras are connected to a box that has the ability to multiplex the signals for the recorder.

- Video signals can be analog or digital. With the software integration of alarm systems and video, an alarm can activate the pan and tilt system of a camera to steer to the alarm area immediately and start running the video recording at real time. A person could actually be tracked within the premises by controlling video and access control points with software.

KEY TERMS

Pinhole Camera

Aberrations

Chromatic Aberration

Telephoto

Wide-Angle

Shutter Speed

Field of View

Panchromatic

Vidicon Tube

CCD Chip

Pan and Tilt

Multiplexer

DVR

NTSC or PAL

DISCUSSION QUESTIONS

1 Name three different types of cameras.

2 How is a telephoto lens related to its angle of view? What about a wide-angle lens?

3   Name an application in the security field where a still camera may be used.

4   What is the difference between a DVR and a VCR?

5   What part of a DVR determines how much recording time it can handle?

6   Regarding film, what is emulsion?

7   What is the basic difference between color and black and white film types?

8   What does it mean when we refer to film speed?

9   If I wanted to control depth of field by making it very broad, what would I make sure to pay attention to?

10   If I wanted to catch fast action but still have a broad depth of field, what is another factor I could adjust?

11   On film, silver halide crystals make up the light areas. What makes up these areas in digital photography?

12   What is a long lens? A short lens? A normal lens?

13   What is meant by the "focal length" of a lens?

14   What is chromatic aberration?

15   What does the term "panchromatic" mean?

RESEARCH QUESTIONS

1   There are two types of color film emulsions: additive and subtractive. Cibachrome™ was an additive type of emulsion. Explain the difference between the two.

2   Can lenses be used interchangeably between still, video, and digital cameras? If so, what conditions must exist? Would the focal lengths always be the same for any given lens? Explain.

3   Are there any types of devices available that will allow a digital (IP) camera to transmit its signal via analog on a coaxial cable? Explain.

CHAPTER 7

Alarm Systems

PURPOSE AND OBJECTIVES

Alarm systems have been around for a long time, and in some respects, have changed very little. The technology has become more sophisticated and compact, and electronics now does most of what mechanical systems used to do, but the operational aspects remain pretty much the same as early systems. The basic system is designed to detect some sort of unauthorized activity and then produce some type of alarm.

■ In this chapter we start with a little bit of history about alarm systems, which teaches us that, at least in principle, early alarms were not so different from the systems used today. There were sensors, some type of control unit, and an alarm

■ With the proliferation of different devices that are now available, there is little that we cannot monitor with an alarm system

■ We will look at the specifications of two commercially available systems, one small and one large, and see the many peripherals used with the systems

A BRIEF HISTORY

In the mid-nineteenth century, in New York City, each district was equipped with a "fire-watch tower." From this tower, a watchman would ring an alarm that had a distinctive sound for the district in which he was working. Later, when the telegraph had been developed, the watchman could use the telegraph to point out exactly where the fire or other disaster was taking place. In Boston, a series of call boxes were set up around the city. When activated, the call box would cause a spinning wheel to trigger relays much like a music box plucks reeds. The relays would cause a telegraph message locating the call box to go to a central station and firefighters would be dispatched.

As for home burglar alarm systems, some were surprisingly similar to those we use today. As early as 1850, magnetic contacts were used as window alarm sensors. The entire circuit consisted of a bell, a battery, and magnetic contacts. A magnet attached to the window or door would hold together the contacts fastened to the adjoining frame. When the portal opened, the magnet would slide away and the contacts would close, causing an alarm bell to ring. Another system consisted of a trip-wire mechanism, and a contraption similar to a mousetrap. When the trap sprung, it would complete a circuit that would ring a bell.

Metal foil was first used in alarm systems during the early 1870s. The foil would be fastened all around glass surfaces. If the glass broke, the foil would (theoretically) also tear open and cause a change in the circuit that would sound an alarm. This foil and principle of operation is still used with some systems, although modern glass break sensors have been developed within the last several years.

Central station operation for alarm recognition took place around the time the telephone was invented. Telephone wiring and central station wiring for alarms had much in common. Thomas Watson, who worked with Thomas Edison and Alexander Graham Bell, also worked for the Holmes Alarm Company where telephone lines were used for the first time in wiring up an alarm central station. Edwin Holmes later became the president of the Bell Telephone Company of New York.

Alarm systems have become more sophisticated in modern times, with a selection of hundreds of different types of sensors. The theory of operation, however, has remained surprisingly constant since the 1850s. We still use a sensor, some method of carrying a signal, and a control unit that provides a battery. An alarm can ring a bell, or notify a central station, or both.

THE BASIC ALARM SYSTEM

An alarm salesperson knocks on your door. He tells you that his crew is installing a system just down the street, and he would like to know if you are interested in considering a system for your house. He tells you that he will even install the system free: no charge for the system or the labor. All you have to do is sign a contract for two years of monitoring for a nominal monthly fee. Here is the system he proposes:

- A control unit, hidden in a closet
- A *keypad*, located close to an entry point of the property
- Front and rear *door contacts*
- One *glass break sensor*
- One *motion detector*
- An *annunciator*, guaranteed to be loud enough to wake up the entire household

All of these parts of the system will be wired with twisted pair wire, or possibly connected by means of wireless sensors depending on the *trade-off* of labor and cost of wireless. Trade-off means that the building would either provide an easy path for wiring (less labor cost) or a difficult path for wiring (labor cost exceeds wireless cost).

The system discussed above is a basic system that can be found in a house on just about every block in every city. Let us look at each component and expand on each a bit.

THE CONTROL UNIT

The main difference from control unit to control unit is determined by system size, capability, and expansion potential. The main difference from control unit to control unit is determined by system size, capability, and expansion potential. Figure 7-1 shows specifications for a small system from Ademco. In order to familiarize the reader with the various components that interface with the systems, comments have been added.

Figure 7–1 Ademco alarm system and accessories ©Honeywell International, Inc.

VISTA-10P

Features

- Six hardwired zones on board, each of which operates as an independent area of coverage. That is, each one can be turned on and off separately
- Sixteen wireless expansion zones totaling twenty-two protection zones
- Eight independent key-fob zones allow two wireless keys to be programmed without using any of the twenty-two zones. The key fobs are similar to those carried to lock and unlock a vehicle. They are operated by just pushing a button, eliminating the need to enter a code
- Thirty-two event log

- Sixteen user codes
- One configurable zone type allows installers to create their own custom zone type
- Two on-board triggers
- Four output devices using a 4204 relay module, which provides four on-board programmable Form C relays. Applications include sounder, strobe light, or an interface to other equipment to provide added convenience

Valuable End-User Features

- Flexible function keys allow single button arming
- One programmable macro key
- Viewable on system keypad display
  - Exit countdown
  - Time and date[1]
  - Event log[1]
- Two schedules
  - Can activate relays on programmed times or on events
  - Latchkey reports to a pager
  - "User Access" time windows
- Chime by zone
- 4286 Phone Module allows system control from any touchtone phone
- Four output devices with multiple actions per device
  - Turn lights on when system disarms with a 4204 relay
  - Flash same lights when system is in alarm with a 4204 relay

Security Dealer Features

- Contains features to reduce false alarms
- Dynamic signaling reduces redundant reporting to the central station when multiple reporting methods are used (digital dialer, AlarmNet radio)

---

1. Requires 6160 Custom Alpha keypad.

Electrical

- Auxiliary power 12 VDC, 600 mA max
- Seven hour standby at 400mA aux load with four amp hour battery
- 16.5 V AC/25 VA transformer
- Alarm output 12 VDC, 2.0 amps max
- For Underwriter's Laboratories (UL) installations, combined auxiliary and alarm output cannot exceed 700 mA

Output Control

- Supports multiple output devices, one 4204, and two triggers

Zones

- Six hardwired zones
- Selectable response: 10 msec, 350 msec, 750 msec
- Sixteen selectable zone types plus one configurable zone type
- Programmable swinger suppression is used to prevent multiple alarm messages from being for the same occurrence

Expansion Devices

- 4204—Up to four relays—15 mA standby (each active relay draws an additional 40 mA)

Accessories

- 4286 VIP Voice Module—220 mA

  With the Vista Interactive Phone Module (VIP) you can perform all the functions of a wall mounted keypad using any ordinary touchtone phone, from home or any remote location. You can check security system status, arm or disarm the system—even operate lights and appliances.

The VIP's high quality voice output verbally identifies open zones and prompts you to take appropriate action.

5881ENL RF Receiver supports up to eight zones—60 mA Receiver—connects to four wire keypad data lines

> **5881ENL**
>
> Up to eight zones
>
> **5881ENM**
>
> Up to sixteen zones
>
> **5881ENH**
>
> Up to sixty-four zones depending on control panel
>
> **5881EH**
>
> Commercial wireless fire receiver
>
> For use with QED control panels only

Approved for UL864d commercial fire installations when used with the Vista 100 control and 5808 wireless smoke detector

■ 5883 Transceiver supports up to sixteen zones—80 mA

■ Supports Eagle 1225 and 1221 boards

Keypads

■ 6160 Custom Alpha (required for programming)—100 mA

■ 6160V Custom Alpha Voice—100 mA

■ 6150 Fixed English LCD—85 mA/40 mA

■ 6150V Fixed English Voice LCD—85 mA/40 mA

■ 6150RF Fixed English RF LCD—85 mA/40 mA

■ 6148 Fixed English LCD—70 mA/30 mA

Agency Listings

■ UL Residential Fire, Burglary, and CSFM

Smoke Detectors

■ Supports four-wire smoke detectors

Communications

- Touchtone or pulse
- Formats supported
  - Ademco Contact ID
  - Ademco 4 + 2 Express
  - Ademco Low Speed
  - Sescoa/Radionics
- 3 + 1, 4 + 1 and 4 + 2 code formats reporting
- Reporting capabilities
  - Split
  - Dual
  - Split/Dual—True dial tone detection
- Low battery reports 11.2 – 11.6 VDC
- AC loss and restoral reporting supported

THE VISTA-250

- Nine style-B hardwired zones
- Up to 241 additional zones by using a built-in polling (multiplex) loop interface
- Up to 250 wireless zones by using 5881 type RF receiver (fewer if using hardwired and/or polling loop zones)
- One power-limited bell circuit delivering 1.7 amps (max) at 12 VDC
- Ability to control eight separate partitions independently, each functioning as if it had its own separate control
- 250 user codes with seven authority levels
- Thirty-two keypad macro commands per system
- Keeps a log of up to 1,000 events
- VistaView-100 CCTV support

- The VistaView-100 module is a CCTV switcher that accepts four video inputs, switching them to two video outputs. The video inputs are compatible with any standard 75-ohm, line-locked video cameras. The video outputs are compatible with any standard 75-ohm video monitor or recorder

- The VistaView-100 also provides a Form-C trigger relay output and an open collector video loss output. The trigger relay output may be used to start and stop recording or to change from time lapse to real time recording. The video loss output indicates when video signals are no longer present on one or more video input

■ Up to sixteen two-wire smoke detectors on zone 1

■ Up to fifty latching-type glass break detectors on zone 8

■ Zone 7 may be used for keyswitch arming/disarming

■ Integrates with PassPoint access control systems to provide event log, scheduling (up to 32 doors), and increased users

- The PassPoint family has been expanded with PassPoint PLUS, the enhanced version of PassPoint Express. Like PassPoint Express, PLUS offers simplicity in setup and maintenance. PLUS is a full featured access control system (see Table 7–1)

Table 7–1 Capabilities of the PassPoint PLUS Access Control System

• 32 Doors	• 2000 Card Holders	• 7000 Event Log
• 66 Inputs	• 33 Relay Outputs	• 32 Trigger Outputs
• 128 Access Groups	• 64 Time Schedules	• 32 Holidays
• Basic Starter Kit Includes Software and Cables, No readers.		

■ Supports V-Plex addressable VistaKey access control (up to 15 doors and 500 cards)

■ Easily programmed and maintained by the newly upgraded Compass Windows-based downloader

■ Up to 96 programmable relays

■ Supports the Ademco 4286 VIP Module

■ False alarm reduction features

New Enhancement

- Up to eight panels
- Two-way RS232 (facility automation software support) optional
- Supports eight numeric pager numbers
- Supports touch screen Advanced User Interface (AUI) (Future)
- Smoke detector reset at keypad
- Group bypass
- Event arming
- Scheduled check-in
- Arm stay (arming the unit while people remain in the area) by group

Additional Features

Basic Hardwired Zones

Provides nine style-B hardwired zones with the following characteristics:

- End of Line Resistor (EOLR) supervision (optional for zones 2–8) supporting Normally Open (NO) or Normally Closed (NC) sensors (EOLR supervision required for fire and UL burglary installations)

  EOLR prevents tampering with the cable and provides a value of resistance that is monitored. If the cabling is cut or shorted, the resistance value will change drastically and an alarm will sound.

- Individually assignable to one of eight partitions
- Up to 16 two-wire smoke detectors on zone 1
- Four-wire smoke or heat detectors on zones 1–8 (power to four-wire smoke detectors must be supervised with an EOL device)
- Up to fifty two-wire latching glass break detectors on zone 8

Polling Loop Expansion

Supports up to 241 additional zones using a built-in polling (multiplex) loop interface. Current draw can total up to 128 mA. Polling loop zones have the following characteristics:

■ Must use RPM (Remote Point Module) devices

■ Supervised by control panel

■ Individually assignable to one of eight partitions

Wireless Expansion

Supports up to 250 wireless zones using 5881 RF receiver (fewer if using hardwire and/or polling loop zones). Wireless zones have the following characteristics:

■ Supervised by control panel for check-in signals (except certain non-supervised transmitters)

■ Tamper protection for supervised transmitters

■ Individually assignable to one of eight partitions

Scheduling

Provides the following scheduling capabilities:

■ Open/Close Schedules (for control of arming/disarming and reporting)

■ Holiday Schedules (allows different time windows for Open/Close Schedules)

■ Timed Events (for activation of relays, auto-bypassing and un-bypassing, auto-arming and disarming, etc.)

■ Access Schedules (for limiting system access to users by time)

■ End User Output Programming Mode (provides twenty timers for relay control)

Eight Partitions

Provides the ability to control eight separate areas independently, each functioning as if it had its own separate control. Partitioning features include the following:

- A common lobby (shared by two or more businesses) partition (1–8), which can be programmed to arm automatically when the last partition that shares the common lobby is armed and to disarm when the first partition that shares the common lobby is disarmed
- A master partition (9), used strictly to assign keypads for the purpose of viewing the status of all eight partitions at the same time (master keypads)
- All zones assignable to one of eight partitions
- Keypads assignable to one of eight partitions or to master partition 9 to view system status
- Ability to assign relays to one or all eight partitions
- Ability to display fire and/or burglary and panic and/or trouble conditions at all other partitions' keypads (selectable option)
- Certain system options selectable for each partition, such as entry/exit delay and subscriber account number

New Enhancement

Allows multiple control panels to be networked together and controlled from any keypad in the system, so the user can:

- Control multiple zones, partitions, and buildings from a central location
- Check status, arm, or disarm any partition from any keypad in the system (based on user's authority level)
- Have a different authority level in each partition and access to different partitions in each panel
- Arm and disarm all the partitions in all the panels they have access to with one set of keystrokes (global arming)

Applications

The Vista-250BP control is well suited for a variety of applications as a burglary control. A diverse line of Ademco initiating devices supports this extremely powerful control. Some of the applications supported are medical and professional buildings, supermarkets, churches or synagogues, office buildings, schools, universities, strip malls, larger residences, and factory or warehouse environments.

Installation

The Vista-250BP alarm system has been designed to mount both quickly and easily. It meets all applicable requirements for UL-Commercial Burglary installations; for instances where the UL-Commercial Burglary requirements demand an attack resistant enclosure, use the Vista-ULKT kit.

Agency Listings Burglary

- UL609 Grade A Local Mercantile Premises and Mercantile Safe and Vault
- UL611/UL1610 Grades A, AA Central Station
- UL365 Grades A, AA Police Connect
- UL985 Household Fire
- California State Fire Marshall (CSFM)
- UL listing 1023—Household Burglar Alarm

Electrical

Here are typical electrical requirements for the system:

- Voltage Input: From Ademco No. 1361 Plug-In Transformer (use 1361CN in Canada) or 4300 Transformer (for X-10 installations) rated 16.5 VAC, 40 VA

- Alarm Sounder Output: 10 VDC–13.8 VDC, 1.7 amps max, (UL1023, UL609 installations), 750 mA less auxiliary current draw (UL985 installations)
- Auxiliary Power Output: 9.6 VDC–13.8 VDC, 750 mA max. For UL installations, the accessories connected to the output must be UL listed and rated to operate in the above voltage range
- Backup Battery: 12 VDC, 4 AH, or 7 AH gel cell. YUASA NP4-12 (12 V, 4 AH) or NP7-12 (12 V, 7 AH) recommended
- Standby Time: four hours minimum with 750 mA auxiliary load using 7 AH battery
- Circuit Protectors: PTC circuit breakers are used on battery input to protect against reverse battery connections and on alarm sounder output to protect against wiring faults (shorts). A solid state circuit breaker is used on auxiliary power output to protect against wiring faults

Main Telephone Dialer

- Formats supported: Ademco High Speed, Ademco 4 + 2 Express, Ademco Low Speed, Ademco Contact ID, Sescoa and Radionics Low Speed
- Line Seize: Double Pole
- Ringer Equivalence: 0.7 B

Cabinet dimensions

- 12-1/2" W × 14-1/2" H × 3" D

COMPATIBLE DEVICES

See Ademco control accessories compatibility chart for complete list.

Auxiliary devices

- 4204 —Relay Module, four form C contacts
- 4204CF—Two supervised output circuits
- 5881 Series—RF Receiver supporting 5800 wireless detectors
- 6160/6139—Alpha Keypad/Annunciator

- 6220S—System Printer used with 4100SM Serial Module
- VA8200—(PLM) Panel Linking Module
- VA8201—(APM) Alpha Paging Module

Two-wire Smoke Detectors (Conventional)

- System Sensor smoke detectors

Horn/Strobes

- System Sensor notification appliances

Manual Pull Stations

- 5140MPS-1
- 5140MPS-2

V-Plex (Addressable) Devices

- 4101SN Single Relay/Zone Module
- 4190SN Remote Point Module—two zones
- 4193SN Two Zone Serial Interface Module
- 4208U Loop Expansion Module—eight zones
- 4208SNF Class A/B Expander Module
- 4209U Group Zoning Module—two/four zones
- 4293SN One Zone Serial Interface Module
- 4297 Isolation/Extender Module

V-Plex (Addressable) Smoke Detectors

- 5192SD
- 5192SDT

Passive Infrared Detectors

- 998MX
- 4275EX-SN
- 4287EX-SN
- QUEST2260SN

V-Plex (Addressable) Contacts

- 4939SN-WH
- 4944SN-WH
- 4959SN, 9500SN

Glass Break Detectors

- 9500SN

Vista Interactive Phone Module

- 4286 Voice Module

Long Range Radio

- Long Range Radio 7720ULF-XX, 7845CZ, 7845C

Upgraded Software

- Upgraded Compass Downloader—Windows compatible

Wireless Devices

- 5804—Wireless Key
- 5804BD—Bi-Directional Key
- 5804BDV—Bi-Directional with voice
- 5804Watch—Wireless Key and full featured wrist watch
- 5816—Door/Window Transmitter
- 5819—Shock Sensor
- 5827BD—Bi-Directional Keypad
- 5849—Glass Break Detector
- 5890—PIR (Passive Infrared)

Access Control

- VistaKey V-PLEX (Addressable) Access Control
- VistaKey-SK Starter Kit
- VistaKey-EX Expansion Kit
- VGM Vista Gateway Module to PassPoint Access Control (by Northern Computers)

CCTV

- CCTV—VistaView-100 CCTV Switcher Module

Commercial Wireless Devices

- 5808LST—Wireless smoke detector[2]
- 5809—Wireless Heat Detector
- 5817CB—Commercial UL Burglary, Universal Contact Monitoring Transmitter

---

2. Not listed for commercial use with the Vista-250BP; residential listing only

■ 5869—Commercial UL Wireless Hold-up Button[3]

■ 5881ENHC

You can see that both the low end and high-end systems described previously offer an extensive assortment of devices that can be attached to the system. In the next section, we will get into more detail about some of these devices.

PERIPHERAL DEVICES

As we have seen, a control unit for an alarm system has many capabilities for adding all types of devices. It is possible to attach sensors that will sense gas, moisture, noise, motion—just about anything imaginable. Some of the more frequently used devices are covered in the following section.

Motion Detectors

Motion detectors come in several varieties. These devices are associated with alarm systems and can be wired or wireless. They can be microwave devices, which usually operate in the "K-Band" (18–27 GHz), infrared devices that sense changes in temperature in a zone, or both, called dual technology sensors. In addition to the variation in sensor technology, the devices can provide different angles of view. For a long, narrow hallway, a user would select a motion detector with a narrow angle of view horizontally (similar to a photographic telephoto lens). For a large, expansive room, a wide-angle unit would be selected. These devices also have angles of view in the vertical plane, so they are very versatile for coverage. For setup purposes, the units usually have a small red light in the front that illuminates when it detects movement within the coverage area. This feature is very handy for setup, but many users erroneously leave this light on during operation. The light function should be turned off to conserve battery power, that is, unless you want people to know they are being detected. Why would someone use a dual technology unit? With PIR (Passive Infrared) detectors, heat from sunshine through a window or radiation from a heat vent sometimes can set off the unit. Adding microwave technology ensures that the unit not only senses a change in temperature for an area, but also

---

3. When used with 5881ENHC Receiver

detects movement using Doppler technology. These units have *tamper switches* that will cause an alarm if someone tries to open the device while it is set.

In the event that a CCTV system is integrated with the alarm system, you can choose to use motion detectors that are associated with the CCTV system. These are sensors that look at pixel changes in the image itself. These motion detectors are very versatile because you can set the field of coverage anywhere within the image area and even adjust the size of coverage area from a very tiny dot all the way up to the full screen. Video motion detectors are great for areas where movement is expected, since those areas need to be ignored.

Glass Break Detectors

Many years ago, glass break detectors consisted of ribbons of metallic tape that were epoxied to the glass surface, usually around the edges of windows and glass doors. Ideally, when the glass broke, a crack would work its way to a taped area and create an open circuit by separating the tape. The tape had a resistance added at the end, and was simply set up as a closed path to the control box. This type of sensor has been used since the 1800s and still can be found in some installations.

The modern glass break detector is a small unit encapsulated in a small plastic box or ceiling housing similar to a smoke detector in appearance. The detector "listens" for the distinctive sound of glass breaking and even stores in its memory, the sounds of different types of glass breaking. In addition to the sound sensor, the detector senses a vibration from the surface it is attached to that corresponds to the sound. If the timing of the glass break sound and vibration are concurrent, an alarm sounds. There is a sensitivity control inside the box, which is set at installation. There is also a tamper switch inside the package.

Photoelectric Beams

Moviegoers are certainly familiar with the photoelectric beams that form a crisscrossed web of invisible light in a room. Devices employing these beams are used indoors and outdoors for many different purposes. The beams, when broken can be set to turn on porch or driveway lights, or with the use of different relays and switches, can trigger almost any type of operation. Many of these beams are also "pulsed," so that they cannot be "copied" unless someone is familiar with the frequency at which the beam pulses. The frequency is set by the installer who has a choice between six to twelve selections.

Gas, Smoke, and Fire Detectors

There are many variations of detectors available for smoke, fire, or gas. Fire detectors are designed to detect a very sudden rise in temperature. Smoke detectors sense impurities in the air, such as those found in smoke. Some of these detectors are dual sensor types, that is, they can sense a sudden change in temperature as well as sense particles in smoke. Gas detectors generally detect carbon monoxide and are mounted in the vicinity of a furnace room. Gas detectors can be designed to sense different types of gas for special applications purposes.

Switches

Many varieties of switches are available. They can normally be open or closed and can be magnetic, pressure sensitive, capacitive, optical, liquid sensing, or by using transducers, activated by anything a person can imagine.

Figure 7–2 shows a variety of sensors and devices that we have been discussing in this chapter.

Alarm Activation

Not long ago, the only way to activate an alarm system was to use a key activated switch at the control panel. Now there are numerous models of keypads available, with the choice mainly determined by style preference. The system also can be activated by a key fob device, similar to one used with automobiles to lock and unlock doors. Systems can even be activated remotely or from inside the premises by using the touchpad of a telephone. Some systems can be voice activated through the telephone. Figure 7–3 shows some of these activation devices.

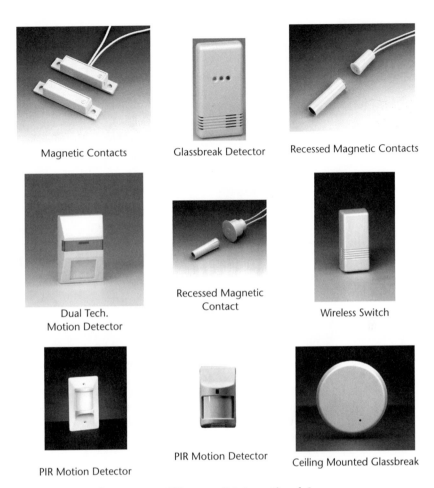

Magnetic Contacts Glassbreak Detector Recessed Magnetic Contacts

Dual Tech. Motion Detector

Recessed Magnetic Contact

Wireless Switch

PIR Motion Detector

PIR Motion Detector

Ceiling Mounted Glassbreak

Figure 7-2 Various sensors ©Honeywell International, Inc.

Integrity of the System

In time, batteries go dead, sensors can develop problems, and wires may open or short. To ensure that the system is intact and operating properly, it monitors itself by *polling*. Polling means sending a signal down the cable—or in the case of wireless, through the airwaves—and then waiting for a response. If no response is received within a specified amount of time, the system is presumed compromised and some type of alarm is initiated. If the system is active, the polling alarm might set off an annunciator, and a signal is sent to the central station. If the system is inactive, a notification would most likely

Figure 7–3   Activation Devices ©Honeywell International, Inc.

show up on the face of the keypad, and the system would not allow itself to be armed without an override. The polling signal itself is usually encrypted or sent via encryption and spread spectrum technology to further ensure *communications security*.

FALSE ALARMS

This chapter would not be complete without information concerning the problem of false alarms. A security professional is responsible for installing and maintaining a system so that the ordinary citizen using it will not be fined for false alarms. The city of New Orleans has developed an extensive program for dealing with false alarms. The case study that follows is a notice published by the city of New Orleans[4] and is very similar to what can be expected

4. http://www.new-orleans.la.us/home/nopd/conten.php?dir=divisions&page=falsalrm.html

from other cities and counties throughout the United States. It contains many elements that could be found in other notices from other jurisdictions. Notice that contact and help information is advertised in order for the pro-active alarm user to be fully knowledgeable about his or her responsibilities regarding false alarms.

FALSE ALARM REDUCTION SCHOOLING

False alarm reduction schools are a fairly new phenomenon. The problem of false alarms is so serious, that many municipalities have formed these schools in an effort to cut back on the number of false alarms in their territory. Voluntary attendance is usually "awarded" a false alarm call without penalty. Other attendees of these schools are people who have had an unacceptable amount of false alarm calls, and must attend the school program similar to the folks who must attend driving schools after too many traffic tickets.

False Alarms
New Orleans Police Department Case Study

False Alarm Reduction Section

- You can now complete the False Alarm Reduction School online to earn one False Alarm Waiver! or

- Tune into the City of New Orleans Government Access Channel #6 to view the program at a time convenient to your schedule (Sunday at 7pm, Monday at 9pm, or Wednesday at 8pm).

In response to an overwhelming number of false alarm calls that waste police resources, the New Orleans City Council enacted a False Alarm Ordinance on May 17, 1997. The intent of this ordinance is to make alarm users accountable for the proper operation of their system to prevent the sending of false alarms.

In 1997 the New Orleans Police Department responded to 615,413 calls for service, of these calls for service 107,651 were alarm calls, accounting for 17% of the Department's total calls for service. Citywide only 2% of these alarm calls were actual burglaries or attempted burglaries, 98% were false alarm calls.

False Alarms
New Orleans Police Department Case Study (Continued)

Responding to false alarms consumes many man hours of the New Orleans Police Department—and costs the City of New Orleans millions of dollars annually. Most importantly, false alarms place the safety of citizens truly in need of police response in jeopardy. False alarm activations divert police from real emergencies and proactive patrol activity.

Citizens must be educated on the prevention and causes of false alarms to successfully partner with the department in this reduction program.

Some of the causes of false alarms are:

- Use of incorrect keypad codes
- Failure to train authorized users
- Weak system batteries
- Failure to secure doors and windows once the alarm is turned on
- Wandering pets
- Failure (businesses) to notify monitoring company of unscheduled openings and closings
- Not requiring the monitoring company to notify persons on the contact list before calling the police

How can I find out more?

Contact the False Alarm Reduction Section to discover how you can benefit from alarm schools, which are offered free of charge.

What are some equipment problems causing False Alarms?

- Improper installation of equipment
- Improper charging of batteries
- Faulty equipment, key pads, batteries, panels, detectors
- Use of unlicensed alarm business installers/monitoring companies and untrained personnel

False Alarms
New Orleans Police Department Case Study (Continued)

Here are some ways to help reduce False Alarms

- Know how to operate and be familiar with your alarm system.

- Make sure that anyone with a key to your home or business knows the alarm code and password.

- Secure doors and windows before turning on the alarm. Make sure the doors are closed tightly when you leave your home or business.

- Make sure you and all of the occupants know your passcode in case the monitoring company calls you because of an accidental activation.

- Make sure your equipment is inspected and maintained by licensed alarm installers. Have your alarm system checked twice a year.

Under the current Municipal Ordinance, penalties for sending false alarms in New Orleans are as follows:

# of False Alarms	Penalty
1 to 3	No fine assessed
4 to 5	$25.00 fine per False Alarm to Alarm System User
6 to 7	$50.00 fine per False Alarm to Alarm System User
8 to 9	$75.00 fine per False Alarm to Alarm System User and Suspension Warning Notification letter will be issued
10 and above	Notice of Suspension issued ("Non-response" by police)

When a burglary or attempted burglary has occurred and a police report is filed, no fees are charged for an alarm activation. If a burglar is apprehended, then the entire community enjoys a reduction in potential burglaries. However, with a growing number of alarms being installed, the false alarm problem will continue to escalate if users are not accountable for the proper operation of their systems.

False Alarms
New Orleans Police Department Case Study (Continued)

When having a burglar alarm installed, make sure of the following:

■ Make sure the company is a licensed company. Ask to see their identification. All licensed alarm agents, installers and technicians carry picture identification with their Louisiana Burglar and Fire License number. Call the State Fire Marshall's Office and verify the company and license number.

■ Ask for documentation on their "False Alarm Rate" and programs in effect to reduce false alarms.

■ Make sure the company has a record of quick service.

■ If you have questions about the company you select or the company you are presently doing business with, call one or more of the following:

● The New Orleans Better Business Bureau

● The Louisiana State Fire Marshall's Office

● The Louisiana Burglar and Fire Alarm Association

● The New Orleans Police Department, False Alarm Reduction Section

False Alarm Reduction School

You can now complete the False Alarm Reduction School online to earn one False Alarm Waiver!

The New Orleans Police Department and the Louisiana Burglar and Fire Alarm Association conduct false alarm reduction schools on a regular basis. These alarm schools are another tool used in reducing alarms in the City of New Orleans. These schools are held every other Thursday, lasting approximately one hour. Attendees receive a certificate that can be used as a waiver for one false alarm fine during a calendar year. If you would like to attend this school, you may call the New Orleans Police Department, False Alarm Reduction Section, and reserve a seat.

A complete copy of the ordinance can be obtained by contacting the police department.

INSTALLER TRAINING AND LICENSING

In many states, it is required that alarm system sales and installation personnel go through a period of training, and obtain a license or certification. There may also be requirements for periodic retraining. Virginia has one of the most complete programs for certifying security and alarm personnel. About two thirds of the nation's states have similar programs that exhibit some of Virginia's requirements. The following case study is a description of licensing and training requirements in the state of Virginia as of November 2003.

**Licensing and Training Requirements for Security Personnel
Virginia Case Study**

Electronic security subjects

The entry level electronic security subjects curriculum for central station dispatcher, electronic security sales representative, electronic security technician and electronic security technician's assistant sets forth the following areas identified as:

- Administration and orientation to private security—1 hour
- Applicable sections of the Code of Virginia and DCJS (Department of Criminal Justice Services) regulations—1 hour
- Overview of electronic security—1 hour
- False alarm prevention—1 hour
- Written examination

Total hours (excluding examination)—4 hours

Central station dispatcher

- Electronic security subjects—4 hours
- Central station dispatcher subjects—4 hours
  - Duties and responsibilities
  - Communications skills
  - Emergency procedures
- Written examination

Total hours (excluding examination) —8 hours

Licensing and Training Requirements for Security Personnel Virginia Case Study (Continued)

Electronic security sales representative

- Electronic security subjects—4 hours
- Electronic security sales representative subjects—4 hours
  - Duties and responsibilities
  - System design/components
  - False alarm prevention

- Written examination

Total hours (excluding examination) —8 hours

Electronic security technician

- Electronic security subjects—4 hours
- Electronic security technician subjects—10 hours
  - Duties and responsibilities
  - Electronics
  - Control panels
  - Protection devices and application
  - Test equipment
  - Power and grounding
  - National electrical code
  - Job safety
- Written examination

Total hours (excluding examination) —14 hours

Compliance agent

- Industry overview and responsibilities
- Regulation review
- Business practices and ethical standards
- Records requirements and other related issues
- Written examination

Total hours (excluding written examination) —6 hours

Licensing and Training Requirements for Security Personnel Virginia Case Study (Continued)

VAC 20-171-360 In-service training

Each person registered with the department as an armed security officer/ courier, personal protection specialist, armored car personnel, security canine handler, private investigator, alarm respondent, central station dispatcher, electronic security sales representative, electronic security technician, unarmed security officer or electronic security technician's assistant, or certified by the department to act as a compliance agent shall complete the compulsory in-service training standard once during each 24-month period of registration or certification.

Compliance agent—In-service training must be completed within twelve months immediately preceding the expiration date. Individuals who fail to complete in-service training prior to the established expiration date may complete in-service training within 30 days after the expiration date if a completed in-service training enrollment application and a $25 delinquent training fee is received by the department.

Instructor—All private security instructors must complete instructor in-service training within twelve months immediately preceding the individual's expiration date.

Hour Requirements—the compulsory minimum in-service training hour requirement by category, excluding examinations, practical exercises, and range qualification, shall be as follows:

- Unarmed security officer—4 hours
- Armed security officer/courier—4 hours
- Armored car personnel—4 hours
- Security canine handler—8 hours
- Private investigator—8 hours
- Personal protection specialist—8 hours
- Alarm respondent—4 hours
- Central station dispatcher—4 hours
- Electronic security sales representative—4 hours
- Electronic security technician—4 hours
- Electronic security technician's assistant—2 hours
- Compliance agent—4 hours
- Firearms Instructor—4 hours
- General Instructor—4 hours

SUMMARY

- In the mid nineteenth century, in New York City, each district was equipped with a "fire-watch tower." From this tower, a watchman would ring an alarm that had a distinctive sound for the district in which he was working. When the telegraph came into use, the watchman could use the telegraph to indicate exactly where the fire or other disaster was taking place. As for home burglar alarm systems, some were surprisingly similar to those we use today. Salespeople sold alarm systems by going door-to-door.

- As early as 1850, magnetic contacts were used as window alarm sensors. The entire circuit consisted of a bell, a battery and magnetic contacts. A magnet attached to the window or door would hold together the contacts fastened to the adjoining frame.

- There were other types of systems consisting of a trip-wire mechanism, and a contraption similar to a mousetrap. When the trap sprung, it would complete a circuit that, again, would ring a bell.

- Metal foil was first used in alarm systems during the early 1870s. The foil was fastened all around glass surfaces. Ideally, if the glass broke, the foil would also tear open and cause a change in the circuit that would sound an alarm. This foil and principal of operation is still used with some systems, although within the last several years, modern glass break sensors have been developed.

- Around the time that the telephone was invented, central station operation took place for alarm recognition. Telephone wiring and central station wiring for alarms had much in common.

- The theory of operation of alarm systems is still surprisingly similar to that of the 1850s. We still basically use a sensor, some method of carrying a signal, and a control unit that provides a battery. An alarm can ring a bell, or be sent to a central station, or both.

- Motion detectors come in several flavors. The devices that are associated with alarm systems can be wired or wireless, and can either be microwave devices, usually operating in the "K-Band," or infrared devices which sense changes in temperature in a zone, or both, called dual technology sensors.

- Citizens must be educated on the prevention and causes of false alarms to successfully partner with their local police in an effort to reduce false alarms.

- Many states require alarm sales people and installers to attend training to become licensed or certified.

KEY TERMS

Central Station

Control Unit

Keypad

Door Contacts

Glass Break Sensor

Motion Detector

Annunciator

EOLR

PIR

Tamper Switch

DISCUSSION QUESTIONS

1 Approximately when did magnetic contacts first appear?

2 Which city first used call boxes for their watchmen?

3 What was an early method of glass break detection? How does the modern glass break sensor work?

4 Name the parts of a very basic alarm system.

5 Besides the possibility of customer preference, why would an installer use a wireless system instead of a wired system?

6 What is an end-of-line resistor, and why is it used? Does a wireless system use an end-of-line resistor?

7 What is polling?

8 What are "zones" in alarm systems? Why would we want zones?

9 If I were to say that a system supports Radionics Low Speed as well as Sescoa, what would I be talking about?

10 What is a dual-technology motion sensor? Why use two different types of technology?

11 What is the purpose of the little red light in the front of a motion detector?

12   What is a tamper switch and why is it necessary?

13   Name three ways to activate an alarm system.

14   How many false alarm calls were there in New Orleans in 1998?

15   What is involved with polling to accomplish "communications security"?

RESEARCH QUESTIONS

1   Virginia's requirements for security technicians are listed in the chapter because they are some of the most comprehensive in the country. Do all states have similar requirements?

2   Some alarm systems allow the user to call home and monitor audio inside the premises. Are there any legal ramifications to this practice?

3   If I wanted to monitor the temperature of a freezer with an alarm system, would it be possible? If so, what type of a transducer would I use? Could you find a transducer for this purpose advertised on the Internet?

CHAPTER 8

Computers and Security Software

PURPOSE AND OBJECTIVES

Security systems have always used simple switches; devices that are either in an "on" state or in an "off" state. Computers make work easier for security system designers because from the microprocessor on up, computers use digital technology. This chapter is about computers and software, not just for the internal circuitry, but also for design, operation, and "putting everything together."

The reader will learn that:

■ A digital signal is in an "on" state or in an "off" state; just like a switch

■ Security systems now use fast, efficient, computer technology; whether an alarm system, an access control system, or a CCTV system, you will find microprocessor chips in the circuitry

■ Personal Computers (PCs) are used abundantly with security systems. The reader will see that computers are taking the "heavy burden" off the security guard who monitors the system

■ Computers are used for designing the security system as well as its operation

COMPUTERS FOR CONTROL

Computers have many uses. They are used for designing systems, for holding and manipulating data, for help in diagnosing problems with the so-called *expert systems,* and for controlling devices and various operations. In the field of physical security, computers are used quite often for control.

THE BADGING STATION

Most large companies, especially those connected in some way to government or government contracting have a *badging station.* This is the place, usually near the human resources office, where employees get their picture taken so it can be put on a badge that also has a bar code, a magnetic strip, or perhaps even an electronic circuit inside. As mentioned in Chapter 1, this badge can be charged with money and used as a Cafeteria Card; it can be programmed with specific access control information and used as a key card, as well as other, more specific functions.

THE ALARM SYSTEM

The alarm system at a facility is set up as a series of closed loops. It may be wired, or it may be wireless using radio frequencies (RF). Further, the system, if it is wireless, may be using spread spectrum or encryption. Devices that are connected along the loops include:

- Door and window contacts, either normally open or normally closed and operated by magnetic forces
- Glass break sensors
- Smoke and heat detectors
- Motion detectors using microwave or passive infrared technology
- Light beams projected from transmitter to receiver
- Keypads or key and lock devices
- Annunciators such as buzzers or sirens

This system has a communicator device in the control box that sends its information to a monitoring center.

THE CCTV SYSTEM

Cameras are mounted throughout the facility. They all have lens types that will provide proper coverage for the surroundings. In hallways, telephoto lenses are used. If there were a window at the end of the hallway, an auto iris lens would be used to adjust for light changes from sunlight at the end of the hall. In a square room, a wide-angle lens may be used, aimed outwards from a corner of the room. An outdoor camera would be in a weatherproof housing. Some of the cameras would be attached to a pan, tilt, and zoom (PTZ) mechanism. The cameras would send their video signals through cabling to a monitoring site. There would be additional cables attached to the cameras that offer panning, tilting, and zoom. Additionally, on this camera circuit, there would be recorders; either video tape recorders (VTRs), or digital video recorders (DVRs) which are instruments of choice now that the prices have become competitive with VTRs. Of course, at the monitor site, there would be video monitors, some showing multiplexed images (perhaps 4-up), and some available via a switcher for showing different views via the pan, tilt, and zoom controls at the monitoring console.

ACCESS CONTROL

Throughout the building, doors are protected by magnetically controlled locking mechanisms, or electrically controlled door locks that are interfaced to an access control device. The device may be:

- A swipe card reader
- A proximity card reader
- A biometric device such as a thumbprint reader, an iris scanner, or a retina scanner
- Any combination of the above

All these devices connect to a computer; they all access databases in order to ensure proper authorization. The computer can be a standalone unmonitored unit or a monitored station. In case of a breach in security, an alarm would sound, and security personnel's attention would be directed to the computer for further information.

GUARD TOUR

The guard tour system may consist of iButtons® and a wand that interfaces with them, or another type of system that has a sensor and wand configuration, and stores information which will later be "dumped" or uploaded to a computer at the end of a shift, or at the end of a tour. This information will show stations and times that the guard physically walked the area.

PUTTING THE SYSTEMS TOGETHER

All of the systems mentioned in this chapter can be set up to be autonomous. All systems used to be set up that way. The monitor, or alarm, or control point usually ended up in one location at a guard station, or at the reception desk at the front entrance, but they were nevertheless, separate systems. Now, with networking technology, large hard disks, fast desktop computers, and the right software:

- The badging station not only makes up an I.D. card, it also sends pertinent personnel data, including pictures, to an employee database. This database contains access privileges, perhaps iris, retinal, or thumbprint info, and historical information.

- The software provides a graphical user interface (GUI) that shows a map of the facility complete with access control points, camera locations, doors, windows, sensitive areas, and anything else the client wants to see.

- Doors and other portals are shown either open or closed. Cameras can be selected for pan, tilt, and zoom, and the GUI will show a video box which can also be displayed on a separate monitor.

- Not only can an alarm sensor be activated via this software, but also real time video can be set up with algorithms to show certain *condition* and *response* situations. For instance, the video can be setup to recognize a carried package or briefcase. It will react when the package has been separated from the person and left unattended for a period of time that can be preset. Many different "what-if" situations can be preset.

- Guard tour can be set up in real time to show the location of any guard using not only the traditional guard tour stations, but also radiolocation devices.

- Instead of hooking all the systems up separately with the traditional twisted pair or coax cable, telecommunications cabling is used to hook up everything *directly multiplexed* to the network via TCP/IP either through a Local Area Network (LAN) or a Wide Area Network (WAN).

- Using a WAN, allows remote control of the facility's security through the Internet, a VPN, or a private telecommunications system.

This list just scratches the surface of possibilities when networking the security system. The only limitations are funding and the imagination.

SOFTWARE

There is an abundance of software on the marketplace for computer and network security: software for firewalls, virus protection, network intrusion detection and such. This chapter is *not* about that type of software. In chapter 7, we mentioned that the types of sensors available have become very sophisticated, and the development of new types of sensors is only limited by imagination and a good engineer. Biometrics is an especially good example of using sensors that measure many different parameters of the human body; but what do you do with this information once it is obtained? This is where the software part comes in. Let us say, for example that a person wishes to enter an office that is protected by a card reader and thumbprint scanner. First, the individual will swipe his or her ID card, the card reader sends the card information to a database, which confirms that the card is active, and the cardholder has permission to enter that office. Next, the person places a thumb on the thumbprint reader, and a scan of the thumb sends information to a database, which has in its files the thumbprints of all cardholders. The software at the database verifies that the cardholder is actually the right person holding the card, a signal goes to the lock mechanism on the door, a buzzer sounds, and the door is opened for the employee. All this happens in just a small fraction of a second. Even though it happens very fast, only recently did it become *fast enough* to handle hundreds or even thousands of people trying to access a portal. Only with the advent of extremely fast computers did biometric devices become viable. A retinal scan used to take milliseconds to operate. Sounds fast, but what we really needed, and now have, are *micro*seconds, or faster.

The software used with security systems is generally sold as a *suite*, meaning it handles more than just one function. For instance, one of the first things that happens to a new employee at a large company is that a picture is taken. The picture goes onto an ID card, but it also goes into a database, along with all the information provided on the employee application. An ongoing history of the employee updates this part of the database constantly. This same software interfaces with various sensor devices within the company's infrastructure. Swiping a card in a reader may send a query to the database, which will return some sort of action, either an alarm or a signal to open a door, or activate a camera. So now we have application software for, say, human resources, that can access the employee database; and we have a different application program that is interfaced to the physical security system, but if necessary, can access the *same* database that the human resources department uses. This software is on a server connected to a LAN or WAN, so it can be accessed remotely. The database may be located in New York, and the door that the employee needs to open may be in Los Angeles. You can see that things have to happen very quickly, especially when biometrics are involved. Just as with network security software, the security *control* software has to have an administrator, usually someone who is familiar with both security and networking. It is becoming increasingly more necessary for the security specialist to have a good working knowledge of TCP/IP, operating systems, routers, hubs, switches, and the like.

With LANS, WANS, remote control, and hundreds of different types of sensors measuring hundreds of different parameters, the day of the security guard sitting at a console, using only his human senses to monitor activity is waning. Security software is being developed and improved on a daily basis doing everything that the human guard used to do; only much faster, with better efficiency and it never sits and reads a newspaper or goes off for a cup of coffee.

A good example of the type of software discussed above is VistaScape's Security Data Management System (SDMS®), which integrates the monitoring and management of security hardware and software products into a single user interface and relational database. SDMS provides a wide area view of specified areas of interest. Unique data transfer and storage techniques help facilitate the rapid retrieval of data on events while analytical tools enable analysis and assessment of security data for pattern analysis, predictive behavior, and more. SDMS can be integrated into existing security infrastructures while maximizing performance of existing equipment and minimizing capital expenditures. Security Data Management System is used at borders, coastlines, pipelines, military bases, harbors, industrial plants, and data centers. SDMS solves complex and demanding security issues of limited spatial awareness, ability to react to threats, cost of manpower, raw data feeds with no option for numerical analysis, system scalability, and remote locations by integrating and enhancing the capabilities of market available security sensor products. SDMS is based on Microsoft technologies running on Intel-based PCs and servers. Its main purpose is to collect data from field sensors and provide the means for storage, analysis, and presentation of security and surveillance data. The system collects data from a variety of market available sensors, which is processed locally to become event records. After formatting to XML and encrypting, all records are transmitted to a centralized location where they are fused into a single data model, analyzed, and archived into a database. End-user applications retrieve data in real-time and display them on a virtual 3-D model of the area under surveillance. Users can interact with the displayed objects bringing up detailed descriptions and viewing live video feeds. They can also define restricted zones and events and set up rules for triggering alarms. SDMS consists of three main software suites, Sensor, Data Center, and Command & Control. Each suite is built using a multi-tier extensible architecture to isolate completely various components, and each component can be improved, replaced, or in the case of optional sub-components, removed without affecting the operation of the remaining parts, thus providing the means for specialized implementations and support.

Figure 8-1 illustrates the data flow in the system.

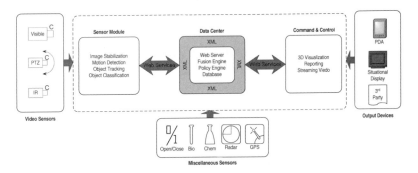

Figure 8–1   Any number or type of sensor can be used to generate data, while any type of device with Web access can view presentation data. Vistacape— figure and above information courtesy of VistaScape Security Systems, 300 Galleria Parkway, Suite 690 Atlanta, GA 30339—above information and excerpts from www.vistascape.com.

GUARD TOUR SYSTEMS

THE VERSATILE IBUTTON

The iButton® is a computer chip contained in a 16mm stainless steel can. Because of this unique and durable stainless steel can, up-to-date information can travel with a person or object anywhere they go. The steel button can be mounted virtually anywhere because it is rugged enough to withstand harsh environments, indoors or outdoors. It is durable enough to attach to a key fob, ring, watch, or other personal items and used daily for applications such as access control to buildings and computers.[1]

Figure 8–2   iButtons © Maxim Integrated Products, http://www.maxim-ic.com, used by permission.

THE CAN AND GROMMET

All iButtons use their stainless steel "Can" for their electronic communications interface. Each can has a data contact, which is called the "Lid" and a ground contact called the "Base." Each of these contacts is connected to the silicon chip inside. The lid is the top of the can and the base forms the sides and the bottom of the can and includes a flange for easily attaching the button to just about anything. The two contacts are separated by a polypropylene grommet.

---

1. Information and excerpts about iButton from the company's website at *www.ibutton.com*.

THE 1-WIRE INTERFACE

By simply touching each of the two contacts you can communicate to any of the iButtons by using their 1-Wire® protocol. The 1-Wire interface has two communication speeds. Standard mode at 16 kbps and overdrive mode at 142 kbps.

THE ADDRESS

Each iButton has a unique and unalterable address that is laser etched onto its chip inside the can. The address can be used as a key or identifier for each iButton.

The iButton product line has been expanded into over twenty different products by adding different functionality to the basic button. Buttons come in the following different varieties:

- Address Only
- Memory
- Real Time Clock
- Secure
- Temperature

HOW DOES INFORMATION GET IN AND OUT OF THE IBUTTON?

Information is transferred between the iButton and a PC with a momentary contact, at up to 142 kbps. You simply touch your iButton to a Blue Dot receptor or other iButton probe, which is connected to a PC. The Blue Dot receptor is cabled to a 1-Wire adapter that is attached to the PC's serial or parallel port. The iButton is also the ultimate information carrier for AutoID and portable applications. All of the latest handheld computers and PDAs can communicate with iButtons.

There are several different types of guard tour systems available that are software based, many using the iButton system.

ARES III WATCHMAN / TOUR GUARD SYSTEM

This watchman system provides an easy to use, reliable proof of security personnel patrols. The system ensures employers that their security personnel are covering their rounds. The M4000 Recorder is in a carrying case with a strap, which makes it easier for the security guards to handle.

In this application the watchman or guard uses his or her assigned "Guard Badge Button" to identify themselves—to start a shift the guard touches his or her badge button to the M4000 recorder. During rounds, the guard carries the M4000 and touches the recorder to designated "Recording Stations" registering station location (i.e. Front Door, Break Room Window, etc.) The system records date and time of the round, along with location. There is an optional Incident Pad that can be used to define conditions at locations (Door Unlocked, Window Opened, etc.) After tour/shift the M4000 data can be downloaded to a PC and reports can then be generated.

DEGGY CONTROLS

A guard tour system is an essential tool for any company that provides guard services.

Security guard tour control means that guards can prove exactly when and specifically where and what they inspected at a client's location, which improves the quality of services. A guard touches the Deggy pen over the Deggy button affixed at certain check points at a client's location. The pen then collects data throughout the guard's tour. At the end of his shift, the pen is downloaded to a computer. A report can easily be printed, showing where, when, and what the guards are doing.

As an option, the pen can be downloaded on the Deggy Remote and data can be transferred through the phone line. Using a supervisor's portable unit connected to a vehicle cigarette lighter adaptor, the pen can be downloaded right on the spot every time a supervisor arrives at a client's site. Once data is collected from many sites, it can be downloaded into a computer to generate reports.

SECURITY MANAGEMENT SYSTEMS

Security Management Systems (SMS) is an Add-On Modulated user friendly, guard tour system. SMS monitors all guard activities and tracks user-definable incidents. SMS integrates a database and a portable reader into a complete, easy-to-use tracking and evaluating system for any security organization. What is unique about SMS is that you can create and design your own personal software program according to your company's needs. You can choose Add-On Modules according to what types of hardware you want to use and according to what types of reports your company and clients will require. Add-On Modules also will include scheduling, inventory, and maintenance just to name a few.

OBJECTVIDEO

ObjectVideo is one of the leading developers of intelligent video security software for physical security applications. Founded in 1998, ObjectVideo generates products that employ an artificial intelligence technology known as computer vision that adds automated threat detection, identification, and notification capabilities to today's video surveillance systems. By enabling computers to "see," ObjectVideo's software significantly reduces false alarm rates while markedly increasing the effectiveness of security professionals. Headquartered in Reston, Virginia, ObjectVideo works with both government and commercial organizations to solve the many complex security challenges facing them today—see the ObjectVideo case study.

ObjectVideo Provides Andrews AFB Security—A Case Study

ObjectVideo Software Helps Air Force Enhance Security for Air Force One

RESTON, VA. December 3, 2003—ObjectVideo™, the leader in intelligent video security software, announced today that it is helping the U.S. Air Force enhance physical security at Andrews Air Force Base (AFB), home of Air Force One. ObjectVideo's software will transform the passive video surveillance cameras at the base into an active system for alerting security personnel to potential threats.

Under the agreement, ObjectVideo will install and maintain intelligent video security software to better safeguard "flightline operations," all procedures, such as maintenance, fueling and loading, that occur when a plane is on the ground. To enhance perimeter and ground security, the Air Force chose ObjectVideo's VEW® (Video Early Warning) software that accurately detects, identifies and analyzes in real time potential threats captured on video.

ObjectVideo Provides Andrews AFB Security—A Case Study (Continued)

"Security technologies at Andrews Air Force Base have to be the best to provide the highest level of protection possible, and nothing compares to the effectiveness of VEW," said Clara Conti, CEO of ObjectVideo. "The security system being installed at Andrews will serve as the model for security at many bases and ObjectVideo is very pleased to be a part."

Andrews AFB is best known as the airfield used by the President of the United States and home base for his plane, Air Force One. The base also provides air transportation for the Vice President, the Cabinet, Members of Congress, military leaders and receives high-ranking dignitaries from around the world. About 20,000 people live and work at Andrews.

ObjectVideo already is supplying technology to the Department of Homeland Security, the Department of Defense, the Department of Energy and the Federal Aviation Administration and a variety of private sector customers. ObjectVideo developers are currently working on the creation of the next generation of VEW under grants from the National Science Foundation and DARPA. Andrews AFB, because of its strategic importance and proximity to senior military leaders, was selected as the site for a program to identify the best tactics, techniques, procedures and technologies to protect forces, classified facilities and military bases from unauthorized entry. The base is conducting the initial testing and evaluation of technologies that later could be used to improve security at other military installations.

ObjectVideo's software combines the analytical capabilities of artificial intelligence with the ubiquitous, unblinking eye of surveillance cameras to extend the effectiveness of government personnel on watch. Applying artificial intelligence to the flow of video images, ObjectVideo's software can distinguish people, trucks, and other objects from background images and then check their actions against preprogrammed rules. Behavior that violates the rules – for instance a man walking too close to a plane—is immediately brought to the attention of security personnel to take action.

The government agencies using ObjectVideo technology say it combines state-of-the-art "computer vision" with open architecture that allows it to work with any video camera. Security can be significantly improved using existing cameras, which saves taxpayer dollars. ObjectVideo software provides much better threat detection, far fewer false alarms, and greater control of resources deployed by an organization.

DESIGN SOFTWARE

Software is used right from the beginning in designing logic circuits and for programming the brains behind the circuits. Early electronic circuits had to be "hard-wired" using discrete components such as resistors, capacitors, inductors, and active devices like diodes and transistors. As electronics became more miniaturized, clusters of components were squeezed together and packaged in small integrated circuits. This allowed for the use of printed circuit boards that only had a few discrete components and a couple of chips on board. Later, even more components were packaged together into large-scale integrated circuits (LSI), and then on even further with application specific integrated circuits (ASICs) which were custom made for specific uses, such as the alarm circuits we are discussing. Now we have programmable logic devices (PLDs) and complex programmable logic devices (CPLDs). These amazing IC chips contain in a small (about 1 inch square) package as many as 70,000 logic gates made up of combinations of transistor circuits. Logic gates are the OR, AND, NOR, and NAND circuits we discussed in the Boolean Algebra section. The really amazing thing about these PLDs and CPLDs is that they are just dumb chips waiting to be programmed using commonly available software (see Figures 8–3 through 8–5). This software, produced by different companies such as Altera® or Xilinx®, besides just programming the chips, can be used for several related functions. Altera's software is called QUARTUS. This software has a graphical interface and compiler as well as a more traditional programming input with compiler. The user can draw a logic diagram using symbols provided by the GUI such as gates (AND, OR, NAND, NOR), inputs, outputs, and so forth. The finished circuit can be tested by the software, checked for design errors, and then compiled. Once compiled, the operation of the circuit can be simulated, and then finally downloaded to the PLD chip. The downloading process is very easy. The chip is plugged into a circuit board, the circuit board is connected to the computer via the parallel port, and the circuit design is downloaded through this pipeline by simply issuing a command.

The PLD chip can then be unplugged from the circuit board and taken to its new home. The design software can also be used as a programming interface. Besides using a method of schematic design capture, a designer can use a programming language such as VHDL or Verilog®. These languages are similar in form to C or C++, and can be used to greatly increase productivity and reduce design cycle time.

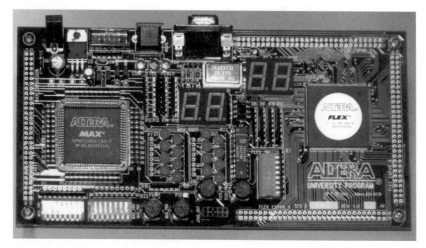

Figure 8–3   Altera's university program board for uploading and testing Complex Programmable Logic devices.

Figure 8–4   A Complex Programmable Logic Device (CPLD).

Figure 8–5   A surface mounted CPLD.

SYSTEM DESIGN SOFTWARE

Hardware design is not the only type of design in which computers are a help. There is systems design, in which many components or parts are put together with the help of a computer. The computer allows an operator to mix, match, and perform many "what-if" situations, which saves reams of paper that would be used on a drafting board.

CAD Software

The very first thing that has to be done when designing a security system for a building is to decide what types of systems will be used and where the sensors and controls will be located. In the case of a new building, blueprints are usually used, but in the case of a pre-existing structure, a new drawing may have to be done if blueprints are not available. After pacing off the premises, taking notes, and measurements, a designer will use Computer Aided Drawing (CAD) software to make final drawings. Of course, some designers still prefer to use a drafting board, paper, and pencil, but software makes the process much easier and faster, especially when it comes to corrections and modifications. There are many different types of CAD software available for all types of budgets. The preeminent CAD software is AutoCad®. AutoCAD software is a 2-D drafting and detailing and 3-D design tool that is used by more designers world-wide than any other CAD software. It provides native DWG file-type compatibility, plus the software can be personalized or programmed or a third-party application added to meet specific design require-ments. AutoCAD integrates enhanced productivity tools, presenta-tion graphics, CAD standards, and more for fast, easy data creation and sharing.

The file type "DWG" is universal and is provided by AutoCad as well as most other CAD software. Here is an assortment of various CAD programs:

- CAD X11—2-D, 3-D for general use in drafting including ANSI standard, surfaces, Gerber, Acrobat, Patran output, and more, by GrayTech

- CADKEY—general purpose, full-featured CAD, favored for mechanical application

- CADopia IntelliCAD—AutoCAD-compatible, by CADopia

- CADVANCE—from FIT Inc.

- DataCAD

- DesignCAD 3-D MAX—offers 3-D modeling, 2-D drafting, and many other features of more expensive, high-end CAD programs. From Upperspace

- FastCAD—by Evolution Computing

- freeCAD—a basic 3-D CAD with advanced motion simulation capabili-ties, suitable for anyone interested in learning to use CAD for free before upgrading to a commercial application

- Generic CADD—this is the website of GenericCadd.com, a CAD dealer-ship that continues to offer support and information for users of this now-discontinued Autodesk program

- Graphite—2-D drafting and 3-D from Ashlar Vellum, available for PC and Mac (replaces Vellum Draft)

- GTWorks—2-D, 3-D mechanical design and drafting, includes ANSI/DOD/MIL standard drafting, surfaces, solids, flat pattern layout, and more, by GrayTech

- IDRAW 2000—by Design Futures

- IGEStoolbox—a standalone, lightweight CAD program for viewing or plotting IGES files without converting files to other formats, cutting sections in surfaces, and transforming and creating geometry. From Cornerstone Technology

- QuickCAD—entry-level CAD, by Autodesk

- MicroStation—industrial strength, very popular (second only to AutoCAD), Bentley Systems, Inc.

- Modular CAD—for resizing and placing modular products: wall storage units, toilet cubicles, washrooms, kitchens, custom cabinets, shelving, racking, and shop equipment, by Leonardo Computer Systems

- PowerCAD Professional—(formerly FelixCAD) offers AutoCAD compatibility and customization, supports paper and model space and xrefs, and includes utilities to convert AutoLISP and ADS program code, menus, dialog boxes, and toolbars. From GiveMePower Inc.

- TurboCAD—full function CAD program, favored by construction, hobbyists

- Vdraft—from SoftSource, DWG-based CAD system

- VectorWorks—from Nemetschek

- VersaCAD—production-level CAD for engineers, drafts persons, and others in the architectural, civil engineering, construction, and mechanical industries, by Archway Systems

System Modeling Software

There are many different software programs available that are used for computer modeling the effectiveness of a security system. Some of them are:

- ASSESS (Analytic System and Software for Evaluating Safeguards and Security), a proprietary model used by the Department of Energy (DOE)

- FESEM (Forcible Entry Safeguards Effectiveness Model). This model uses a simulation to analyze forced entry along an assumed path by an adversary with an assumed set of attributes

- ISEM (Insider Safeguards Effectiveness Model). Similar to FESEM, but no longer generally in use

- SAFE (Safeguards Automated Facility Evaluation). Selects most vulnerable paths through a facility

- SAVI (System Analysis of Vulnerability to Intrusion). Provides a comprehensive analysis of all adversary paths into a facility

- SNAP (Safeguards Network Analysis Procedure). Requires the analyst to model the facility, the guard force, and the adversary force

- EASI (Estimate of Adversary Sequence Interruption). A simple, easy-to-use method of evaluating physical protection systems performance along a specific path and under specific conditions of threat and system operation

PROTECTING THE COMPUTER

We have been talking about using the computer with physical security systems to enhance performance, but there are times when we want to protect the computer, itself. Companies keep all of their information on data hard drive systems. The information covers all aspects of the business—business plans, finances, products, marketing plans, past performance, budgeting, and forecasting, among other things. The compromise of this information can devastate a company, so it is very important that it be protected. Information security guidelines provide for layers of protection in the form of access privileges, but what about protecting computers and networks from eavesdropping?

All devices that have operations running at the speed of radio frequencies (RF), give off electromagnetic emanations. Manufacturers must keep this radiation down to a certain level according to FCC rules and regulations. These regulations cover such things as electromagnetic interference (EMI), and electromagnetic compatibility (EMC). Complying with these rules and regulations and staying within proper limits will ensure that the computer, monitor, or other peripheral will not interfere with other equipment that is located in close proximity. Unfortunately, this same compliance will not protect the system from being compromised by means of "reading" the electromagnetic radiation that still exists. A scientist named Wim van Eck expanded on the fact that electronic equipment produces electromagnetic fields, which may cause interference to radio and television reception. In 1983, he found that interference is not the only problem caused by electromagnetic radiation. It is possible in some cases to obtain information on the signals used inside the equipment when the radiation is picked up and the received signals are decoded. Especially in the case of digital equipment, this possibility constitutes a problem, because remote reconstruction of signals inside the equipment may enable reconstruction of the data the equipment is processing. Engineers have long been aware of the fact that this problem existed, but they felt that only an expert with very expensive equipment would be able to "listen in" on this radiation. Wim van Eck demonstrated that with the use of only about $10.00 worth of equipment, he could read the radiation off of a computer's cathode ray tube (CRT) from a distance of several meters. For this demonstration van Eck only concentrated on the CRT but wrote that other internal emanations from a computer could be picked up in the same manner. The CRT eavesdropping by this method became known as van Eck hacking. Of course, a much simpler method of getting information from a CRT screen would simply be to watch it through a pair of binoculars! Getting back to radiation, keyboards give off electronic radiation (and can also be watched with binoculars). Wires that connect components emanate, so do routers, hubs, switches, you get the idea. The government has formulated a set of standards known as Tempest.

Tempest guidelines provide for protection against electromagnetic "leakage," usually by enclosing equipment in an electromagnetically shielded "box." This box is often made up of matrices of copper wire and other materials that will keep radiation inside. This box may be slightly bigger than the computer, or it could be the size of a room, or an entire building! Originally, Tempest provided for the protection of electrical equipment such as radios, computers, and even electric typewriters, but more recently, has been expanded to include optics. There have been papers written about picking up light reflected from a computer screen and reformulating information from that. Now procedures for protecting work areas include special window films that will suppress RF radiation and light in the infrared and ultraviolet wavelengths that are commonly used with lasers. Although it is a very weak method of eavesdropping, laser beams can be aimed at windowpanes, or interior articles such as picture frames, and the vibrations are reflected back using Doppler methods, to pick up room conversation and other noises. Locations of equipment in rooms should be carefully planned to keep outsiders from simply looking in and watching what is going on. Outside landscaping can also be designed to protect against snoops.

SUMMARY

- Security systems have always used simple switches; devices that are either in an "on" state or in an "off" state. Computers make things easier for security system designers, because computers use digital technology.

- Most large companies, especially those connected in some way to government or government contracting, have a badging station.

- The alarm system at a company's facility is set up as a series of closed loops. It may be wired, or it may be wireless using radio frequencies. Further, the system, if it is wireless, may be using spread spectrum or encryption.

- Cameras send their video signals through cabling to a monitoring site. There are additional cables attached to the cameras that offer pan, tilt, and zoom. Additionally, on this camera circuit, there would be recorders; either video tape recorders or digital video recorders which are the instruments of choice now that the prices have become competitive with VTRs.

- Throughout a secure building, doors are protected by magnetically controlled locking mechanisms, or electrically controlled door locks that are interfaced to an access control device.

- The possibilities derived from networking the security system are limited only by the human imagination.

- Software used with security systems is generally sold as a suite, meaning it handles more than just one function.

- With LANS, WANS, remote control, and hundreds of different types of sensors measuring hundreds of different parameters, the day of the security guard sitting at a console, using only his human senses to monitor activity is waning. Security software is being developed and improved on a daily basis doing everything that the human guard used to do, only much faster, and with better efficiency.

- Software is used right from the beginning in designing logic circuits and for programming the brains behind the circuits.

- The very first thing that has to be done when designing a security system for a building is to decide what types of systems will be used and where the sensors and controls will be located. After pacing off the premises, taking notes, and taking measurements, a designer will use Computer Aided Drawing (CAD) software to make final drawings.

- There are many different software programs available that are used for computer modeling the effectiveness of a security system.

■ All devices that have operations running at the speed of radio frequencies (RF) give off electromagnetic emanations.

■ A scientist named Wim van Eck expanded on the fact that electronic equipment produces electromagnetic fields, which may cause interference to radio and television reception. In 1983, he found that interference is not the only problem caused by electromagnetic radiation. It is possible in some cases to obtain information on the signals used inside the equipment when the radiation is picked up and the received signals are decoded.

■ The government has formulated a set of standards known as Tempest. Tempest guidelines provide for protection against electromagnetic "leakage," usually by enclosing equipment in an electromagnetically shielded box.

KEY TERMS

Badging Station

Normally Open (NO)

Normally Closed (NC)

Digital Video Recorders (DVRs)

Swipe Card Reader

Proximity Card Reader

Integrated Circuits

Application Specific Integrated Circuits (ASICS)

Programmable Logic Devices (PLDs)

Complex Programmable Logic Devices (CPLDs)

Computer Aided Drawing (CAD)

Electromagnetic Interference (EMI)

Electromagnetic Compatibility (EMC)

Van Eck Hacking

Tempest

DISCUSSION QUESTIONS

1 Besides having a picture taken for a badge at the *badging station*, where else does the video information go?

2 What do we mean when we speak of multiplexed images on a monitor?

3 What is the difference between a DVR and a VTR?

4 Define PTZ.

5 What is a guard tour?

6 What do you suppose the difference is between a *swipe card reader* and a *proximity reader*? Do some research on the Internet, and discuss distances in relation to proximity card readers.

7 Discuss how a biometric reader operates.

8 There are several "intelligent" CCTV systems available. Discuss why they are *intelligent* compared to a plain old CCTV camera.

9 Why would anyone want to hook up an alarm system to a WAN?

10 What is CAD, and why would we use it in the physical security business?

11 The chapter stated that an alarm system at a company is set up as a "system of closed loops." What does that mean?

12 What type of information do you suppose would be stored on a guard's "wand" as she makes her rounds?

13 What is a GUI?

14 What is a Security Data Management System (SDMS)?

15 What is QUARTUS?

RESEARCH QUESTIONS

1 Distinguish between the following: Computer, CPU, Microprocessor, and Microcontroller.

2 What is the difference between an analog computer and a digital computer? Are analog computers still in use? For what?

3 Does the server computer of an alarm system have to be located on the premises? Explain.

Low Tech Tools, Small Tools, and Methods of Use

PURPOSE AND OBJECTIVES

We have already discussed the abundance of marvelous high tech equipment available for use in the security industry, such as spectrum analyzers, non-linear junction detectors, time-domain reflectometers, etc. Such high tech equipment has become a necessity, but what would we do without screwdrivers, pliers, wire strippers, and wire pulling equipment? This chapter deals with some small special purpose, and so-called "low tech" equipment, without which we would be in a terrible bind.

■ We will review some tools that are provided specifically for the security and "home entertainment" industries

■ You will learn about purpose and use of some lower cost tools and equipment that can be found in the toolkits of most service engineers

■ The chapter will describe the operation of some simple, "low tech" devices

THE BASIC TOOLKIT

An example of a very useful toolkit for the security engineer would be the Jensen Tools® JTK-45 toolkit shown in Figure 9–1. This kit contains the following tools in a zippered soft case:

Cable cutter, 8"—This is a cutter that is somewhat more "heavy duty" than the cutter that is integrated into some pliers. It has large jaws that are designed to cut through wire bundles of up to about 1/2" in diameter.

Can Wrench—The can wrench is a specially designed wrench that is used to open telephone company equipment panels, telecommunications pedestals, and cabinets. It has deep nut drivers on each end that are 3/8" and 7/16" by 1-1/8" deep.

Hemostat, Straight, 6"—The hemostat is actually a surgical clamp that is also very useful for electronics work (see Figure 9–2). It is a locking type of scissors clamp that can grip small parts.

Hex key set, fold-up (9), .050-3/16"—This is an entire set of hexagonal wrenches that fold into a jackknife type of mechanism.

Knife-driver, electrician's—A utility jackknife that also has a screwdriver.

Pliers (2): chain nose with cutter, 6"; Diagonal cutter, 5"—A small wire cutter.

Pliers (2)—shear cutter, flush; insulation.

Skinner, 6"—A tool designed to strip insulation from wires.

Scissors, strip-jaw and electrician's—This particular pair of scissors has a small notch built into one of the blades that can be used for stripping wire insulation.

Screwdrivers (4): Phillips #1, #2; slotted 5/16 × 4"; cabinet slotted 3/16 × 6".

Screwdriver, Phillips, pocket clip, #0.

Screwdriver, slotted, pocket clip, 1/8".

Screw starter, double-ended, Phillips/slotted—These "screw starters" have spring clips located at the end of a slim rod that can hold a screw head, thereby allowing a person to start a screw in a very tight location.

Socket set, 1/4" drive 14pc.

Wire stripper, stranded 16-26 AWG.

Wrench, adjustable, 6".

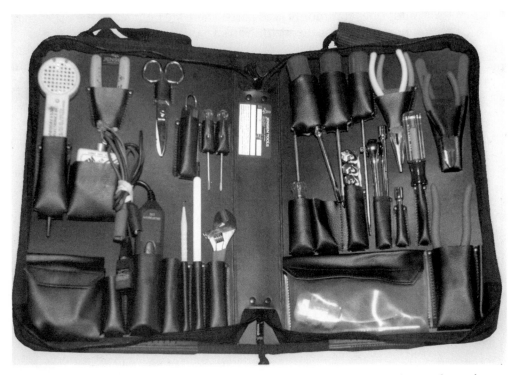

Figure 9–1 Jensen Tools' JTK45 toolkit, a favorite among telecommunications and security technicians.

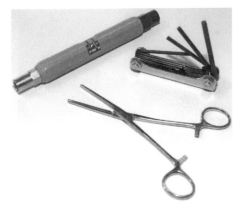

Figure 9–2 Can Wrench, HexKeys, and Hemostats.

The kit also contains several pockets in the zippered bag that can be used for miscellaneous parts such as splices, door magnets, batteries, and other commonly used parts. There are holders on the pallet that are available for the technician's favorite tools that may not be included in the basic kit, such as a splicing tool. The outside of the case has large pouches that are handy for carrying a telephone butt-set, and/or other test equipment such as digital multimeters or LAN analyzers.

SPLICES

Very often, it becomes necessary to splice wires together, whether for a telephone wire connection, or for alarm wiring. Figure 9–3 shows some very handy splices manufactured by 3M that provide for a strong, low resistance splice. The crimping pliers shown in Figure 9–4 have the exact gap set in them for setting the splice without damaging the plastic housing or causing the wires themselves to be damaged. Red (UR) Connectors provide three openings for 19–26 AWG wire, ideal for pigtail and load coil splice applications. Yellow (UY) Connectors are used for 22–26 gauge. Green (UG) Connectors are for tapping onto 19–26 AWG wires. This only applies to solid conductor wires. Crimping pliers are specifically designed for these button type connectors and include a side wire cutter.

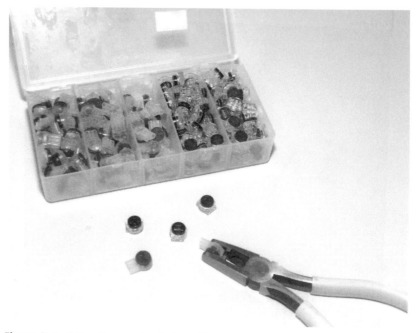

Figure 9–3   3M splices and splicing pliers.

Figure 9–4   Closeup of the splicing pliers.

ELECTRICAL TESTERS

A digital multimeter (DMM) can be used as an electrical tester, to check whether there is voltage on a wire pair, and whether it is high enough to be dangerous. The DMM, however, is fairly large, and usually cannot be carried in a shirt pocket. A tester such as the Fluke® Voltalert AC Voltage Detector can be carried like a pen. This is a very easy device to use. Just touch the plastic tip to a control wire, conductor, or outlet. When it glows red, you know there is voltage on the line. This device is available in two voltage ranges: low voltage at 24-90VAC, and high voltage at 90-600VAC. The price is in the low twenty dollar range.

MAGNETIC PROBE

A magnetic probe similar to the electrical tester just discussed is also available. This "Mag-Probe"® will detect magnetic fields around transformers, coils, armatures, solenoids and relays as well as perma-nent magnets. Red lights glow, indicating the presence of static (DC) or fluctuating (AC) fields. These probes can even indicate north or south magnetic poles. For micro relays and reed switches such as the type found in security electronics, a high sensitivity probe is avail-able. These probes cost approximately $35.

POWER MONITORING

Something frequently encountered in security work, and most electronics in general, is the intermittent problem. Many times, these intermittents can be blamed on glitches in the electrical system. A very useful, but not inexpensive, tool is the *power monitor*. A good example is the Power Investigator®, which will find and explain problems and even suggest solutions. This unit is plugged into an outlet and left for a few hours. It examines power quality for nine types of problems and counts each event type (up to 65,000) It downloads a report telling you in plain English the causes of problems and their effect on electronic equipment. A solutions report is printed detailing how to correct the problems. The output is provided via a built-in parallel port. The unit will work on AC lines from 80V to 300V, 40 to 400Hz. The unit is small at about 7" × 4.5" × 2.25". The price is around $450.

CABLE AND NETWORK TESTERS

In Chapter 4, we mentioned cable testers that performed just about every test needed for certification of cable after it has been installed. The tester mentioned; the DSP-4300, although excellent, is also very expensive. A less expensive alternative would be the Microscanner Pro®. This device costs about $400–$550, depending on features ordered. This is a cable verification and troubleshooting tool designed specifically for home networking and IT network managers, and it also has many handy features for the security installer. It can test both coaxial and all twisted pair cable and even troubleshoot any other two-wire network like speaker wires, security networks, or telephone cabling. It measures length and distance to fault, using true time domain reflectometry for the most accurate reading. The TDR can be used to inventory cable or perform job costing on installed cable. The unit produces and tests a wiremap for crossed and split pairs on twisted pair cables and finds opens and shorts on all cabling. It has four different toners for finding hidden cabling. With room/office identifiers, you can easily determine routing at the patch panel, and document twisted pair and coax networks easily. A great feature is the detection of active 10/100 networks. It will identify whether the network is running at 10 or 100 Mbps, and identifies if it is half or full duplex capable. It will flash hub port lights for identification (see Figure 9–5).

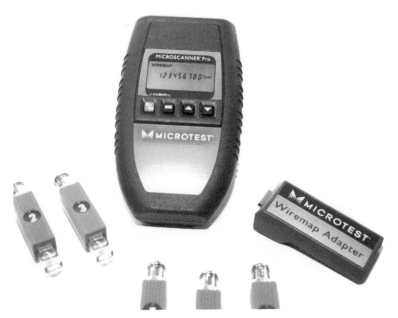

Figure 9–5   A Microtest wiremapping tool.

UNDERGROUND CABLE LOCATOR

We can use a TDR to determine the distance to a fault on an underground cable, but we need another special purpose tool to determine the routing of underground cable. This tool would be the *underground cable locator*. A good example of this device is the Cable-Tracker® by Psiber. This device uses dual frequencies, either 2 KHz or 33 KHz, and works by connecting the built in transmitter to the cable and following the audible signal. The 2 KHz frequency is best for cables and pipes. It uses a direct connection and reduces false coupling with adjacent lines. The 33 KHz frequency is used to apply the signal by induction, or for high resistance lines. The higher frequency also jumps insulators and rubber gaskets often found in water and gas distribution systems. The wand receiver picks up signals and can be held waist high to ease back strain. This unit is in the $500 price range.

TONE TESTER

One of the most useful testers in a security engineer's kit is the *tone tester*. This device is used for tracing lines. Patch panels can be a nest of identical looking wires. To trace one individual wire from a connector back to a patch panel could be impossible without a tone tester. This device is designed for technicians installing and maintaining CATV, CCTV, and security systems. It will identify untagged or mislabeled drops. A transmitter injects a tone onto any coax terminated with an F connector, or twisted pair and distribution cables with an adapter. It will send a signal through splitters, traps, and directional couplers, and will indicate continuity and presence of voltage on the line. The receiver can pick up the tone on terminated and unterminated cable via induction. Progressive Electronics, a communications company, markets the 620K Security/Alarm kit, which is designed specifically for security and alarm techs. It operates as a continuity tester on NO and NC circuits, giving an audible tone when it detects an alarm condition (see the case study courtesy of Progressive Electronics).

Testing Switches Using the Continuity/Discontinuity Function—A Progressive Electronics Case Study

Testing alarm switches for continuity/discontinuity with the Model 620 is achieved using the RED and BLACK test leads connected to the loop pair. No other test equipment is required to perform this operation. With its magnetic back plate, the Model 620 can be mounted to the control panel door or cabinet.

To test a Normally Open switch

Method 1

Attach the RED and BLACK test leads to the loop pair that has been disconnected from the control panel. Move the slide switch to the "N.O." position. If the alarm switch is in the normally open condition, no signal will be heard. Move to the location of the alarm switch and close the switch. The tester will produce a distinct audible signal. The Model 620 will continue sounding until the switch is returned to its normally open position.

Method 2

Attach the RED and BLACK test leads to the loop pair that has been disconnected from the control panel. Move the slide switch to the "N.O. LATCH" position. If the alarm switch is in the normally open condition, no signal will be heard. Move to the location of the alarm switch and close

Testing Switches Using the Continuity/Discontinuity Function—A Progressive Electronics Case Study (Continued)

the switch. The tester will produce a distinct audible signal that will continue to sound even after the switch is returned to its normally open position. In the "latching" mode, the captured occurrence will continue to sound until the "RESET" button on the Model 620 is depressed.

 NOTE The Model 620 will not detect a switch closing in a normally open switch with a resistor in parallel. Testing a normally open circuit with a resistor in parallel is possible using the tone feature (see section "Testing the Switches Using the Tone Function.")

To test a Normally Closed switch

Method 1

Attach the RED and BLACK test leads to the loop pair that has been disconnected from the control panel. Move the slide switch to the "N.C." position. If the alarm switch is in the normally closed condition, no signal will be heard. Move to the location of the alarm switch and open the switch. The tester will produce a distinct audible signal. The Model 620 will continue sounding until the switch is returned to its normally closed position.

Method 2

Attach the RED and BLACK test leads to the loop pair that has been disconnected from the control panel. Move the slide switch to the "N.C. LATCH" position. If the alarm switch is in the normally closed condition, no signal will be heard. Move to the location of the alarm switch and open the switch. The tester will produce a distinct audible signal that will continue to sound even after the switch is returned to its normally closed position. In the "latching" mode, the captured occurrence will continue to sound until the "RESET" button on the Model 620 is depressed.

 NOTE The Model 620 is designed to withstand accidental connection to energized circuits (24 VDC or 110 VAC). When a connection is made to these energized circuits, the Model 620's internal speaker will produce a distinct "buzz." DO NOT ATTEMPT TO PERFORM TONE OR TEST FUNCTIONS ON AN ENERGIZED CIRCUIT.

Applications Note

High resistance intermittent faults, commonly known as "high swingers," are often difficult to locate and result in numerous call backs for service technicians. Poor quality mechanical connections and damaged conductors

Testing Switches Using the Continuity/Discontinuity Function—A Progressive Electronics Case Study (Continued)

can be identified by using Model 620 to check continuity/discontinuity in the "Latching" mode (see section "Testing Switches Using the Continuity/Discontinuity Function.") Moving along the circuit path while agitating the conductors and alarm contacts will often cause a weakened circuit to fail. The Model 620 will audibly capture that occurrence (> 100µS) and identify the general area of the failure. Examples of this process would include shaking closed doors, pounding on walls where cable drops have been installed, carefully tapping window glass, etc. As a technician becomes more familiar with the Model 620, "high swingers" will become easier to locate using this process.

Testing Telephone Circuits

To test for the presence of Central Office battery (telephone service), use the Alarm Circuit Tester in the OFF position.

1   Connect the modular plug to an RJ-11 telephone jack or connect the red test lead to the ring side of the circuit and the black lead to the tip side.

2   Note the condition of the Light Emitting Diode (LED) on the face of the tester.

   ● A bright green LED indicates a working line with correct polarity battery.

   ● A bright red LED indicates a working line with reversed polarity battery.

   ● A flashing red and green LED indicates a ringing line.

   ● No LED indicates an in use, "off hook," condition or no service provided.

Maintenance

The only service requirements for the Model 620 will be a periodic 9-volt battery replacement. Remove battery cover on back of the tester and replace with any standard 9-volt battery.

 NOTE Move the slide switch to the "TONE" position and listen for a soft tone from the Model 620's internal speaker to confirm proper switch setting and tone function. At the point where the identification is to be made, touch the tip of the probe to the insulation of the suspect conductor(s). Reception of tone will be strongest on the subject conductor(s). Normally Closed switches must be opened to perform this function.

Testing Switches Using the Continuity/Discontinuity Function—A Progressive Electronics Case Study (Continued)

Testing Switches Using the Tone Function

The Model 620 can be use in conjunction with an inductive amplifier (probe) to test the operation of alarm switches. Progressive Electronics' Models 200EP and 200FP are ideally suited for this application. Disconnect the loop pair from the control panel. Connect the RED and BLACK test leads to the loop pair. Move the slide switch to the "TONE" position and listen for a soft tone from the Model 620's internal speaker to confirm proper switch setting and tone function. Move to the switch under test and activate the probe. Scan the switch with the probe tip noting the presence and level of tone.

Testing Switches Using the Continuity/Discontinuity Function

Testing alarm switches for continuity/discontinuity with the Model 620 is achieved using the RED and BLACK test leads connected to the loop pair. No other test equipment is required to perform this operation. With its magnetic back plate, the Model 620 can be mounted to the control panel door or cabinet.

To test a Normally Open switch

Method 1

Attach the RED and BLACK test leads to the loop pair that has been disconnected from the control panel. Move the slide switch to the "N.O." position. If the alarm switch is in the normally open condition, no signal will be heard. Move to the location of the alarm switch and close the switch. The tester will produce a distinct audible signal. The Model 620 will continue sounding until the switch is returned to its normally open position.

Method 2

Attach the RED and BLACK test leads to the loop pair that has been disconnected from the control panel. Move the slide switch to the "N.O. LATCH" position. If the alarm switch is in the normally open condition, no signal will be heard. Move to the location of the alarm switch and close the switch. The tester will produce a distinct audible signal that will continue to sound even after the switch is returned to its normally open position. In the "latching" mode, the captured occurrence will continue to sound until the "RESET" button on the Model 620 is depressed.

CABLE CHECKER

In addition to using a digital multimeter or other test instrument for continuity checks, another handy instrument is the *cable checker* (Figure 9–6). This device will instantly check continuity and mapping of many different multi-strand cables. The tester has numerous plugs and connectors, and tests and checks the pin-outs of a wide variety of cable used in computers, phone lines, LANs, and security systems. The checker sequences wire-by-wire, showing exactly how the cable is wired. It quickly determines whether the cable is good, or how it is wired for duplication.

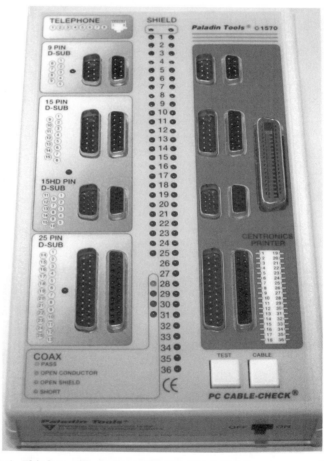

Figure 9–6   This box will check continuity of just about every type of computer cable.

THE BUTT SET

The *butt set* or 2-way speakerphone test set is just a telephone
handset replacement with added features that can be attached to any
line pair and used to listen in on it, whether a phone line or a line
used in conjunction with a security system. The butt set is a very
versatile instrument that is a high impedance device for safe operation on a data line, and has a built in speaker for hands free operation. Figure 9–7 shows an analog model, but there are also digital
units available to test Digital Subscriber Line (DSL) or other types of
digital lines.

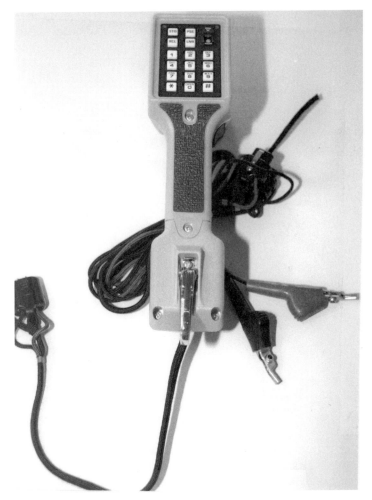

Figure 9–7   Harris TS-22 Butt Set

CRIMPERS

Paladin Tools All-in-One Telephone Tool®

This tool cuts, strips, and crimps modular telephone wires and plugs. It cuts and strips flat line cord up to eight conductors wide. It crimps handset connectors, RJ-11 and RJ-45 plugs with no die change.

Paladin Tools Wire Ferrule Crimp Tool®

This tool (Figure 9–8) is designed to crimp both insulated and non-insulated wire ferrules. It is made of steel construction and has ergonomic handles for low effort operation. A fixed steel die system eliminates the need for purchasing additional dies. The range of this tool is 10-24 AWG.

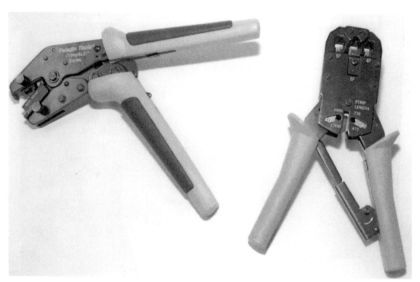

Figure 9–8 Crimping tools with dies installed for various types of telco connectors.

TELESCOPING POLES AND LINE CASTERS

Telescoping fiberglass poles such as the Gopher Pole® will stretch out to 22 feet long from a collapsed length of 52 inches. This push-pull installation tool is used for installing wires over long spans or hard to reach areas such as suspended ceilings, sub floors, crawl spaces, and attics. The unit has an "s-hook" at the end, which can be used to drag cable from the near end, or grab cable from the opposite end.

Another handy instrument is the Cablecaster®, which is a plastic gun, the same type kids use with suction cup darts. This gun has a fishing reel attached and the dart has line attached to it from the reel. Shooting the dart will shoot a line through hard to reach spaces, such as suspended ceilings, rafters, and sub floors. It will launch the dart up to 50 feet to the cable supply access point, pulling a durable mono filament line. The cable is attached to the dart, and pulled back with the Cable Caster take-up reel. An integral flashlight holder on top will accommodate a Mini Maglite®.

TAPES

Fish Tape

An absolute necessity for a security engineer is at least one reel of *fish tape*. Ideal Industries offers several different types of fish tape (figure 9-9), either metal or non-metallic. The tape is optimized for use in conduit runs that have difficult cable placement characteristics such as multiple bends, elbows, and junction boxes. It also has the ability to deliver true omni-directional pushing performance so it can handle bends and changes in plane without hanging up or deforming within the conduit and it will not break or rust. The dispensers offer 100 or 50 feet of tape.

Under Carpet Tape

Under carpet tape is a 25-foot long annealed, stainless steel, 3/4" wide tape with one end curled up and the other rounded. This allows the user to run wire or cable between the padding and the carpet. Under carpet tape is a very practical solution for when the home or building is on a concrete pad and you are unable to fish, or pull wire through the walls and ceiling.

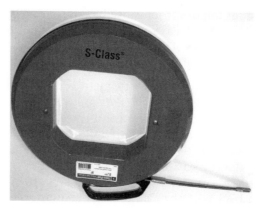

Figure 9–9 "Fish" tape.

SECURITY SCREWDRIVER KIT

Jensen Tools® sells a 30-piece security screwdriver kit. This kit contains bits that are necessary for use on specialized security equipment. The types of bits are Torx®, security torx, security hex, and spanners.

RUNNING CABLE

One problem area when installing a wired security system is running the cable from one component to another. Fortunately, there are many tools and "tricks of the trade" used to accomplish this sometimes difficult task. One method used quite often to get cabling from one side of a room to another, is to remove the molding (very carefully) at the bottom of a wall, using a pry bar. Prior to removing the molding, a sharp pencil is used to draw a line on the wall at the top of the molding. Once the molding is removed, the drywall is cut away from just under the pencil line to the floor. This will expose the bottoms of wall joists, which can now be "notched" or have holes drilled just inside the outer surface. The cable is run inside the holes or notches. New pieces of drywall are cut to cover the exposed joists, and the molding is then reattached.

There is new cable available now that is so thin and flat, it can literally be attached directly to the wall, and painted over, and it will barely be noticeable; this can be done at the very top of the molding. As an alternative, the flat cable could be routed under carpeting, between the carpet and the floor pad. A metallic tape tool (discussed previously) is available for this operation.

Another useful trick for routing cable, in this case vertically, from one building level to another, is to remove molding at the top level. Then, drill a hole at the bottom of the lower level's wall large enough to insert the tape of a tape measure and to feed it into the hole in the shape of a "U" where it will snug up against the joists in the wall. Then, dangle cable down inside the wall from above, where molding was removed, between two joists. By pulling the tape out through the hole in the wall, the cable will be pulled along with the tape out through the hole. The only problem with this particular trick is that you typically cannot do it at an outer wall due to insulation between wall joists.

We talked about using dart guns and extender poles for cable runs in false ceilings. Keep in mind that these techniques are used in crawl spaces below a building, as well. Occasionally, there are horizontal sections of 2 × 4 that are installed between joists, and it is necessary to get a cable through this barrier. There are very long drill bits available (usually about four feet, or more, in length), that are flexible, and with the use of a supplementary holder, these bits can actually be bent *into* a wall from top or bottom to drill through barriers. Usually, these drill bits have holes through the end so they can also be used as wire pullers. This type of drilling will necessitate making a hole in the wall, so you should develop your plaster-patching skills. Fortunately, there are kits available for doing this type of hole patching that allow the technician to do a great repair job with little effort.

WIRELESS

After doing a few cable runs, technicians usually develop a great admiration for all the new advances in wireless networking. Wireless used to be very susceptible to noise, eavesdropping, and several other problems, however with modern methods of cryptography, and spread spectrum methods such as direct sequence spread spectrum or frequency hopping, wireless has become a very viable alternative to cabling. Wireless also used to have limitations on distance, but again, with modern advances in repeater methodology, antenna design, and digital signaling, wireless can sometimes cover even greater distances than cabling.

SUMMARY

- High tech equipment has become a necessity in the security industry, but what would we do without screwdrivers, pliers, wire strippers, and wire pulling equipment?

- Often, it becomes necessary to splice wires together, whether for a telephone wire connection, or for alarm wiring. Red (UR) Connectors provide three openings for 19–26 AWG wire, ideal for pigtail and load coil splice applications. Green (UG) Connectors are for tapping onto 19–26 AWG wires. This is applicable to solid conductor wires only. Crimping pliers are specifically designed for these button-type connectors and include a side wire cutter.

- There are compact electrical testers available in two voltage ranges: low voltage at 24–90VAC, and high voltage at 90–600VAC.

- There are cable testers that perform just about every test needed for certification of cable after it has been installed. These devices can test both coaxial and all twisted pair cable and even troubleshoot any other two-wire network like speaker wires, security networks, or telephone cabling.

- The TDR can be used to inventory cable or perform job costing on installed cable. The unit produces and tests a wiremap for crossed and split pairs on twisted pair cables and finds opens and shorts on all cabling.

- One of the most useful testers in a security engineer's kit is the tone tester. The device is used for tracing lines and checking continuity.

- The cable checker has numerous plugs and connectors, and tests and checks the pin-outs of a wide variety of cable used in computers, phone lines, LANs, and security systems. The checker sequences wire-by-wire, showing exactly how the cable is wired.

- Under carpet tape allows the user to run wire or cable between the padding and the carpet.

- One problem area in installing a wired security system is running the cable from one component to another. A metallic type of tape is available for this operation.

KEY TERMS

Can Wrench

Hemostat

Splice and Crimping Pliers

Power Monitor

Underground Cable Locator

Tone Tester

Cable Checker

Butt Set

Fish Tape

DISCUSSION QUESTIONS

1   Name splicing activities that would call for different *types* of splices in a security installation.

2   If a technician spliced two wires along with a third tap, what would be the color of the 3M splice used?

3   If an open circuit along a wire was suspected as a problem, and the wire ran in an underground plastic conduit, which two tools would be used to locate the open?

4   What is the purpose of *room* or *office* identifiers?

5   What is a good alternative to a DMM for quickly checking whether there is voltage on a wire? Why would a technician want to use this alternative?

6   What is a power monitor used for?

7   If a technician was working with a wire pair at a workstation and wanted to determine where those wires were at the patch panel on the other side of the building, which tool would she use?

8   How would you run a wire under a carpet for about twenty feet?

9   What would be a good way to pull wire through a jumble of wires atop a false ceiling? What is an alternative method if there was less wire scattered everywhere?

10   Why do some very long drill bits have a hole through them at the drilling end?

11   What is a "hemostat?"

12   Why would a technician want a "digital" butt set?

13   A butt set has a *high impedance input*. Why is that?

14   What is the use of a cable checker?

15   What are the ranges of a Voltalert tester?

RESEARCH QUESTIONS

1   Where did the name, *Torx* come from?

2   Why is a fiberglass or wooden ladder better to use in many situations than a metal ladder?

3   What is the advantage of a Phillips or square head screw over a slotted screw?

CHAPTER 10

Locks, Keys, and Access Control

PURPOSE AND OBJECTIVES

The Bastille, the Tower of London, and Alcatraz are all places designed to keep people in. Fort Knox, the Skunk Works, and CIA Headquarters are places designed to keep people out. Both classes have something in common: in addition to fences, guards, and walls, these places employ locks and other types of access control devices. This chapter focuses on locks and access control devices.

After completing the chapter, the student will have a basic knowledge of:

■ Lock and key types

■ Various access control devices and how they work

■ Combinations of access control devices used for increased security

A special thanks to the U.S. Department of Defense and authors Eric Elkins and Mike Farrar, whose comprehensive public domain information on locks and access control is used extensively in this chapter.

BACKGROUND

According to the U.S. Department of Defense[1], access control is used to ensure that only authorized personnel enter a designated area. Covert threats refer to a person who is not authorized to be in the facility who tries to enter using false credentials or bypass methods. Insider threats refer to employees with legitimate access to a facility who try to compromise an asset. The insider may or may not have legitimate access to the asset.

The assumed goal of an unauthorized outsider is to compromise an asset without being noticed. Access control aims to keep unauthorized intruders from entering areas where they should not be. For the insider compromise, an access control program limits access to assets within controlled areas to people who need to be in the area. Regardless of whether the access control equipment is mechanical or electronic, control of the devices (locks, keys, and access cards) that allow approved entry into a secure area is important to ensure that integrity of the system is maintained.

LEVELS OF PROTECTION

Four levels of protection can be applied to covert and insider threats. The levels of protection and their associated access control strategies are as follows:

Low-Level requires a single access control device, such as a keyed lock, a combination-operated lock (mechanical or electronic keypad), or an electronic entry control device, such as a card reader. Each of these admits any bearer with the authorized credential (key, card, or combination) to the controlled area.

Medium-Level requires two access control devices. The two access control elements should identify the individual and authorize entry into the facility. Two primary approaches to access control exist. The electronic entry control option consists of a card reader and a keypad, onto which a personal identification number (PIN) can be entered. A key and electronic keypad for PIN entry is another alternative. A guard or receptionist can also verify identification visually, based on identification credentials, in addition to one of the access control elements described for low-level protection. Access should

---

1. User's Guide UG-2040-SHR, User's Guide on Controlling Locks, Keys, and Access Cards, DoD Lock Program, Naval Facilities Engineering Service Center, Port Hueneme, CA.

be monitored at a central processing unit for this level of protection. Challenging procedures to prevent tailgating (gaining access by closely following a person with proper credentials) should also be required at this level.

High-Level requires three access control elements, incorporating biometric identification devices, such as thumbprint readers, in addition to the two required for medium-level protection. Mandatory monitoring of access at a central processing unit is required at this level of protection. Strict procedures or single pass equipment, such as sensors or optical turnstiles, to prevent tailgating must also be used at this level.

Very High-Level requires three access control elements, as described for high-level protection. As with high level, access is monitored at a central processing unit at this level of protection. The major difference with this level is that in addition to other precautions, anti-passback (referring to the prevention of an authorized individual passing an access card to an unauthorized person) and tailgating prevention in the form of mantraps and full-height turnstiles are used to ensure compliance with access control requirements.

LOCKS AND KEYS

Locks and keys were around long before the birth of Christ. They are mentioned often in the Old Testament of the Bible and in mythology. Locks initially were large, crude, and made of wood, however, the principle of operation was similar to the locks of today.

The first wooden locks most likely were created by several civilizations at the same time. Records show locks in use over 4,000 years ago in Egypt. Secured vertically on a doorpost, the wooden lock contained movable pins or *pin tumblers*, which dropped by gravity into openings in the crosspiece or *bolt* and locked the door. The lock was worked by a wooden key with pegs or prongs that raised the tumblers enough to clear the bolt so it could be pulled back. This method of locking is similar to modern pin tumbler locks. The first metal lock appeared sometime around 900 A.D. and is credited to artisans in England. These simple bolts were made of iron with wards, a type of obstruction, fitted around the keyholes to prevent tampering.

The first use of wards is credited to the Romans, who devised barriers to "ward off" the entry or turning of the wrong key. Wards were notched and cut into decorative designs, and warding became a basic locking mechanism for more than a thousand years.

> **Before Locks and Keys in India**
>
> In India, royal valuables were sealed into large blocks of wood, which were placed on small islands or submerged into surrounding pools of the inner courts of the palace. Here, they were protected by several crocodiles kept on starvation rations so they were always hungry. Going into the water meant certain death.

PADLOCKS

The first padlocks were known in early times to merchants traveling ancient trade routes to Asia and Europe. Padlocks were used throughout the centuries to lock prisoners and possessions. They were usually made of iron, bronze, or brass and were rugged in construction. However, internal locking mechanisms were often simple and easy to pick.

As *lock picking* became an art around the eighteenth century, the locksmith met the challenge of the thief with increasingly complicated locking mechanisms. Among the new improvements were keys with changeable bits, curtains that close out around keyholes to prevent tampering, alarm bells combined with the action of the bolt, and "puzzle" or ring padlocks. These padlocks developed into dial face and bank vault locks, operating without keys and known as combination locks. The early combination padlocks were Asian and had three to seven rings of characters or letters that released the hasp when properly aligned. The dial locks were similar in operation, and both types were set to unlock to words or patterns of numbers known only to the owners or responsible people.

LOCKS IN AMERICA

In the days of Colonial America, the "key" to unlock the door of the house often hung on the outside of the door as a length of cord or string. Doors were latched on the inside with a wooden bar, with one end of the bar dropping into a slot. The string was attached to the bar and was threaded through a small hole to the outside of the door. To the visitor, the dangling string was an immediate welcome. Pulling the string raised the bolt and opened the door. This lock and key became the origin of our expression of hospitality, "the latch-string is always out."

In the 1700s, locks were few in the colonies and most were copies of European mechanisms. In the following years, there was a growing demand for sturdy door locks, padlocks, and locks for safes and vaults, and so the lock industry in America had its start. Each native locksmith had a unique idea about security, and between the end of the eighteenth century and the mid-twentieth century, American lock manufacturers patented about 3,000 different varieties of locking devices.

KEY CONTROL

Now that we have some history about locks and keys, let us get back to learning how to control these devices. The U.S. Department of Defense says the primary purpose of a lock and key or access credential control system is to control access to lock cores and keys or to access control credentials that permit access to a particular building or structure. Key and access control systems can be simple or complex, depending upon user requirements. As a minimum, lock and key or access control systems require a key or credential inventory, issue records, and a procedure for returning the key or access control credential once the user no longer needs it. When control of keys or access control credentials is abandoned or lost, reestablishing security can be time consuming and expensive, especially for conventional lock and key systems. It is the responsibility of the enterprise to develop and carry out a policy for controlling locks, keys and access credentials. For general security, lock, key, and access control is usually part of a comprehensive security and loss prevention plan.

DESIGNATED KEY CONTROLLER

The designated key control person is responsible for the operation and general function of the enterprise's lock and key control program. This person typically reports to the senior manager of the facility on all matters related to the lock and key control program. Specific duties should include the following:

- Determining the location and category of all locks at a facility
- Determining the status of all keys currently in use
- Maintaining key storage, including selecting containers, key rings, and key tags, among other things
- Ensuring that all key storage is used properly and in accordance with directives and instructions
- Identifying restricted or critical areas
- Recommending areas for common security and master keying
- Choosing key custodians
- Setting up lock and core rotation schedules
- Setting up locations for code storage and, if available, computer program acquisition for lock and key code control
- Identifying qualified locksmith(s) for use by the enterprise
- Developing log procedures and forms for daily use
- Ensuring that lock and key procedures are known throughout the enterprise through educational programs

AUTOMATED KEY CONTROL

Paper-based key control systems are time consuming. Reports other than those which can be contained on a single record sheet require a significant amount of time to produce.

Computer-based programs track keys and users and produce reports about the number of keys in the system, users, locations, and check-out/check-in data. Other programs are available to aid in core/lock rotation and maintenance, pinning/key cutting codes, and cylinder/core locations. Still others can interface with electronic locking systems to activate and deactivate locks remotely and provide specific access control for spaces and key storage.

Computerized record-keeping programs can store, arrange, search, and analyze data and automatically produce reports based on the data. These programs typically have built-in report forms customized by the user and search features to isolate and arrange input data into specialized formats. The record-keeping programs list keys by location hook numbers, as well as by lock locations. Other programs link key-cutting machines direct to computers for cutting keys.

Available programs include the following:

- KeyTrak
- The KeyWatcher by Morse
- KEYSURE
- InstaKey
- TracAccess by Supra
- Key Systems Key Monitor
- KRM by Locksoft
- Key-Z by Morse
- Key Trail by HPC

ELECTRONIC ACCESS CONTROL

Before starting an access control program, the security manager should make a survey of all access control locations throughout the facility with emphasis on:

- Priority of assets protected
- Requirements for access to the assets
- Access control credential reissue schedules
- Enclaving requirements
- Status of access control training
- Schedules for periodic meetings to reevaluate requirements

PROCEDURES

Access Control Centers. For large enterprises with extensive electronic access control requirements, it may be necessary to set up an Access Control Center where the daily access control credential issuing and recording can take place. There should be adequate personnel to provide access control services. The issue point for access control credentials should be located where it will not interfere with emergency personnel, such as dispatchers or operators.

Blank *access control cards* and materials should be stored in a security container with access limited to the security manager and an alternate. Treat blank access control cards in the same manner as sensitive documents. Do not allow unauthorized access to blank materials.

Records Management. Electronic access control systems normally include software programs that allow the tracking and management of access control credentials. The database may contain information on badge authorization and can include employee number, name, address, telephone, motor vehicle registration, status, issue date, return date, authorization center, portal restrictions by time zones, entry/exit status, and tracking. A commentary section may also be used for emergency call lists and other safety-related information. Computers containing personal and classified data of this nature should always be secure.

Lockout Procedures. When an electronic access control unit (credential reader, electric strike, or magnetic lock) fails or a credential denies access to the user, an incident report must be made to the security manager or to the manager's designee. An effective access control program should have established procedures for entrance into a building or office when the access control system fails. Any forced entry or bypassing of the electric lock should be documented and witnessed by two or more people. The security manager should make provisions to secure the area immediately.

Personnel Termination. Access codes should be immediately removed or canceled when personnel are terminated. This is particularly important if the employee had access to restricted areas.

Access Control Credential Disposal. Used or obsolete access control credentials should be secured until properly destroyed, especially if they are also used as identification badges. Credentials must be destroyed in such a way that they cannot be used or copied. A cross-cut shredder is a good method for destroying credentials.

Maintenance of credential readers is normally not required other than periodic cleaning of the credential swipe path (not required for proximity sensors). Electric strikes need routine periodic maintenance and lubrication, similar to mechanical locking devices. Magnetic locks require little maintenance. Credential readers and electric strikes exposed to natural elements or harsh environments should receive maintenance more often.

COMPONENT PARTS OF AN EFFECTIVE ACCESS CONTROL SYSTEM[2]

For access control to work effectively, the access control system must be selected, designed, and integrated to meet the security objectives of the enterprise. In addition, an effective mechanical or electronic access control program must be in place so integrity is not compromised. Earlier, we discussed how to set up a lock and key and/or electronic access card control program. The following description of measures can be applied to the design of an effective access control system. However, in-depth design and integration of access control systems is a complex issue that is beyond the scope of this chapter.

DEFENSIVE MEASURES

The layout of a building can be used effectively to defend against covert and insider threats. Because experts anticipate many different situations in developing industry guidelines, seeming contradictions may occur. Apply the guidance regarding layout where appropriate to the specific situation.

BUILDING LAYOUT TO ADDRESS ACCESS CONTROL THREATS

To limit the number of visitors who must be supervised or escorted, locate facilities with large visitor populations separate from protected assets. Consider using on-site personnel to provide monitoring capability or locate protected assets in common areas where the asset or access to the asset is visible to more than one person. This decreases the likelihood that unauthorized personnel can gain undetected access to an asset. To reduce the number of access locations that must be monitored, minimize the number of entrances into controlled areas. Building layout considerations also include allocating adequate space for key/access control centers.

Because insiders work around the assets, simply setting up controlled areas is not always sufficient. If all employees within a controlled area do not need access to all assets, compartmentalize the assets within the controlled area. For example, if sensitive activities occur in half of a building, that area should have controlled

2. Component Parts of an Effective Access Control System is from User's Guide UG-2040-SHR, Naval Facilities Engineering Service Center, Appendix D.

access. When only a few people in the controlled area need access to a particular asset, place that asset in a room within the controlled area and limit access to only those with an established need. Compartmentalization, when used with a two person rule (no single individual can have access to an asset without the knowledge or presence of a second person) provides more security protection for critical information and assets.

NOTE The assessment of alarms from an intrusion detection system (the sensor contact installed on the access-controlled entry point to detect the opening of the door without authorization) may be done by guards or with closed circuit television (CCTV).

ACCESS CONTROL SYSTEMS

Access control systems employ various techniques to verify authorization. These include visual verification of credentials by security personnel, electronic confirmation of credentials from information known or held by an approved individual, and the use of electronic biometric identification. Throughput rate refers to the average number of individuals who can pass through an entry point during a period of time and is an important factor in the design of an access control system to minimize inconvenience to the user. Large throughput rates can be handled with multiple access control units. Examples of access control devices and procedures are described below.

PERSONNEL-BASED SYSTEMS

Receptionists or security personnel can be effective access control, especially for activities with a small staff. For personnel-based systems, locate security posts at the controlled area entrance. Install electric strikes or magnetic locks on entry points that security personnel can activate after verifying identification.

Various types of mechanical and electronic equipment can be installed to allow access to controlled areas not requiring the presence of security personnel. Keys, electronic access control cards or push button mechanical/electrical combination locks are sufficient for low-level access control. Higher levels of protection require secondary credentials, such as a PIN or *biometric certification*, with a card reader and keys/key cards. In addition, strict procedures or equipment must be set up to prevent tailgating. When an authorized individual enters the facility, then passes the card to an unauthorized individual for access using the same card, this is called *passback*. This can be controlled by using software designed to detect passback conditions. The various types of equipment are described below and are presented in the order of increasing effectiveness.

BADGING SYSTEMS

Badges are entry credentials that must include a photograph of the authorized individual who is issued the badge. The individual keeps the badge and wears it at all times within the facility. Security personnel check identity by comparing the photograph on the badge to the wearer's face. When a controlled area is compartmentalized, the badge should identify specific areas of access. This is usually done using code numbers or colored stripes. Security identification badges have low to medium effectiveness as access control devices in large facilities, because badges are easily forged and procedures used to challenge access (of individuals without badges or those with counterfeit badges) are often ineffective. When combined with an electronic access control system, however, badges become an effective method for controlling access, because counterfeiting is minimized and bypassing an access control device is difficult without extensive knowledge of electronic systems and use of sophisticated card-duplicating equipment.

Visitor badges represent a significant vulnerability for badge-based access control systems. Visitor badges should be strictly controlled, and the use of commercially available, self expiring, and time limited visitor badges is recommended. Before visitor badges are issued, authorization must be checked and identification verified by picture identification, such as a valid driver's license.

BADGE EXCHANGE

Badge exchange can be used to provide more effective access control. In this method, an individual receives a primary security identification badge. A second badge, different from the first or with different access coding, is kept inside the controlled area at all times. When access is required, security personnel exchange the second badge for the individual's primary badge. The individual wears the second badge while in the controlled area. A similar badge exchange takes place as the individual enters each compartmentalized area within the restricted area. When the individual leaves, the exchange process is reversed. This procedure makes counterfeiting difficult, because the intruder would have to gain access to the exchange badges as well as the primary badge.

EQUIPMENT-BASED SYSTEMS

Mechanical Locks

There are two major categories of mechanical locks: keyed locks and push button locks.

Keyed locks are the most common and least expensive way to secure doors. Key control and key accountability are critical issues if keys are used. The beginning of this chapter explained the procedure for setting up a lock and key control program.

Mechanical push button locks include a keypad on which an access code is entered, activating the lock to open the door. These locks are fairly inexpensive but have a high cycle rate. The high cycle rate means that they take a relatively long time to operate; therefore, they should not be used on entry points requiring a high throughput rate. One advantage of using access codes is that, unlike keys, they cannot be lost and subsequently found by unauthorized individuals, unless the access code has been written down. The primary disadvantage is the ease with which the access code can be passed to unauthorized people or covertly compromised by simple observation of the entry process.

Electromechanical Locks

Electromechanical locks include an electronic keypad connected to an electric strike, lock, or magnetic lock. When the access code is correctly entered, the strike or lock releases to open the door.

AUTOMATED ACCESS CONTROL SYSTEMS

Automated access control systems grant or deny access, based on prior approval of authorization criteria encoded into an electronic access control card. This authorization approval sequence is information that communicates with the equipment in a format acceptable to the electronics and provides the criteria for entrance or exit. In general, a multidoor automated access control system is composed of a central controller, an enrollment console, an event video or hard copy display, and entry points controlled by a coded credential and reader. The primary advantage of these systems is that they are difficult to bypass, compared with conventional lock and key systems. If a badge is lost, it can be voided easily by deleting identification data from the system. The central processor constantly monitors the condition of remote readers, and access activities are logged on a permanent record.

Stand-alone access control systems are battery powered, and the controller and enrollment components normally consist of a hand-held palmtop or laptop computer. Single door systems are mainly used at locations where access control is the primary requirement and integration with an alarmed response is not necessary. These stand-alone systems are easy to use, simple to install, and inexpensive because they do not need the installation of data transfer and power lines.

ACCESS CONTROL CARDS

Access control card systems are classified according to their resistance to copying, decoding, and duplication. Electronic equipment designers and manufacturers are making major strides in developing innovative devices for access control. New security technology is reaching the marketplace on an almost daily basis. Currently available card systems of low, moderate, and high resistance to copying, decoding, and duplication are described and listed by category as follows:

Low Resistance

The *Hollerith Card* is a low resistance access control card. Information is stored on it using punched holes, similar to those on a computer keypunch card. The amount of information that can be stored is quite limited and the available storage space is even less when printing or a photograph is required on the card.

A *Magnetic Stripe Card* is characterized by a strip of magnetic material containing encoded information. The stripe data is encoded in what is called an Aiken Code. The standards for this encoding relate to the relative position of information on the stripe. Magnetic Stripe Cards are classified as high-energy or low-energy, depending on the encoding energies (resistance to magnetic interference) used with this medium. The high-energy types are less susceptible to accidental erasure from contact with magnetic fields.

The *Electric Circuit Card* is essentially a printed circuit that can be plugged in. The card can present a limited number of unique codes that are values of continuity of electrical pathways on the card. The cards are decoded and simulated easily with inexpensive tools that are unique to them. This type of card is encoded in the factory but may be assembled by users.

Bar Code Cards have bar codes (a set of parallel thick and thin black lines) printed directly on access control cards. These lines form a light versus dark pattern that is interpreted by an optical reader or scanner as a code number. This method provides the least expensive, easiest-to-use system in electronic access control identification.

Moderate Resistance

Metallic Strip Cards consist of a matrix of metal (usually copper) strips that are laminated to a badge core. The presence or absence of strips can encode a moderate amount of information. The card is factory-encoded but may be assembled locally to add custom artwork and photographic images.

Magnetic Spot Cards are laminated, and each card incorporates a sheet of ferromagnetic material with strongly and permanently magnetized spots on the core material. Exercise caution when placing these cards next to bank cards or magnetic tape/stripe media because the other cards are susceptible to erasure. The Magnetic Spot Card is manufacturer-encoded but may be assembled on-site for photograph or custom printing additions.

Optical Cards have rows of spots or lines that change under specific illumination, meaning they are optically encoded. Generally, optically encoded cards contain spots or lines that absorb, transmit, or reflect infrared or another specific light spectrum. This makes up the unique code that is facility-specific as well as card-specific. The encoding is manufacturer-processed, because custom printing must account for the specific ink colors that are critical to the read technique.

High Resistance

Active Electronic Cards are essentially miniature transmitters that contain an individual code, which is sent when energized by the reader. This medium is characterized by a limited amount of information storage.

Capacitance Access Control Cards contain an array of capacitor plates that are connected or disconnected in a specific pattern. This pattern is the limited information code.

Proximity Access Control Cards are essentially tuned (passive) antennas, laminated within the core of a card. The card reader spectrum generates a weak radio signal, which is attenuated and reflected to the reader as specific information. The information on the card can be decoded.

Wiegand Access Control Cards contain a series of small parallel wires laminated within the card. These wires are made from ferromagnetic materials that produce a sharp change in magnetic flux when exposed to a slowly changing magnetic field. Placing the wires above and below a critical centerline determines the specific information in binary code. This technology is factory-encoded and, therefore, impossible to erase and difficult to alter or duplicate.

A *Contact Memory Button* is a computer chip armored in a stainless steel can that usually resembles a button. These chips have up to 64K of computer memory that can store text or digitized photos. This information can be downloaded or updated as often as needed with a simple, momentary contact with the reader. These buttons are ideal for applications in which information needs to travel with a person or an object. They can be used to provide access, carry essential information during a process, or serve as an electronic asset tag. Contact Memory Buttons are used similarly to Smart Cards, but the memory buttons are packaged for durability so they can be used in rugged or harsh environments, like on outdoor guard tours, in the elements.

As the name suggests, a *Mixed Technology Access Control Card* combines various technologies, including Proximity, Magnetic Stripe, microprocessor (Smart Card), Wiegand, etc. Mixed Technology cards can be used on a variety of readers, which eliminates the need for carrying many cards at a facility with different reader systems. These cards also make it unnecessary to retrofit a facility to take advantage of new technologies, such as Smart Card technology. Smart Cards make biometric verification faster and more practical by storing the information on the card, rather than in a computer.

BADGE READER

For the cards discussed in the previous section to be effective, the information encoded on a badge must first be decoded or read. This information is then transmitted to a processor that grants or denies access based on a comparison of the encoded information with authorization files.

A badge or card reader is composed of a card sensor and an electronic interface. The card sensor detects the presence of the coded credential and reads the data. The electronic interface converts the data read by the card sensor into the proper format and sends it to the controller. The controller also returns a command to energize a relay that allows access.

Two types of readers are commercially available. The first type has both the card sensor and the electronic interface housed in one unit. The second type of reader has a separate card sensor and electronic interface. The card sensor is mounted separately from the electronic interface and is connected by a short cable. State-of-the-art readers contain microprocessors or large-scale, integrated circuits that can perform many other sophisticated functions such as data communication, line supervision, fail-safe operation, and PIN verification.

SECONDARY CREDENTIALS

All card access badges are susceptible to alteration, decoding, duplication, and loss. The degree to which the technology and associated procedures resist these threats is important to the integrity of the security system. For more critical access verification needs, additional verification systems, requiring either a code be entered on a keypad or a physical characteristic confirmation, may be advisable as a backup to card-only access authorization. The second verification is to minimize the vulnerability associated with insider collusion and lost or stolen cards. Examples of secondary verifications are personal identification numbers, photographic image match-ups to personnel files, hand geometry, fingerprints, handwriting, speech, weight, and other biometric characteristics.

Secondary systems, with the exception of biometric systems, are less secure than coded credentials. This is due to the easily read identification media and the wide latitude needed to accommodate variations due to environment, stress, and other data-entry errors that may deny access to authorized users. A PIN is the most commonly used secondary verification system because of the relative ease with which it gets an accurate specific data entry and the immunity of this data to environmental influences.

The use of a secondary means of access authorization should be limited to selected mid-level security applications, because throughput rates and cost concerns need to be controlled. Systems currently available to commercial users display various error rate data that should be considered in the design analysis phases of access control system development. There are many options available for secondary credential systems.

Personal Identification Number systems provide a keypad on which the PIN can be entered. Usually, the PIN is not stored in the central controller's memory but is derived from the credential identification (ID) numbers, following some encryption algorithms. In this case, the reader matches the entered PIN with the calculated number to validate the coded credential before it sends the data to the central controller. The preferred method is a system that either assigns a PIN or allows users to select their own PIN that is not related to the badge ID number. Personal identification numbers are vulnerable to covert discovery by unauthorized personnel by visual observation of the keypad entry sequence or poor control of code numbers by users.

Hand geometry is a distinct measurable and individual characteristic that measures the relative finger length of the user and compares measurements taken at the access point to those stored in a central computer. Systems using hand geometry are characterized as having medium to high resistance to tampering.

Signature verification has been used for many years by the banking industry. However, signature comparison methods are susceptible to forgery. Automated handwriting verification systems have been developed that use handwriting dynamics, such as velocity, acceleration, and pressure as a function of time. Statistical evaluation of this data shows that an individual's signature is unique and reasonably consistent from one signature to the next. Systems have been developed that use from one to three axes of dynamic measurements. Transducers, which change mechanical motions (e.g., pen pressure or stroke speed) to electronic signals, can be located in either the writing instrument or tablet. Like hand geometry, signature verification has a medium to high level of resistance to counterfeiting.

Speech can be validated easily and is well suited to automated data processing. Speech measurements that are useful for speaker discrimination include waveform envelope, voice pitch period, relative amplitude spectrum, and vocal tract resonant frequencies (formats). High-end systems have a high resistance to counterfeiting; however, some low-end systems can be fooled with high-quality recordings.

Fingerprints have been used as a positive personnel identifier for more than one hundred years and are still considered one of the most reliable means of distinguishing one individual from another. The art of processing human fingerprints for identification has been greatly improved in recent years by the development of automated systems. These systems, which rely on pattern recognition of one or more fingers and computerized data processing, are frequently used in access control. All fingerprint identification systems require accurate finger positioning and pattern measurement for reliable identification. Some problems occur with individuals who do not have clearly defined finger ridge patterns or who have had an injury to the identifying finger. Fingerprint systems have a high resistance to counterfeiting.

Palm print recognition systems measure features of the palm, identify the pattern of blood vessels below the surface, or both. Palm print readers are easy to use; however, they are more cumbersome than fingerprint readers, and some practice is required before their use becomes natural to the user.

Eye scanning systems measure the retina or iris and are highly resistant to counterfeiting. More advanced systems use a charge-coupled device camera, which is unobtrusive and requires little action on the part of the user. Because the scan involves shining a light into the retina, one potential problem with these devices is that they may irritate the user's eye when used on a routine basis. Employees have shown resistance to eye-scanning systems for this reason.

ELECTRIC DOOR LOCKS

Locking hardware that is compatible with automated access control systems includes electric strikes, electric bolts, electric locksets, and electromagnetic locks. Each of these devices is available with one of two features, termed "fail-safe" or "fail-secure," and configured in either alternating or direct current in a range of 6 to 240 volts. The design of an automated access control system must take into account variables that are related to entry point use and the application of local and national fire, life safety, and electrical codes. Many different types of electric door locks provide different ranges of accessibility and security.

One of two operations can take place with electric door locks during a power failure. These operations are termed *fail-safe* and *fail-secure*. If the power fails, the lock becomes either safe and allows access/exit or secure and remains locked. These operations are usually applied based on fire code, electrical code, or activity regulations. These codes and regulations assume that, in the event of an emergency (fire or other catastrophe), the individual seeking to exit may not be capable of rapid thought and logical reasoning and thus requires a simple, usually entirely mechanical, means of exit. The spirit of this requirement is to assure that speedy exit is possible without reading directions or depending on electrical or electromechanical devices that may fail because of the emergency condition. From a security viewpoint, this option must be clearly addressed since it can create vulnerability if procedures are not in place to prevent reentry during alarm conditions.

The *electric strike* is the most frequently used electric lock. It comes in various sizes and can replace existing mechanical locks without much difficulty. The strike, which is the electrically controlled portion of the lock, is mounted in a doorframe (jamb) and does not require wiring through the door itself. The electric strike contains a bolt pocket, which is the indent that holds the protruding latch bolt or dead bolt secure in the frame. To open, the strike rotates away from the pocket, providing a path for the bolt to escape. This rotating side is called a pivoting lip or keeper. This device provides a depression or channel that fits the bolt or latch of the lock. The channel catches or releases the bolt, depending on the lock status. Issues that must be considered when selecting an electric strike include composition of the doorframe, size and shape of the latch bolt, holding force, and potential for abuse of the door lock. Heavy-duty strikes are recommended for access control systems in which potential abuse or high traffic volume is an issue. Options for electric strikes include:

- A latch bolt monitor indicating if the bolt is extended into the strike
- A lock cam monitor indicating if the strike is in a locked position
- Sensors indicating whether the door is shut
- An interlock feature to allow only one door in a series to be unlocked at a time, as in mantrap or energy-conservation foyer applications

The *electric bolt* is a long pin that is fitted on or in the jamb or the door and, when activated, protrudes or swings into a strike plate on the adjoining surface. The deadbolt will not give way with spring action and once it is locked in place, cannot be retracted until the electric "unlock" signal is given. This device is used for interior door applications, because the electric bolt may not meet certain safety code regulations for exit doors.

An *electric lockset* provides positive locking by pushing a solenoid-operated bolt or rotating bar into a hole in the door edge. Another choice is the electric key-in-knob (or key-in-lever) lock, which electrically releases the knob, allowing retraction of the bolt. Critical alignment is required between the bolt and the locking strike opening.

The *electromagnetic lock* consists of an electrically powered magnet and a steel plate. The magnet is mounted to the doorframe in alignment with the steel plate to provide a strong or hardened area in which to apply magnetic force. Most of these devices are inherently fail-safe (open during power failure), because power is interrupted to unlock, while some are fail-secure (remain locked during power failure) because they preserve power with backup battery supply. Minor variations in door alignment and problems associated with door settling and warping can be overcome using this device. Pairs of doors can be secured by a single device, if both swing in the same direction (outswing or inswing).

CENTRAL CONTROL UNIT

The central control unit refers to the main computer that processes and controls information on electronic access control authorization and verification. The central control unit consists of one or more processors and associated peripheral equipment. A typical central controller consists of a microprocessor, read-only memory (ROM), random-access memory (RAM), and magnetic storage memory (disk or tape). The microprocessor carries out the computer program stored in the ROM. The RAM contains the access authorization data associated with the enrolled credential number. During normal operation, the central controller receives the incoming credential ID number from the access/entry reader or remote controller and compares it to the numbers stored in memory.

The central controller may also compare the time and location of the requesting credential against the time zone and the area authorization allotted to it. If all information is correct, the central controller gives a go-ahead command to the reader or remote controller and energizes a relay to unlock the door. The central controller records the credential identity number, the date, the time of day, and the reader or door number through which access took place. Conversely, if any information is incorrect, the system rejects the credential, entry is not allowed, and the system issues an appropriate warning message. The time for one transaction is usually less than three seconds. Depending on the system design, there are many techniques for transmitting data between the reader and the central controller. The most common technique is to transmit the data digitally. Such data can be transmitted for a distance of one mile or more without degradation. In addition, by using a modem or cellular interface, data can be passed on for an unlimited distance.

REMOTE CONTROL UNITS

The remote control unit is the part of the access control system that translates communications and performs interface tasks between credential readers, electric door locks, and the central control unit. This intermediate device is usually subject to distance constraints and is often located in a position to accommodate line length from readers and the central control unit. The role of a controller includes interpretation of coded information to the central control unit. The controller may also supply conditioned power to the reader.

ENROLLMENT CONSOLE

The enrollment console is the device used to launch the authorization status of an encoded badge. The enrollment console may contain information on badge authorization and can include badge number, employee number, name, address, telephone number, motor vehicle registration, status, issue date, return date, authorization center, and entry point restrictions by time zones, entry/exit status, and trace. A commentary section may also be included for emergency call lists and other safety-related information. Enrollment equipment and equipment used for transferring the data to the central control unit must be located in a secured area. The enrollment console usually consists of a keyboard, badge reader, and a video display terminal. Changes of high authorization levels must be password-protected or software-protected in order to prevent unauthorized use of the system. Passive software protection should be included in all system functions to preserve integrity of the total system. Components of the enrollment console include a central processor and printer.

CENTRAL PROCESSOR

The central processor makes decisions based on information files entered at the enrollment console. It also communicates with remote controllers and checks the encoded information input against the existing files. The central processor approves access based on the filed authorizations and creates a historical file of attempted accesses and the manipulations of the existing files. This history may be recorded electronically in computer storage media or printed on paper for later review.

Other functions performed by the central processor depend upon the system design. At one extreme, only minimal capability is assigned at the entry point and reader. In this case, data is transmitted to the central control unit, and the central processor makes all decisions. At the other extreme, significant capability is assigned at the entry point and reader, and decisions are made locally, which allows faster processing and entry. In all cases, reader status and alarm status signals are sent to the central processor and then transferred to the information display in the guard station.

PRINTER

The printer is an output device that provides a hard copy record of activities reported by the central processor. Printers should have enough speed and appropriate buffer to avoid information omissions from overload by the much faster system electronics. Security systems do not generally require letter quality printing, so faster printing can be selected for this operation.

ACCESSORIES

Accessories may be added to the basic system in order to extend or improve its capabilities. Three types of useful accessories are multiplexers, alarm-switch monitors, and computer interface modules.

MULTIPLEXERS

A multiplexer accepts input from several readers, patches the signals together, and sends the combined signals to the controller. The multiplexer also receives commands from the controller, then separates the information and routes the separated commands to the appropriate readers. The multiplexer serves as a concentrating point and is used in conjunction with a remote cluster of readers. Because the multiplexer amplifies the signal, the distance between the controller and the readers can be longer than a system without a multiplexer.

ALARM SWITCH MONITOR

An alarm switch monitor checks the status of several switches and reports any change of switch status to the controller. The monitor also enables the card access system to function as an alarm monitoring system, since it can report events not associated with personnel access, such as an open door that should have closed automatically. Security operations requiring separate access and alarm monitoring control functions will need two distinct systems to be developed during the design phase.

INTERFACE MODULE

The computer interface module ties the card access system to an existing computer system. It converts the output of the controller into a proper format and sends it to the host computer. By integrating the card access system into the computer system, the output of the card access system can be stored in a permanent file, or it can be processed and displayed in compatible format.

AUTOMATED ACCESS CONTROL SYSTEM FUNCTIONS

Computer-based systems allow flexibility in controlling and removing repetitive tasks from guard responsibility. These systems can instantly check authorized access data against the access requests and record the event. This automation permits greater efficiency of guard personnel, while potentially reducing the number of fixed posts required and improving the security of the facility.

ACCESS AUTHORIZATION/VERIFICATION AND REPORTING

Approval for personnel to access a specific entry point requires advanced approval and system enrollment. Approval or denial of access also requires the system to check for any limitations associated with the encoded credential at the time of each access request. The system performs without prejudice on a repeatable basis. Approval of entry is reduced to a routine task that requires human intervention only in the event of exceptions. The access control system will note and report exceptions and operator-initiated actions. In this system, human failures or errors are controlled, while high throughput for verified access approval is preserved. Use of closed-circuit television and/or voice communication at each access control point allows immediate assessment of exceptions or operator error.

MULTIPLE AREA AUTHORIZATION

Access authorization can be as general as system-wide approval or as specific as an individual entry point. Authorization files should include the appropriate classification of an entry point if it is associated with the perimeter of controlled or restricted areas. The entry point should be assigned the classification of the restricted area and access allowed only to people with authorized access to the area and based on need-to-know principles.

TIME ZONING

Access authorization can also be based on time. Access may be approved only if the individuals are approved for access during the specific time period in which they attempt to enter. Time codes may also be designated to preclude all access during specific time periods (such as at night or weekends) assigned to an entry point. Thus, some individuals and certain areas may be excluded from access based on defining time periods. This feature could be used for established regular working hours or closed hours at a facility. The criteria include time of day, day of week, and an eight-day calendar (with holidays scheduled as the eighth day).

FAIL-SAFE/FAIL-SOFT

Not to be confused with Fail-Safe/Fail-Secure

If communication between the controller and the central processor is lost, the default parameters within the system are exercised. Two schemes are available to address this problem. The first, fail-safe, bans all access, even if the criterion of correct facility code is met. The fail-soft scheme, also referred to as degraded mode, normally grants access on correct facility code entry. A caution must be observed: few systems in the degraded mode record access information for later transmission to the computer when the communication line is restored.

OCCUPANT LISTING

An occupant listing is an internal software function that can process entry information and allow access by area, maximum number or load of personnel, or enforcement of the two person rule (which states that no individual can access an asset without the knowledge or presence of a second person). Specific reader configurations and entry and exit readers must be used with anti-passback or tailgate (or piggyback) prevention controls in order to ensure that accurate data is gathered. The computer can compile valid lists only if all entries and exits are indicated. Requirements such as safety and the two-person rule can be effectively controlled with manipulation of this information. This feature can also play a role in evacuation plans and evacuation assurance.

ANTI-PASSBACK

Anti-passback refers to the denial of access or exit approval in the event of two successive "in" or "out" access requests. This denial prohibits the unauthorized use of a single card by two people until exit readout is accomplished. This avoids an event in which one individual gains access and, while inside, "passes back" the access credential. Tailgating or piggybacking is a fault in automated access control systems in which two people gain access with one card at the same time. A single authorized card is used and approved, but two people enter during the entry point access time window. This problem is critical in sensitive facilities, particularly if duress situations are a threat. The problem can be addressed by using a rotary gate or turnstile connected to and controlled by the access control system or by an interlocking mantrap with direct visual security surveillance. Closed-circuit television assessment, in addition to access control at entry points, the less effective "light beam break," and personnel counting devices with appropriate alarm/delay features, should also be used for these applications.

GENERAL AUTOMATED ACCESS CONTROL APPLICATIONS

Several factors directly affect the successful operation of an electronic access control system. System designers must be familiar with limits and constraints.

Selecting an access control system involves almost as many factors as there are potential applications. Selection generally concerns off-the-shelf commercial systems, and there are two primary considerations: first, the capabilities of the proposed equipment, in terms of local security/use requirements, and second, the experience and capabilities of the installation firm regarding support of the equipment throughout its life cycle. These two factors need to be considered together, because poor installation and service can cancel the benefits of the most detailed design process. Maintenance must be examined as part of the life cycle cost of the system.

The standard features of the automated access control system enhance security operations, particularly in instances when the equipment outperforms humans in repetitive functions. This creates a more secure environment, because it allows the humans to focus on the areas where they can achieve greater efficiency. The definition of access, based on area, access point, time zone, holiday schedule, loading, two person rule, and the subsequent recording of the information relative to use, can be essential. Automation of electronic alarm processing within one control center provides a single source of information about the facility or activity security. Other software enhancements, such as automated guard tours and patrols, redundant life safety system monitoring, security trace, data encryption, and centralized control and reporting, can improve the versatility of the system. The ability of the system to call up electronic commands that will address detected events with specific details, telephone numbers, and prioritized sequences further reduces the margin for error by reducing the requirements for human judgment.

Design of the access control system should take into consideration an expansion capability of at least 25 percent with minimum hardware and software additions. The best systems permit additions of equipment to meet expansion, without obsolescence of existing hardware. Modular enhancements in hardware capability permit maximum configuration until the central processor is outgrown and additional or different processors are required. State-of-the-art processing equipment is designed to be set up in building blocks, with logical breaks, to meet individualized usage. Off-the-shelf modules that are oriented toward system enhancement often provide the required capabilities cost-effectively.

The access level designed into a system is based on the security requirement of the protected area, verified need for access through a particular entry point, and the resistance to defeating the identity verifier that is required at that entry point. The design at the requirements phase should identify all entry points scheduled for control and determine the number of authorized personnel who use each entry/exit control point. The configuration of each control point is determined based upon peak throughput requirements, mostly at shift changes. The throughput rate is the average number of individuals who can pass through an entry point during a specific period of time. Normally, the throughput rate is specified in personnel per minute. The employment of positive barriers, such as turnstiles or other access limitations, determines the number of readers required to process legitimate access conveniently. Card credentials alone typically require three to five seconds per card when configured properly.

In normal operation, automated access control systems provide a given level of security by restricting unauthorized access. Although this level of security may normally be sufficient, equipment failure can decrease security to an unacceptable level. Failure of critical equipment may cause total system failure. Efforts must be made to minimize both the impact of system failure and the associated repair time.

SUMMARY

- An access control program will limit access to controlled areas to authorized personnel only.

- The primary purpose of a lock and key or access credential control system is to control access to lock cores and keys or to access control credentials that permit access to a particular building or structure.

- Key and access control systems can be simple or complex, depending upon user requirements. Lock and key or access control systems require, at a minimum, a key or credential inventory, issue records, and a procedure for returning the key or access control credential once the user no longer needs it.

- When control of keys or access control credentials is abandoned or lost, re-establishing security can be time consuming and expensive, especially for conventional lock and key systems.

- For large enterprises with extensive electronic access control requirements, it may be necessary to establish an Access Control Center where the daily access control credential issuing and recording activities can take place.

- Blank access control credentials should be stored in a security container with access limited only to the security manager and an alternate.

- Electronic access control systems normally include software programs that allow the tracking and management of access control credentials.

- An effective access control program should have established procedures for entrance into a building or office when the access control system fails.

- Access control system failure at the access portal normally requires repair or replacement of the electric lock, strike, and/or reader.

- For access control to work effectively, the access control system must be selected, designed, and integrated, to meet the security objectives of the enterprise.

- Large throughput rates can be handled with multiple access control units.

- Visitor badges represent a significant vulnerability for badge-based access control systems.

- Automated access control systems grant or deny access, based upon prior approval of authorization criteria encoded into an electronic access control card.

- Access control card systems are categorized according to their resistance to copying, decoding, and duplication.

- Locking hardware that is compatible with automated access control systems includes electric strikes, electric bolts, electric locksets, and electromagnetic locks.

- The central control unit refers to the main computer that processes and controls information regarding electronic access control authorization and verification.

- The remote control unit is the component of the access control system that translates communications and performs interface tasks between credential readers, electric door locks, and the central control unit.

- Computer-based systems can instantly check authorized access data against the access requests and record the event.

- The access control system will note and report exceptions and operator-initiated actions.

KEY TERMS

Pin Tumblers

Bolt

Lock Picking

Access Control Cards

Electric Strikes

Biometric Certification

Passback

Eye Scanning

Fail-Safe

Fail-Secure

DISCUSSION QUESTIONS

1   How does the U.S. Department of Defense define access control?

2   Regarding access control, how many levels of protection are there, and how many access control methods does each level call for?

3   When was the principle of pin tumblers first used with locks?

4   Who in the security hierarchy ensures that all key storage is used properly and in accordance with directives and instructions?

5   How should blank access control cards and materials be stored? Why?

6   How many people should be witness to any forced entry or bypassing of an electric lock at a secure location?

7   To what does the term, "automated key control," refer?

8   According to this chapter, what is a good method for destroying credentials?

9   When controlled areas are compartmentalized, how are badges coded for access?

10 Would a Wiegand Card be considered a proximity card? Explain your answer.

11 What is the principle of "badge exchange"?

12 What does the term, "stand alone" mean in regards to an access control system?

13 Explain fail-safe and fail-secure operations.

14 Differentiate between electric bolt, electric lockset, and electromagnetic lock.

15 Refer to question 13. How does a fail-safe/fail-soft system differ from a fail-safe/fail-secure system?

RESEARCH QUESTIONS

1   Assume you have to install a biometric device at a secure machine shop. There is a lot of oil and grease present. You have a choice of installing a hand geometry reader or a fingerprint reader. Which do you choose, and why?

2   What is a *slam hammer*, and what is its use?

3   Compare and contrast a *code-operated lock* with a *combination lock*.

CHAPTER 11

Technical Surveillance Countermeasures

PURPOSE AND OBJECTIVES

Up to this point, we have been discussing ways to secure an area. We have discussed alarm systems, CCTV, access control, and theories for planning and surveying physical security. But what if an area already has been compromised? What if surreptitious radio transmitting equipment, covert CCTV equipment, or wired microphones have already been installed in an area? How would we locate and disable these devices? Would we *want* to disable the devices? This chapter covers Technical Surveillance Countermeasures (TSCM) and will help answer those questions based on the security requirements of different facilities.

By the end of this chapter, the student should have a basic knowledge of the following:

- What types of equipment are used to locate covert surveillance devices

- How TSCM equipment is used

- Steps taken to perform a TSCM "sweep"

- Strengths and weaknesses of various TSCM equipment and practices

WHO NEEDS TSCM

Many people think that TSCM is only useful in the James Bond world of government; that only the top spy agencies like the CIA or the NSA have a need for this type of work. It is true that the government has many secrets to protect. In matters of national security, national governments are always trying to learn the secrets of other countries, while simultaneously instituting efforts to protect their own secrets. Government agencies such as the U.S. Department of State "sweep" their facilities on a regular basis. How regularly depends on the security sensitivity of the various facilities and the threat potential at each. The commercial world also has many secrets to protect, and likewise, there are those who constantly try to steal said secrets. As an example, let us focus on the automotive world. Isn't it amazing how similar the new car designs look from company to company, even when they have never before been introduced to the public? A great deal of spying occurs in the commercial world. Therefore, there is definitely a need for TSCM in both the public and private sectors. There are few differences between equipment and practices used in the public and private sectors that we will discuss later in the chapter. This chapter does not mean to infer that companies regularly spy on each other, but there are good companies and there are some that border on "not so good" (frankly, some go way over the edge). We will not name companies in this book for obvious reasons. It should be mentioned that a "bad" company rarely takes it upon itself to spy on others. Usually, the company is approached by an "agent," who offers to sell or obtain valuable competitive information. The reader should be aware that there is also a completely legitimate business of "competitive intelligence," and many companies are in this business of providing information that is developed from open public sources.

METHODS OF ESPIONAGE

There are many different forms of espionage. You have probably read or watched news stories about people who were caught stealing secrets or covertly photographing sensitive documents. Most of us have heard about the "moles" who are planted into groups to conduct intelligence operations. Then there are the eavesdroppers who plant microphones or transmitters, tap phones, or, in a more recent technological advancement, tap onto the Local Area Network to monitor email. Technical Surveillance Countermeasures is about finding the work of these eavesdroppers. A TSCM technician must be very well rounded: an investigator, a technology expert, and an electrician all in one. Anyone working in TSCM must have good knowledge of construction techniques, know about acoustics, and just be plain curious and innovative.

EAVESDROPPING METHODS

The eavesdropper uses many different methods, from the very simple to the very complicated. When people think about being "bugged," their first thoughts go to complicated electronic devices, phone taps, and even satellite surveillance. Eavesdropping can be simple or sophisticated, depending on the setting and security that must be overcome.

LISTENING

The most basic of all eavesdropping methods is simply listening with the human ear. An eavesdropper may be in a room next door, with an ear to the wall. The eavesdropper may be standing nearby or sitting in the booth behind his target at a restaurant. When discussing sensitive matters, it is important that a person be aware of her surroundings and who might be listening to the conversation. Eavesdroppers will take advantage of existing helpful structures before planting devices that would not normally be in the area. Whether in a home or in a corporate environment, there is usually some type of duct work for heating or air conditioning that leads into the desired room or office. This duct work can carry sound much farther than it will travel in open air. Eavesdroppers can attach a transducer right onto the duct to amplify any sound vibrations that travel through the duct work. A transducer is simply a device that will convert one form of energy to another. In this case, a transducer called a microphone converts mechanical vibrations into electrical energy. Some microphones pick up sound via airwaves striking an internal disk, which then vibrates at the same rate as the airwaves. The Acoustic Leakage Detector, shown in Figure 11–1, is a device that uses a small peg attached to a disk to measure sound vibrations. The peg is touched to the duct work and carries vibrations through the peg to the disk. The disk then vibrates against material that changes in resistance from being compressed to

Figure 11-1 An acoustic microphone. Notice the peg that juts out of the diaphragm side.

expanded (very minutely, of course), and then produces varying electrical signals. These electrical signals are taken to an amplifier where they are amplified enough to hear or be recorded from a "line output."

Some microphones, such as *gun microphones,* are very directional in nature and can be aimed at a target from a significant distance. In combination with headsets and an amplifier, these gun mics can be very effective. Look at the sidelines during a football game and you will see people using these microphones. Do you think they could be used to try to overhear conversations from the other team? Also, notice how the coaches all hide their mouths with a paper when calling plays or giving directions to their players. In combination with a good pair of binoculars, a lip reader can be a very effective eavesdropper. So, lesson number one for the TSCM novice: analyze the outer perimeter of the target area very carefully. Is there a place where vibrations from inside sound can be picked up? Could a lip reader use a telescope to look through a window and accomplish his goal? Of course, an eavesdropper could operate without the use of any sophisticated equipment in many other scenarios as well.

MICROPHONES AND WIRES

Now we get into some technology. As previously mentioned, a microphone is a device that picks up sounds and converts them into electrical energy. There are all sizes of microphones available in the marketplace, from large studio quality mics to those that are smaller than a button—some much smaller. There are also different types of microphones that an eavesdropper can use, depending on circumstances.

A *Carbon Microphone* operates on the principle that vibrating a diaphragm at the mouthpiece will vary resistance in a circuit, varying the amplitude of an existing electrical current. There are carbon granules behind the diaphragm that, when compressed by diaphragm pressure, will be packed more tightly and will lower resistance in the circuit. When the diaphragm moves away, the granules are packed more loosely, and the resistance goes up. These mics will produce a hiss at high frequencies but have good audio response. They get down to about half an inch in diameter.

The *Capacitor* (or *Condenser*) *Microphone* has a very good frequency response, little distortion, and little internal noise. The front end consists of two plates of a capacitor of about 40–50 picofarads. A fixed charge is accumulated on the diaphragm, and as sound waves hit the diaphragm, the pressure causes small changes in the spacing of the capacitor plates, varying the capacitance. Resulting signal voltage then goes from the mic to the line. Frequency response is better than a carbon mic at about 20–20,000 Hertz.

The *Electret Microphone* is a very small capacitor microphone that uses a thin, foil "electret" plate and is a favorite among eavesdroppers. The frequency response is about 50–15,000 Hertz. Because of the electret plate, the capacitance of this mic is about three times that of an ordinary capacitor mic. It has a very low impedance and can be attached directly to a transistor amplifier. Later, when we talk about bugs, it will be apparent why the ability to attach a mic directly to an amplifier is an advantage.

Though early microphones tended to be omni-directional in nature, all microphones can now be designed to have varying directional patterns. These microphones can be hidden almost anywhere. All the eavesdropper has to do is figure out a way to get the mic's electrical

Figure 11–2   Detail of a "bug"—notice the Electret microphone attached directly to the circuit board.

signal to his location. One way to get that signal through is by using a wire. An eavesdropper can run the wire personally or use wire that is already available. One job requirement of a TSCM specialist is to look for wires that do not belong in the area. If some are found, they can be "listened to" by attaching an audio amplifier and listening in. CAUTION—before attempting this, the technician should use a voltage tester to make sure the wires are safe to work on. Even the regular electric wires strung throughout a house or office can be used to carry an audio signal. TSCM devices are available that enable the user to "listen" to these wires. Any wire in the eavesdropper's target area can be used to carry a signal from a microphone to a listener. This includes the electric wires (as mentioned), phone wires, and speaker wire. Actually, speakers themselves are easily converted to microphones; when using sophisticated amplifiers, the speakers do not even have to be converted. Audio speakers can be used as microphones just as they stand; they are not very efficient, but they do work. Always suspect speakers, and get them out of sensitive areas; this especially includes speakers and microphones found in telephones.

It is important to "think outside of the box" when doing TSCM work. One way of carrying electrical signals from a microphone to a destination 10–15 feet away is to use a clear metallic paint. The leads of the mic, hidden on a curtain rod, are painted over, and then a straight line is painted along the window frame and down inside the floor molding, where a wire is connected by painting over it. This may not be completely feasible, but this type of paint is available, and it will conduct electricity.

When looking for wires, it helps to think like an eavesdropper. Where would it be most advantageous to *plant* a microphone—perhaps near a project manager, or maybe a CEO, or possibly a chief engineer? It often helps to research what a company does before performing the TSCM survey. Of course, in the world of security, it is not always possible to find out exactly what a company is working on, but it is helpful to talk with the hiring contractor, who may be able to point out the most vulnerable areas within the building.

THE PHYSICAL SEARCH

Now that we have discussed wires and microphones a bit, let us get into the *physical search*. This is generally the first step in a TSCM survey and is considered to be a *non-alerting* procedure. This means that the search should not alert anyone—especially an eavesdropper—that a technician is looking for hidden eavesdropping devices. Usually, the hiring contractor provides some sort of cover story to justify the presence of the TSCM technician. The physical search usually starts out outside the building. The technician looks at the outside environment and such things as entry and exit points, not just for people, but also for wires, duct work, chimneys, windows, and such. The field of view from windows should be checked out. The TSCM technician should look *into* each window to see what can be viewed from outside. Shrubbery should be checked out to find potential hiding places for recorders, cameras, and people. Telephone and electric company equipment should be located, as taps into telephone lines and electric wires can be made outside in equipment boxes without any need for the eavesdropper to enter the building. The TSCM technician should also take into account whether wires from utility companies enter the building from above or below (underground). During the outdoor survey, the technician should look inside the various equipment "boxes" to see if there is anything that does not belong. Later, a more elaborate test can be done with tone tracing equipment and a device called a TDR to check if there is anything attached (tapped) to runs of wire that go to these utility boxes.

After a good look around outside, the technician does a walk around the inside of the building, this time looking for areas and devices that need to be more closely checked at a later time. During this survey, the technician jots down the presence and location of phone and network outlets, false ceilings, wire ducts, false floors, locations of phone and network "closets," and frame rooms. The technician may want to carry a ladder and flashlight to look above false ceilings and may even want to check out wires in those ceilings using a digital multimeter and audio amplifier. If anything suspicious is noted such as noise on a wire, the noise signals can be traced later when the walk around is completed. At this initial stage, the walk around is *non-alerting*, so if there is an eavesdropper in the area, he will not be aware that we are searching for his handiwork. The idea is to give the eavesdropper as little notice as possible, so he will not shut down his operation. During this walk around, the technician will want to find several central points that will later provide circular, overlapping areas to check out with a spectrum analyzer, to check the radio frequency (RF) environment.

After the initial walk around, a very intense and concentrated physical search should take place. At this time, the technician can use a non-linear junction detector. As discussed in Chapter 4, this instrument will help to find eavesdropping devices, even when they are turned off. The non-linear junction detector is an *alerting* device. It transmits a microwave signal from its antenna. The antenna of the NLJD looks like a Bissell floor sweeper, and is *swept* over areas such as walls, pictures, seat cushions, other furniture, and other things in a room where one would not normally expect to find any electronic devices. If there is a positive indication from a seat cushion, a technician has reason to believe that there may be a pressure activated on-off switch or something similar, hidden in the cushion. A positive indication over a picture frame would also be a good thing to check out further. The range of an NLJD is dependent on the output power of the *signal generator,* which is a part of the device. A microwave signal is transmitted, and then a built-in receiver listens for an RF response. If a response is received, it means a non-linear junction may have been activated to generate a signal. Government NLJDs are permitted to have a greater power output than commercially available equipment. Non-linear junction detectors are available in a variety of power outputs ranging from an output below 25 mW to the restricted government version with an effect power output of over 2 W. Some versions have been produced with an effective radiated power (ERP) of over 5 W, but this power range can be dangerous. Since a commercial device would typically have an ERP of around 5-10 mW, the sweeping part of the antenna should be held closely (within a few inches) over the target area. NLJDs are very helpful for finding hidden "bugs" in walls, chairs, picture frames, and so forth, but they are virtually useless in an area where there are numerous electronic devices present. In these areas, the best physical search instrument is the eyeball used in combination with a great deal of experience.

INSIDE WALLS

Eavesdropping devices can be placed inside walls in a couple of ways. One way is to plant the bug during construction, as was done at the U.S. embassy in the former United Soviet Socialist Republic in the early 1980s. Another way is to cut a hole into the wall, plant the equipment, and then repair the wall. To guard against the latter method, the TSCM technician will use an ultraviolet light to detect plaster repairs on the wall. For bugs implanted during construction, a non-linear junction detector can be used, as we have discussed previously. In addition to the NLJD, the technician can use a portable x-ray machine to check out a "positive signal." Eventually, the wall in question may have to be opened up for a direct look, so the TSCM technician should be well versed in plaster repair. It is much better to have good equipment to locate bugs in walls than to punch holes in the sheetrock any time there is a suspicious reading! There are obvious places inside a wall to look, such as power outlets, phone jacks, and network jacks. Faceplates should be removed and with the use of a flashlight and dental mirror, or better yet, a fiber optic camera and monitor, each and every wall opening should be checked out. This is a long, tedious job, but *must* be performed. These places are perfect for hiding a transmitter, and they even provide a built-in power source. In the case of a phone jack, the power source is a battery source straight from the phone company, which will not fail, even in the event of an electrical brownout. The electrical and phone company devices found in these niches should also be checked. There is a radio transmitter device that looks and works just like a regular electrical outlet, but is physically about a half inch deeper. These are completely illegal, but can be purchased at any of a number of spy shops in major cities throughout the United States or through magazine ads.

The physical search part of a TSCM inspection is the most time consuming, and probably the most important part of the whole process. Surprisingly, the least amount of technology in the TSCM process is used during this phase. Because of this part of the TSCM procedure, the technicians should be experienced, well trained, and very diverse in their knowledge of construction, electronics, engineering, acoustics, communications, antenna theory, and common sense.

THE RADIO FREQUENCY (RF) PHASE

It may not be convenient for an eavesdropper to run wire, or use available wires. If an eavesdropper is going to use a wireless method to get information from one point to another, she will probably use either radio frequency, or light waves. Light waves can be very effective, especially with laser devices, which are just outside the range of human vision, but these devices basically rely on line of sight receivers. RF devices can use a broad array of frequencies, some depending on line of sight, but others that can transmit for many miles in multiple directions, through walls, roofs, and into outer space, depending on the properties of the frequency and equipment. We can discuss properties of various radio waves forever—there are books and even encyclopedias devoted to the subject. For the purposes of TSCM, it should be noted that lower RF frequencies tend to transmit farther than higher frequencies, higher frequencies tend to have a range limited to line-of-sight. Lower frequencies usually require higher power and bigger transmitting antennas than higher frequencies.

What does an eavesdropper typically require?

- A short antenna—the shorter, the better
- Low power
- A tiny device
- Low energy consumption of device
- Privacy

■ Transmitting distance just great enough to get to the listening post—no less, no more

■ Ability to hide or disguise the transmitter

Can the eavesdropper get all of this at once? Probably not, but technology is getting her closer. Let us look at each need.

The short antenna would require high frequency, or alternatively, inefficiency with a lower frequency. High frequency calls for more line-of-sight than low frequency.

Low power is a given. The eavesdropper would not *want* high power because she would transmit too far, and she probably would not be able to find a source of high power anyway.

Tiny physical size is increasingly becoming a reality. With current technology, a *bug* can be totally self contained in a single chip, and can even have a built in buffer that we will discuss a little later.

Low energy consumption is very important for a device that runs on battery power. Probably less important for a bug connected to a phone line, or through a transformer, connected to the power line.

Privacy—this means the transmitting frequency should be one that a casual radio listener cannot inadvertently tune in to on his commercial radio. This could also mean using some sort of encryption or communications security (COMSEC) method.

Transmitting distance. An eavesdropper may have a recorder set up to record transmissions remotely, a radio repeater set up at a nearby location, or there may be an actual listening post nearby such as a van with an antenna on top. The eavesdropper wants the signal to get at least that far, but no farther. The farther the radio wave travels, the more susceptible it is to interception.

The ability to hide the bug could take the form of size or disguise. Earlier we mentioned the disguised electrical outlet, but there are also many other "disguised" bugs—from teddy bears to plaques and seals in embassy buildings.

In theory, the physical inspection phase of the TSCM inspection will turn up some of these devices. One thing to keep in mind is that an eavesdropper will often plant a device (or a couple of them) in areas where she knows they will be found during a good physical search. She will hope that the TSCM technician will be fooled into a state of complacency thinking that he has accomplished his task.

The next phase, the RF phase, will search for active devices that are transmitting at any number of different frequencies. Usually a spectrum analyzer is used for the beginning of the RF phase. A map of the area under observation is used to determine where to set up the spectrum analyzer(s). Depending on the size of the area, perhaps only one location will be used. If the area is large, such as a corporation headquarters building, perhaps there will be a dozen or more setups, either concurrent, or one by one. There are a couple different schools of thought in regards to using the spectrum analyzer. Some technicians like to use sophisticated high reliability antennas to pick up every available signal in the area so that it may be listened to and analyzed. Using these sensitive antennas allows the technician to use very large circles of coverage, and thereby cut down on the repetition. Other technicians go in the opposite direction. They use small circles of coverage, and use the worst, most inefficient antennas available, in order to pick up only the strongest signals. I knew one very good technician who liked to use an unbent paper clip plugged into the center conductor antenna connector of his spectrum analyzer. This cuts out a lot of operator error, as the theory is that a nearby bug will produce the strongest signals in the area. It is extremely important that the circle(s) of coverage are smaller than when using a larger antenna when using this procedure. Although there will be a great deal of repetition in searching through the RF spectrum this way, the sweep will be fairly quick each time due to the small amount of signal reception.

As for the frequencies that should be "swept," many technicians will now go as high as 40 or even 110 GHz. Three gigahertz used to be somewhat of an unwritten standard, but with new 802.11 networking technology, the frequencies have climbed higher than the 802.11(b) 2.4 GHz range. Of course, once a technician starts sweeping beyond about 900 MHz, he would not want to keep using that paperclip antenna!

FLOODING AND SNUGGLING

There is a technique used by eavesdroppers called *RF flooding*. I ran into this type of technology in the 1960s, and it is still being used these days, although the technology has evolved substantially over the last 40-some years. A special transmitter can be hidden and will lay dormant until it is bombarded with electromagnetic radiation of a previously programmed frequency. Similar to smart cards used for parking garages, the transmitter has a built in antenna with a resonant frequency that is the same as the flooding frequency. When the device is "flooded", or bombarded with radiation of a designated frequency from a nearby radio transmitter it is activated and will send its transmission, which is usually real time audio or digital information that was being held in a buffer. If the eavesdropper is really sophisticated, he can disguise the flooding frequency to look (on a spectrum analyzer) like a video signal or something similarly unsuspicious. He could also then *snuggle* the answering frequency up next to one of the parts of the flooding signal. Snuggling is something that many eavesdroppers do without all the elaborate disguises as well. The eavesdropper will snuggle or try to hide the transmission of his bug next to a stronger signal. For instance, TV signals have a video component with an audio component located a short cyclic distance from it. The flooding frequency could be within the "video" component, and the returned, snuggled frequency could be hidden next to the so-called "audio" component of the signal. The video component could even have a "test pattern" active, and the audio component could have a solid tone modulation. At his listening post, the eavesdropper will use a very sensitive receiver with a narrow filter to retrieve the snuggled signal. Because of the possibility of snuggled transmissions, the TSCM specialist should use a spectrum analyzer with a very good *resolution bandwidth*. Resolution bandwidth is the smallest bandwidth within which the spectrum analyzer can discern a signal.

SPREAD SPECTRUM

There are relatively new technologies that make it very difficult to rely on a spectrum analyzer alone to test whether or not there are bugs transmitting in the nearby vicinity. One of those technologies is spread spectrum. Developed by the actress, Hedy LaMarr, spread spectrum technology itself is not new. It was first used during the World War II era. The use of spread spectrum in bugs, however, is recent. There are two varieties of spread spectrum, each making it very difficult to "see and hear" a frequency on a spectrum analyzer. The Direct Sequence Spread Spectrum method (DSSS) takes a signal and *spreads* it out over a broad range of frequencies, perhaps of about a 3–6 MHz range. This has the effect of taking an already low power signal, and making it almost imperceptible at any given single frequency within the spread range (time to throw away that paper-clip antenna). The other spread spectrum method is Frequency Hopping Spread Spectrum (FHSS). This is less frequently used for a bug because the receiver has to be in sync with the transmitter as it changes frequency of transmission at a very rapid rate, perhaps ten hops per second up to hundreds or perhaps thousands of hops per second.

It is possible with current microprocessor capability to build a bug that will take audio that it is "listening to" convert it from analog to digital, and put it into a buffer. The buffer will only release the digital information for transmission periodically. Perhaps a "burst" would be sent out randomly, approximately every twenty minutes, and that burst may only last for about one third of a second, or less. It would be highly coincidental for a TSCM technician to pick up that transmission on the spectrum analyzer, and the transmission would be unrecognizable since it would be digital in nature. These types of "burst" bugs have not been very common yet in the commercial world, but the technology does exist, and it is probably just a matter of time before they proliferate.

So, with all this new technology, do we give up on using the spectrum analyzer? No, of course not, but we do supplement its use with some other types of equipment.

BROADBAND RECEIVERS, WATERFALL PATTERNS, AND RECORDERS

In Chapter 4 we discussed REI's CPM 700 broadband receiver and indicated how useful this equipment is as a search receiver. We set up a Known Sound Source, such as a CD or tape, and then "walk" an area with the CPM700. The strongest nearby signals will be captured. When we hear our sound source, we know there is most likely a radio transmitter very close by. This instrument is usually used in concert with a spectrum analyzer. The spectrum analyzer will show you that a bug may be present in the area because of the RF energy, but the CPM 700 will be used to actually aid in *finding* the location of the bug. The CPM 700 also has a recorder interface, so it can be used as a stationary instrument attached to a sound activated recorder. If a "burst" of RF such as that described previously, takes place, the CPM 700 will capture that noise on tape. In this case, we will not hear a sound source, but a skilled technician will recognize the "signature pattern" of this burst noise, and suspect that there may be a bug nearby. A very careful physical search will be necessary in this event. Some other features of this very versatile piece of equipment are an audio amplifier that can be used to "listen" for audio on wires where it does not belong, and an interface that can safely attach to electrical lines to listen for audio that rides on a *current carrier*. Of course, there are other broadband receivers that can be set up similarly with a recorder to listen for burst bugs.

For spread spectrum, whether direct sequence or frequency hopping, a sensitive receiver with a very good antenna and a *waterfall display* should be used. Ideally, the technician should be able to attach a printer that will print out the graphics of the waterfall display. The waterfall display is a picture of a very broad band of frequencies (think of the paper printout having low frequencies on the left side of the paper, and high frequencies on the right) where shaded patterns indicate radio activity. With a printout like this, a DSSS pattern would show up as an "unbroken line" printed across a frequency span (perhaps around 6 Mhz.) An FHSS pattern would look like a series of "small dots" contained within a frequency span.

SUMMARIZING THE RF PHASE

To sum up, the RF phase consists of setting up a spectrum analyzer, slowly scanning through ranges of frequencies from very low (around 10 KHz) up to as high as 110GHz, using a range of antennas. If a "positive response to a sound source" is detected, the technician will follow up with a walk around the area, using a broadband near-signal receiver to locate the bug. In a large area, the spectrum analyzer will be moved, and the procedure will be repeated throughout the area. The *concentric circles of coverage* with the spectrum analyzer should be planned out earlier before getting to this phase. In order to locate burst bugs or spread spectrum signals, receivers with waterfall displays, printers, and receivers with recorders should be set up to monitor an area for a period of time (at least several hours.)

TELEPHONE LINES

Books have been written about analyzing phone lines, so within this chapter, we will just touch briefly on the subject. First, a bit about where phone lines, and the voltage and current on them, come from.

THE LOCAL LOOP

A phone company central office has the ability to handle about 10,000 telephone lines. Beyond the central office are other exchange offices with even greater capability, but for our purposes, we will limit ourselves to the central office's local network, and to the facility for which we are performing TSCM services. The local network is the configuration in which telephones in homes and businesses are connected to central offices. Locally, there are wire pairs that fan out from a place called the wire center into a serving area. Serving areas vary greatly in size, from an average of about 10 square miles in cities to about 120 square miles in rural areas. More than one central office is often required for a serving area in urban locales, but one central office is usually sufficient in rural areas. An average wire center in an urban area will serve 40,000 subscriber lines and 5,000 larger trunks. City exchanges are usually of higher call capacity than the rural exchanges.

Telephones are connected to the exchange, which contains signaling equipment, switching equipment, and batteries that supply direct current to operate the phones. Each telephone is connected to this central office through a local loop of two wires called a wire pair. One of the wires is called T (for tip) and the other is called R (for ring.) The T and R designations refer to the *tip* and *ring* parts of the plug, which used to be manually operated at switchboards.

Switches at the central office are activated by tones from the telephone to connect the calling phone to the called phone. When the connection is established, the two telephones communicate over connected loops using the battery supplied current from the central office. When the handset of the telephone is resting in its cradle, the weight of the handset holds the push buttons down and the switches in the handset are *open*. This is called being *on-hook*. In this position, the circuit between the telephone handset and the central office is open. The ringer circuit in the telephone is always connected to the central office, however. A capacitor blocks the flow of direct current from the battery, but passes the alternating current (AC) ringing signal. When the handset is taken off the cradle, the push buttons come up and the switch in the phone *closes*. This completes the circuit to the central office and current flows in the circuit, creating the *off-hook* condition. The on-hook, off-hook, and hang-up terms come from long ago when the receiver was a unit that actually "hung" on the telephone set's hook when not in use.

TELEPHONE PARAMETERS

Table 11–1 lists the various voltages, currents, and resistances on a phone line.

Table 11–1 Voltages, Currents, and Resistances on a Phone Line

PARAMETER	TYPICAL VALUE	TYPICAL LIMITS
Battery Voltage	–48 VDC	–45 to –100 VDC
Operating Current	20 to 80 mA	20 to 120 mA
Loop Resistance	0 to 1300 ohms	0 to 3600 ohms
Ringer	20 Hz, 90 VRMS	16 to 60 Hz, 40 to 130 VRMS

TELEPHONE CABLES

The early (to mid 1900s) makeup of cable used by the phone company was one that had the conductors covered with paper or pulp insulation, which was then protected by a metallic sheath. A Plastic Insulated Conductor (PIC) has been in use since the 1950s. The plastic is certainly stronger than the paper that was used previously. *PIC cables* are produced in "air core" and "gel filled" configurations. Air core cable has conductors placed inside a metallic sheath, which is then covered with a plastic (polyethylene) jacket. This cable is still used but has problems with water from the ground when it is buried. To overcome this problem, a petroleum jelly based compound has been used to fill the available air spaces inside the cable. The new designator is called "filled cable."

Recall from Chapter 2 that a capacitor has two conductors separated by an insulator. Telephone cable pairs also have two copper conductors with a plastic insulated material separating the conductors. Therefore, all telephone cables have capacitance. To reduce this capacitance, the cable pairs are twisted together during the manufacturing process so that the amount of capacitance can be held down to 0.08 microfarads per mile. Small wire sizes such as 26 gauge have more twists per square foot than larger wire. The wire pairs are consistently balanced for capacitance. This balance of capacitance is extremely important, because a capacitance imbalance will create cross talk between telephone cable pairs. Remember that cross talk is the transferring of energy from one cable to another due to capacitance or inductance from a magnetic field created around a length of wire in which an electric current is flowing. On long cable runs, *build-out capacitors* are frequently installed on cable pairs. The purpose of these devices is to adjust the capacitance of a cable pair. Likewise, for runs exceeding 18,000 feet, *load coils*, which look similar to build out capacitors, are installed to control induction in an effort to aid voice quality over the line.

COLOR CODING

It is important that a TSCM technician be familiar with the color coding used for telephone company cable. The system of colors is based on a 25 pair grouping of conductors and is a simple matrix of 10 colors in various combinations. Table 11–2 lists the basic colors.

Table 11–2 Basic Color of Telephone Cable

RING (–)	TIP (+)
Blue	White
Orange	Red
Green	Black
Brown	Yellow
Slate (grayish)	Violet

In a 25 pair cable, there will be five of each color. Table 11–3 shows how the pairs are organized.

This series can continue by making up 25 pair binders. In the first group of 25, the binder would be a Blue/White ribbon; the second would be an Orange/White ribbon, and so on, and so forth.

When checking a residence, a TSCM technician will typically analyze the wires starting from the phone company's *pedestal box* and continuing on through the residence. At the pedestal box there is usually a cable containing about 25 pairs broken out to individual terminals where the residential wiring would then be connected. This pedestal box is a very handy place for an eavesdropper to attach a tap, without ever having to enter the residency.

Table 11–3 Color Pairs in a 25 Pair Cable

Pair 1	Blue/White
Pair 2	Orange/White
Pair 3	Green/White
Pair 4	Brown/White
Pair 5	Slate/White
Pair 6	Blue/Red
Pair 7	Orange/Red
Pair 8	Green/Red
Pair 9	Brown/Red
Pair 10	Slate/Red
Continue to Pair 25...	x.../Black, x.../Yellow, x.../Violet

At a business, a TSCM technician may start at the frame room for the building, where hundreds or even thousands of wire pairs may be entering the building. These wires would be attached to *110 blocks* (Figure 11–3), which contain connector tabs, or *66 blocks* (Figure 11–4),

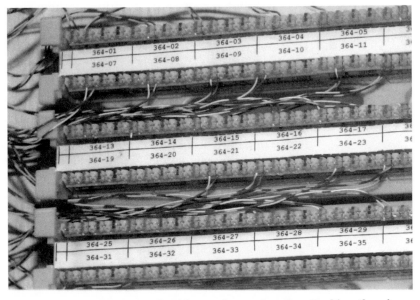

Figure 11–3   110 block detail—this panel uses plugs for attaching the wire.

Figure 11–4   66 block detail—a punch-down tool is used with this type of connection panel.

which have numerous punch down terminals. Inside wiring is then crimped onto corresponding tabs, which essentially connect the inside wiring to the telephone company's wiring. Of course, there are many other types of equipment associated with the entry of these wires, but as previously mentioned, there are entire books devoted to this subject.

THE RESIDENTIAL CIRCUIT

Wire pairs from a pedestal box are brought to the residence via an underground run or wire pairs from an overhead telephone line run down to the residence. At the residence, the wires are connected to one side of a protector block. This protector block may have terminals for one or two wire pairs. The block is not only used as a patch panel, but also has fusing configurations to protect the residential wiring from any current spikes from the outside, such as a lightening strike. Once inside the house, the wire pairs may take on different colors. Pair one may be green and red, and pair two may be yellow and black. More recently, the telephone company has been using a three pair cable for the inside with the colors as seen in Table 11–4.

Table 11–4 Three Pair Cable Coloring

RING (–)	TIP (+)
White	Blue
White	Orange
White	Green

The cables inside the residence can be run in parallel, in a loop around the house, or using different wiring configuration combinations.

Terminal equipment such as telephones, modems, answering machines, and fax machines are attached to the cable(s) at outlets throughout the residence.

ANALYZING THE PHONE LINES

There are many variations of tests a TSCM technician can use to check telephone cabling. Here is just one suggested procedure:

1 Disconnect the cables at the protector block.

2 Put a tone on the wire running to the pedestal box or telephone pole.

3 Go to the pedestal box, or pole, and determine which pair has the tone. Physically check the connection out, and make sure it is not bridged to another wire pair inside the pedestal box—make sure to look at the back side of the terminal block.

4 Use a TDR on the pair from both sides to make sure there are no anomalies on the cable. Run the TDR check from both ends with and without terminators.

5 Disconnect all equipment from the cabling inside the house, paying attention to alarm systems, and being sure to notify alarm companies when appropriate. At this point you should have essentially very long wire pairs that are open on both ends.

6 Using a high quality digital multimeter, measure the resistance of the wire pair(s.) The reading should show an infinite resistance. It is extremely important that a very good quality DMM with the ability to

read very high resistances be used for this step. A high impedance tap across a wire pair would show up as infinite on a low quality DMM.

7   The technician will analyze the wire pairs throughout the residence with a TDR to get a "look" at the cabling.

8   At this point, many TSCM technicians will use a supplementary telephone analyzer (Figure 11–5) to perform several tests. The telephone analyzer allows the technician to perform tests on all possible wire pair combinations. The instrument will also be used to check out the individual telephones in the residence.

Figure 11–5   A battery controlled telephone analyzer—the switches along the right side (toggles and knobs) allow the operator to test every variation on multiple line cabling.

Once the technician has taken a good look at the cabling, the individual telephone sets, fax machines, and telephone answering devices can be checked out as well. The technician should physically look inside these devices to see if anything appears to be modified or if there is anything inside that should not be there. Many circuit boards are reworked at a manufacturing plant before being put on the line for assembly, and these reworked boards may have wire *bridges* soldered onto paths on the board. Unless the client wants to spend the high hourly wage for the TSCM technician to analyze this wire bridge, the phone should simply be replaced (unless, of course, it is a very expensive phone!) After all of the phones and other equipment have been physically checked out, the whole system can be put back together, and the telephone analyzer can be used again to check each device while it is connected to the circuit. At this point, on-hook electrical characteristics and off-hook parameters will be checked. Any device connected to the circuit will require current, and will drop a certain amount of voltage. The problem is that the amount may be very miniscule and sometimes even impossible to detect. This is why many different overlapping types of tests are conducted. Some devices even lay dormant until an activating signal is received. Such is the case with the so-called infinity bug or *harmonica bug* as it is sometimes called. The bug is activated by calling the phone from a remote location, and then playing preset tone combinations. Once upon a time, eavesdroppers used a harmonica for this, although now they can just use the Dual Tone Multi Frequency (DTMF) tones from the phone's keypad. One operation that the telephone analyzer will perform is the injection of hundreds of tone combinations to see if there may be a tone-activated bug present. We have mentioned a few tests, but there are many more that go well beyond the scope of just one chapter in this book. A TSCM technician is familiar with many tricks used by eavesdroppers, but also has to keep himself updated on a regular basis.

THE COMMERCIAL ENVIRONMENT

Tests performed at a commercial facility are similar to those described earlier as pertaining to a residence. Of course, a commercial environment has many false ceilings, perhaps even false floors, and hundreds of feet of cable running throughout the building that would hardly be found in a residential setting. One can see that in the commercial building the physical search would be much more difficult and time consuming, but even more critical than in a residence. All phases, whether physical search, RF sweep, telephone analysis, or LAN/WAN should be done in sections. A logical plan should be developed ahead of time to break the facility into "zones," and then move from zone to zone, securing each.

COMMERCIAL PHONE LINES

Commercial facilities, unless small, generally do not have the same protector blocks that are found at residences. When the telephone company cable enters the building, it goes to a large series of fuse blocks for protection, and then is routed either to a large series of *110 blocks* or *66 blocks*, where it will make connections to other locations throughout the building. The room containing all this equipment is usually referred to as a "frame room," and cable runs will go from the frame room to equipment closets, which look like small-scale frame rooms and are located on each floor level. There may be PBX equipment installed in any of these rooms enabling analog cabling to enter the PBX boxes, and digital cabling to exit and then be connected, once again via terminal blocks, to cable runs throughout the building. Cables are subsequently connected to terminal equipment (phones, faxes, modems, etc.) During the physical search, the TSCM technician will spend a great deal of time analyzing all of the various equipment components located within these various frames rooms and closets. It will be very important that the technician not only check out the front of the terminal blocks, but also the rear, which may require some disassembly and reassembly. Of course, the technician will have to be familiar with the various types of PBX equipment in use, and all of the modules, cables, and test or input/output equipment that may be attached to the unit. The company networking equipment (LANs and WANs) may also be in these rooms or adjoining rooms.

LANS AND WANS

TSCM technicians used to be able to get along without having to learn a great deal about computers, other than to consider them as terminal equipment just like telephones. Now, the outside world is invited into every company's information bank via the Internet. Most companies would not be able to conduct business without an internal network or Local Area Network (LAN), and a connection to the outside world or Wide Area Network (WAN) via modems, Internet Service Providers (ISPs), telco lines, and other cable connections. It is important that the TSCM technician have a very strong working knowledge of the components that are used with these LANs and WANs for their connections and protection. Hubs, switches, routers, gateways, firewalls, and DMZs can be bugged or tapped just like telephone lines. A LAN analyzer set to so-called *promiscuous mode* can literally read every piece of email that travels through the line to which the analyzer is connected. This analysis equipment, in this configuration, is sometimes referred to as a *sniffer*, and can be software or hardware. It is important that the TSCM technician have devices to "look at" the cabling to see what is attached. The RF spectrum also contains digital transmissions from wireless networks such as 802.11(a), (b), (g), and Bluetooth. Many TSCM technicians who have been in business for years have found themselves going back to school to learn about information security during the last several years. Many technicians are lulled into a state of false security when they see that a facility is cabled using fiber optic. Some believe that fiber optic is totally safe from tapping. They are wrong. It is more difficult to tap fiber optic than copper, but it can be done. The way to look for a tap on fiber optics is with an Optical Time Domain Reflectometer or OTDR. The TSCM technician should also have Optical Spectrum Analyzers to break down multiplexed signals, and Optical Power Meters to check gains and losses in his inventory. With LANs and WANs, the cost of business has gone up tremendously. This equipment is very expensive.

FINDING A BUG OR TAP

Depending on the situation and the location, there are different protocols to follow if a bug or tap is found. In the commercial world, a TSCM technician should take pictures, document actions in detecting and reporting the device, and notify appropriate law enforcement authorities. These devices can be booby-trapped, so it is best to let law enforcement handle a found device.

In the government arena, a decision would be made as to whether the bug *should be removed*. If there is a possibility that the eavesdropper would not be alerted, perhaps false information could be fed to the opposition, assuming you know who is listening on the other end.

SUMMARY

- Technical Surveillance Countermeasures (TSCM) operations are designed to determine if surreptitious radio transmitting equipment, covert CCTV equipment, or wired microphones have already been installed in an area.

- There are "eavesdroppers" who plant microphones, transmitters, tap phones, and, more recently, tap onto the Local Area Network to monitor incoming and outgoing email. TSCM is about finding the work of these eavesdroppers. A TSCM technician must be a skilled investigator, a technology expert, and an electrician, and must also be able to think like an eavesdropper and be creative in their searches.

- The physical search usually starts on the outside of the building, locating vulnerable vantage points as well as possible points of entry.

- After a good look around outside, the technician does a walk around the interior of the building.

- It may not be convenient for an eavesdropper to run wire, or use available wires. For the purposes of TSCM, it should be noted that lower RF frequencies tend to transmit farther than higher frequencies; higher frequencies tend to be limited to line-of-sight. Lower frequencies usually require higher power and bigger transmitting antennas than higher frequencies.

- The eavesdropper will *snuggle*, or try to hide the transmission of his bug next to a stronger signal. At his listening post, the eavesdropper will use a very sensitive receiver with a narrow filter to retrieve the snuggled signal.

- Spread spectrum technology itself is not new. The use of spread spectrum in bugs, however, is a recent development. There are two varieties of spread spectrum, each making it very difficult to "see and hear" a frequency on a spectrum analyzer. The Direct Sequence Spread Spectrum method (DSSS) takes a signal and *spreads* it out over a broad range of frequencies, perhaps of about a 3–6 MHz range. The other spread spectrum method is Frequency Hopping Spread Spectrum (FHSS) where the signal hops across a range of frequencies.

- A phone company central office has the ability to handle about 10,000 lines. The local network is the configuration in which telephones in homes and businesses are connected to central offices. Locally, there are wire pairs that fan out from a place called the wire center into a service area. An average wire center in an urban area will serve 40,000 subscriber lines and 5,000 larger trunks. Telephones are connected to the exchange, which contains signaling equipment, switching equipment, and batteries that supply direct current to operate the phones. Each telephone is connected to this central office through a local loop of two wires called a wire pair. Switches at the central office are activated by tones from the telephone to connect the calling phone to the called phone.

- Wire pairs run underground into a residence from a pedestal box, or wire pairs run from an overhead telephone line to the residence. At the residence, the wires are connected to one side of a *protector block*. This protector block may have terminals for one or two wire pairs. Once inside the house, the wire pairs may be a different color. Terminal equipment such as telephones, modems, answering machines, and fax machines are attached to the cable(s) at outlets throughout the residence.

- In the commercial environment, the room containing telephone, LAN and WAN equipment is usually referred to as a *frame room*, and cable runs will go from the frame room to *equipment closets* throughout the building, which look like small-scale frame rooms and are located on each floor. Any of these rooms may contain PBX equipment where analog cabling enters the PBX boxes, and digital cabling exits and is connected, once again via terminal blocks, to cable runs throughout the building. The cables are subsequently connected to terminal equipment such as phones, faxes, and modems. During the physical search, the TSCM technician will spend a great deal of time analyzing all of the various equipment components located within. The company networking equipment may also be in these rooms or adjoining rooms.

■ Hubs, switches, routers, gateways, firewalls, and DMZs can be bugged or tapped just like telephone lines.

KEY TERMS

Eavesdropper

Acoustic Leakage Detector

Gun Microphone

Carbon Microphone

Capacitor (or Condenser) Microphone

Electret Microphone

Physical Search

Non-Alerting

Radio Frequency (RF) Phase

Flooding and Snuggling

Resolution Bandwidth

Current Carrier

Waterfall Display

Tip and Ring

On-Hook

Off-Hook

PIC Cable

Build-Out Capacitor

Load Coil

110 Block

66 Block

Pedestal Box

Harmonica Bug

Promiscuous Mode

Sniffer

DISCUSSION QUESTIONS

1   What is the purpose of Technical Surveillance Countermeasures?

2   What is the most basic of all eavesdropping threats?

3   Why would a coach on the sidelines of a football game want to cover his mouth when he discusses strategy with another coach?

4   What is a "carrier current" device?

5   Explain "snuggling."

6   Why would a spy flood a target area with RF?

7   What is the use of an acoustic leakage detector?

8   What is a transducer?

9   What type of device would show division of frequencies in a wavelength division multiplexed fiber optic?

10   What kind of device would show a tap on a fiber optic?

11   Of what use is a protector block?

12   Why do we find "66 Blocks" in equipment closets?

13   Why would a spy use a "sniffer"?

14   How does a harmonica bug work? Why is it called a harmonica bug?

15   What do you think the most important part of a TSCM procedure is, and why?

RESEARCH QUESTIONS

1   Why is digital communications difficult, if not impossible, to hear on a communications scanner?

2   Why would a TSCM technician make sure to wave his near-field antenna in both vertical and horizontal directions as he sweeps an area?

3   Can a telephone ever be considered to be safe? What about Secure Telephone Units (STUs)? Why or why not?

CHAPTER 12

Putting It Together with Risk Analyses and Physical Security Surveys

PURPOSE AND OBJECTIVES

Now that various parts of a security system have been discussed, it is time to discuss how they work together to form different types of systems. We say *different* types because each situation is unique, and that is why we have *risk analysis procedures* and *physical security surveys*. Although we cannot cover every type of security need that could exist, we can discuss the methodology of discovering what these needs might be, and how to cover them. As we shall see:

■ The risk analysis will pertain to the mitigation of potential threats to the system

■ The *physical security survey* will cover the *physical* components of a system that already exists

A GSA VIEW OF SECURITY IN THE WORKPLACE

The following is from the U.S. General Services Administration, and is an excellent outline of things to look for while conducting a physical security survey, whether at a government facility or a facility in the private sector:

OFFICE SECURITY

Both government offices and private sector facilities can be targets for theft, unlawful entry, kidnapping, bombings, forcible occupation, and sabotage. Effective barriers, both physical and psychological can reduce the likelihood of these threats. The following guidelines will help analyze an office security profile and suggest measures to reduce target potential.

CONDUCT A CRIME PREVENTION ASSESSMENT

The first step toward an effective security program is a complete, professional assessment of security needs. In the case of a government office, the nearest Federal Protective Service (FPS) office can arrange for a risk assessment to be performed on your government-owned or leased office or building.

Since most crimes are directed toward individuals or offices that have little or no security planning in place, take stock of existing security measures and possible weak points. A comprehensive crime prevention assessment should ask:

- What is your target potential?
- What is the prevailing attitude toward security at this location?
- Who is responsible for the overall security program?
- How are security policies enforced?
- When was the current emergency preparedness plan (including fire, power failure, and disaster) developed?
- What resources are available locally and how rapid are the response times for fire, police, and ambulance?

- What kind of physical security systems and controls are presently used?
- Do the available security resources, policies, and procedures meet the potential threat?

RISK MANAGEMENT

Risk management is the process through which the relative risk of harm to a general support system or major application is evaluated, mitigated, and continuously monitored. A team led by the system owner and consisting of other interested parties first performs a risk assessment for all new systems and systems undergoing major modification. The risk assessment team identifies existing controls and additional controls needed to provide adequate security for the system and reduce the risk to a level that is acceptable to the system owner. The system owner then performs periodic vulnerability testing of the controls to monitor the continued adequacy of system security.

RISK ASSESSMENTS AND HOW THEY HELP SECURE RESOURCES

A risk assessment is a methodical identification and measurement of threats to a system or information processed or stored by the system, vulnerability of the system to the threats, or the probability, or risk, that a given threat could exploit the vulnerabilities.

A system owner, in consultation with the Security Manager and other interested parties, must use the results of this evaluation to determine appropriate countermeasures that will prevent or mitigate risk to an acceptable level. The Designated Approving Authority at a facility determines risk as outlined in company policy. The Security Manager can assist by providing the system owner with a risk assessment methodology, and by providing assistance in interpreting the risk assessment results and suggesting possible cost-effective security countermeasure alternatives.

BUSINESS CONTINUITY AND DISASTER RECOVERY

In the process of performing a risk analysis, attention should be given to *business continuity* plans and *disaster recovery* plans. Business continuity refers to the prevention of interruptions to normal business activity from natural or man-made disasters such as:

- fire, explosion, or environmental disaster
- blackouts or brownouts
- communications or long-term network failure
- sabotage, bombings, or attacks from inside
- terrorist actions

Any disruption to normal business activities could cause financial loss that may never be overcome. The business continuity plan is designed to enhance a company's ability to minimize the cost associated with the disruptive event. The number one priority of business continuity or disaster recovery is the safety and security of people. Personnel always come first.

If business continuity is the predecessor of an event, disaster recovery is the successor. If something has already happened to affect business continuity, disaster recovery outlines plans for getting back to business as soon as possible. Disaster recovery plans develop guidelines for what is to be done before, during, and after, any event that causes losses to the business. The objective is to provide the ability to return to business, perhaps at an alternate site if necessary, until the original business site is brought back to operational capacity, and minimize loss to the company.

With regard to alternate sites, there are generally three types that are considered for business continuity:

The *Hot Site*—a fully configured (twin) facility that has all the necessary functioning equipment to *immediately* get back to business. The software and application programs would be at this site from backups that were performed on a daily basis at the original site. This type of site requires constant maintenance and updating of records, programs, and data. This is by far the best solution to get back to business almost immediately, but it is also extremely expensive to maintain.

The *Warm Site*—this has some of the traits of the hot site, but is not as "up to date." Applications would have to be installed, and backed up data would have to be brought in from somewhere else. There would not be a full complement of workstations, so some equipment installation would be necessary. In a warm site, there would be a time lag before the operation would be back in action, but maintaining the site would not be as costly as with a hot site.

The *Cold Site*—this is the most common type of site. It is usually a facility that is owned by the company and can be used in an emergency, but has no equipment, hardware, or data on site. There is power and HVAC, but workstations would have to be brought in and all applications and data would have to be installed. The length of time to get back to business would be quite extensive, perhaps measured in terms of months. Cost is the only real advantage in using this type of site.

THE RISK ANALYSIS TEAM

Many risk analysis projects fail because the team consists purely of upper level management personnel. Subject matter experts should be brought into the process as well as internal personnel who operate different systems and company applications because they are experts in fields that will be directly related to the risk analysis. The risk analysis process should be considered a part of the business process and should be conducted by a trained facilitator who can move the process along without biasing it. The risk analysis process itself should take only days, not weeks or months.

There are both quantitative and qualitative types of analyses. Qualitative seems to be the most commonly used because the team does not get bogged down with accounting processes, and the necessity of coming up with a number for each asset. Whichever analysis is used, the procedure remains consistent:

1   Identify assets to be considered.

2   Determine the risk, threats, and concerns.

3   Prioritize.

4   Either implement corrective controls or accept the risk.

5   Monitor the effectiveness of controls if implemented.

A very popular type of risk analysis is called a FRAP (Facilitated Risk Analysis Procedure.) The process of a FRAP involves analyzing one segment of business operations at a time, and convening a team that consists of managers, technical staff, and a facilitator. The sessions follow a standard agenda, which the facilitator is responsible for moving along in a timely fashion. The team brainstorms to identify threats and vulnerabilities, analyzes the effects of these threats and vulnerabilities, and then prioritizes them. Since the process is qualitative in nature, there is no need to assign a "number" or dollar figure on each potential threat for prioritization. Instead, the members use their experiential knowledge.

In order to make sure that the FRAP will move along in an organized and timely manner, a pre-FRAP meeting is generally held during which a scope statement and a visual model of the process (possibly in flowchart form) are produced, the team is established, the agenda for the meeting is determined, and there is an agreement on key definitions such as risk, control, impact, and vulnerability.

Although FRAP is a very popular process, it is not the only type. Another process that could be used is a multi-step process in which

1 Scope is determined.

2 The team is assembled.

3 Threats are identified.

4 Threats are prioritized.

5 The total threat impact is analyzed.

6 Safeguards are identified.

7 Safeguards are prioritized.

8 A cost-benefit analysis is performed.

9 A risk analysis report is produced.

PRIORITIZING

Prioritization has been mentioned several times, so it would be helpful to mention some formulas that are frequently used in risk analyses.

The Annualized Loss Expectancy or Exposure (ALE)

To identify risk and plan budgets, it is sometimes helpful to annualize loss expectancy for threats that have a significant chance of occurring such as certain natural disasters.

Single Loss Expectancy × Annualized Rate of Occurrence = Annualized Loss Expectancy or

$$SLE \times ARO = ALE$$

For example, the preceding formula shows that the ALE for a threat with an SLE of $200,000 that is expected to occur once every hundred years (1/100) is $200,000 divided by 100, which equals $2,000. This helps the process of prioritizing. The terms SLE, ARO, and ALE are used quite frequently in risk analysis.

FREQUENCY OF RISK ASSESSMENTS

System owners should begin an initial *risk assessment* during the initiation stage of new systems, or in the design of major modifications to existing systems. The risk assessment should be completed in the implementation stage of a system life cycle before the system security plan is finalized in order to ensure that the security plan identifies and addresses residual risk to the system (that risk which was not eliminated by implementation of countermeasures.) The risk assessment is a key consideration in the certification and accreditation of systems before placing them in operation. In addition, updating the risk assessment of systems periodically during the operation and maintenance stages helps maintain an acceptable level of risk throughout the life of the system. System owners should perform risk assessments of operational systems when making significant changes to a system as well as at least every three years.

Once a risk assessment has been completed, follow up with local law enforcement to act on the findings. For example, publicize phone numbers and make sure everyone knows whom to contact in case of an emergency.

Here are some general suggestions that may increase overall security:

■ Install key-card access systems at main entrances and on other appropriate doors.

■ Issue access control badges, with recent photographs, to all employees and authorized contractors.

■ Upgrade perimeter control systems with intercoms and closed circuit monitoring devices.

■ Keep master and extra keys locked in a security office.

- Develop crisis communication among key personnel and security office involving intercoms, telephones, duress alarms, or other concealed communications.

- Have a backup communication system, such as two-way radio, in case of phone failure.

- Locate executive offices near the inner core of the building to afford maximum protection and avoid surveillance from the outside.

- Arrange office space so unescorted visitors can be easily noticed.

- Have staff follow strict access control procedures—do not allow exceptions.

- Keep important papers locked in secure cabinets.

- Keep offices neat and orderly to identify strange objects or unauthorized people more easily.

- Empty trash receptacles often.

- Open packages and large envelopes in executive offices only if the source or sender is positively identified.

- Keep closets, service openings, telephone, and electrical closets locked at all times. Protect crucial communications equipment and utility areas with an alarm system.

- Avoid stairwells and other isolated areas. Try not to ride the elevator alone with a suspicious person.

- Do not allow employees to work late alone or on a routine basis.

- Keep publicly accessible restroom doors locked and set up a key control system. If there is a combination lock, only office personnel should open the lock for visitors.

KEEP AN EXECUTIVE INFORMATION FILE

The security office should maintain an emergency contact file for immediate access to key personnel. The file should contain personal information to be used in case of emergency such as:

- home address and telephone number

- family members; names, ages, descriptions

- school schedules, addresses, phone numbers

- close relatives in the area; names, address, phone numbers

- medical history and physician's name, address, phone number
- local emergency services; ambulance and hospital phone numbers
- any code words or passwords agreed upon

SET UP SECURE AREAS IN THE BUILDING

You may wish to consider maintaining one or more *secure rooms* on work premises. This area can serve as a retreat in case of intrusion or other danger. The room should be equipped with:

- steel doors and protected ventilation system
- first aid equipment
- phone and backup communication equipment
- fire extinguishers
- bomb blankets and hardened walls
- sand bags
- emergency tool kit
- extra food and clothing
- large flashlight and batteries
- firearms (if permitted under established policy)

PHYSICAL SECURITY IN A FRONT LINE OFFICE

Before requesting a security survey, your agency may want to do a "crime assessment" of the risks you and your coworkers may encounter in your workplace. Are your customers likely to experience high levels of stress or tension? Do members of the general public who come into the office tend to be argumentative? Have there been threats or incidents of violence involving the public in the past? Have employees themselves become violent or threatening?

If your front-line office fits this profile, your agency needs to take immediate steps to help make your workplace fully secure. There are some simple changes that you can make to your front-line office that will help improve its security. Issue all employees photo identification cards and assign temporary passes to visitors—(who should be required to sign in and out of the building.) Under certain conditions, officers (or contract guards) should be required to call offices to confirm an appointment and/or to request an escort for all visitors—such as customers, relatives, or friends. Rearrange office furniture and partitions so that front-line employees in daily contact with the public are separated from customers and visitors by "natural" barriers—such as desks, countertops, and partitions. Brief employees on what action to take if a threatening or violent situation occurs. Establish code words to alert coworkers and supervisors that immediate help is needed. Provide an under-the-counter duress alarm system to signal a supervisor or security officer if a customer becomes threatening or violent. Establish an area in the office for employees and/or customers to escape if they are confronted with violent or threatening people.

PHYSICAL SECURITY FEATURES IN A CUSTOMER SERVICE OFFICE

- single public entrance to customer service area
- reception desk immediately inside public entrance
- silent, concealed alarms at reception desk and on employee side of service counter
- barrier between customer waiting and work areas
- service counter with windows between employees and customers
- window in supervisor's office from which supervisor can view customer service
- access-control combination locks on access doors
- closed circuit television camera mounted for monitoring customer service activity from a central security office for the building

THE PHYSICAL SECURITY SURVEY

The very first thing a physical security specialist has to know about the company she will be surveying is what they do and how it is done. The specialist should be familiar with the type of business, and should perhaps even consider bringing a business expert into the operation. Building security may appear to be very similar from business to business, but may require quite different methods for similar operations. For instance, a manufacturing type such as an auto manufacturer in Detroit where hundreds of people may have to go through an entrance in a very short period of time will need a fast access control device, whereas a research and development facility at a major university may only have a few people enter every hour, and can use a slower method of access control. In most situations there will be a need for entrance security, visitor control, perimeter security; a need for video and motion detection throughout, and a need for access control, whether very sophisticated biometrics or simple lock and key. Each business, however, will have unique requirements for protection of their proprietary information and their methods of doing business. A company that produces contact lens solution will be quite different from a welding shop in requirements for protecting the *process*, and this is where expert advice will be an absolute necessity for the physical security specialist. In the case of a manufacturing environment, the physical security specialist should familiarize herself with the entire operation from raw material to finished product. For a company such as an accounting firm, the layout of various departments should be studied, and the specialist must learn which physical areas of the facility are more sensitive than others from a security standpoint. In other words, where are the safes located? Where are the computer servers and data storage located? Is there a need for segmented access control?

The physical security specialist should analyze the operations of a company around the clock. Security requirements may be quite different at two in the afternoon than at two in the morning. Requirements will certainly be different if a company closes down at night and over the weekend. The security specialist should make it a point to actually visit the location several times during day and evening hours, and during weekends.

INITIAL STAGES OF THE SURVEY

Prior to *walking* the facility or facilities, the physical security specialist should obtain drawings, aerial photos, blueprints, and any other written aids that may be available for the survey. If none of these aids are available, the specialist should do her own drawings and sketches before performing an in-depth survey. Areas of importance include:

- outside landscaping and topography
- the facility's perimeter (fence, barriers, gates)
- entrances and exits
- neighboring buildings and perimeter devices

- roadways
- storage, utility, and operations buildings
- locations of all windows, skylights, chimneys, and utilities entrance points
- existing alarm, access control, and CCTV

Non-security personnel should be interviewed to get an idea of what *they* feel is important to protect, and what *they* feel are the weak links in the system. Because of their familiarity with the daily routines, the non security employees of a company can offer very important insights. They may be able to point out areas that can be annotated on the sketches for further study.

According to the United States Geological Survey (USGS), "a physical security survey is an in-depth analysis to determine the extent of security measures that will be needed for protecting personnel, property, and information. An inspection is a check or test against a certain set of standards or regulations to ascertain whether a security program or facility meets those standards or regulations. It is used to evaluate the implementation of regulations, the security awareness of employees, security administration, and existing internal management controls. It should be used as a tool by the security manager to carry out his oversight responsibilities."

The senior facility manager will use the physical security survey to determine the type and extent of security controls needed for the facility or areas. Each type of physical security survey will include a security evaluation (threat assessment) that addresses the criticality of operations, the vulnerability of the facility or area, and the probability of compromise of the personnel or property contained therein. In those cases where the senior manager does not provide a physical security survey, the security manager or facility manager should conduct a survey of the facility.

According to the United States Geological Survey, perfect or absolute security is always the goal of those responsible for security of a facility or activity, but such a state of absolute security can never be fully obtained. There is no object so well protected that it cannot be stolen, damaged, destroyed, or observed by unauthorized individuals. A balanced security system provides protection against a defined set of threats by informing the user of attempted intrusions and providing resistance to the would-be intruder's attack paths. This resistance must be consistent around the entire perimeter of the protected area. There are four main security elements that must be properly integrated in order to achieve a balance of physical security.

Detection. This is the process of detecting and locating intruders as far from the protected areas as possible. Early detection gives the user more time for effective alarm assessment and execution of pre-planned response.

Assessment. Assessment is determining the cause of the alarm or recognizing the activity. This must be done as soon as possible after detection to prevent the intruder's position from being lost.

Delay. Intruders must be delayed long enough to prevent them from achieving their objectives before the response force can interdict them.

Response. A response force must be available, equipped, and trained to prevent the intruders from achieving their objective. The response time must be less than the delay time if the response force is to intercept the intruders before they achieve their objective.

PLANNING AND ADMINISTRATION

Planning for security should be an integral part of any function or project undertaken. The most efficient and cost-effective method of instituting security measures into any facility or operation is through advance planning and continuous monitoring throughout the project or program. Selecting, constructing, or modifying a facility without considering the security implications to employee safety and assets protection can result in costly modifications and lost time.

At a minimum, a physical security program should include:

- a physical security survey of each facility to evaluate the security of that facility for protecting personnel and assets, including classified or sensitive information
- periodic inspections of facilities to ascertain whether a security program meets pertinent standards or regulations
- a comprehensive and continuing awareness and education effort to gain the interest and support of employees, contractors, consultants, and visitors
- procedures for taking immediate, positive, and orderly action to safeguard life and property during an emergency

FACILITY PROTECTION

The extent to which the facility needs to be protected is determined by the senior official or manager of the enterprise based on the results of a comprehensive security survey.

1   Perimeter protection is the first line of defense in providing physical security for personnel, property, and information.

2   The second line of defense, and perhaps the most important is interior controls. The extent of interior controls will be determined by considering the monetary value and criticality of the items and areas to be protected, the vulnerability of the facility, and the cost of the controls necessary to reduce that vulnerability.

3   The cost of security controls normally should not exceed the monetary value of the item or areas to be protected, unless necessitated by criticality or national security.

PLANNING PROTECTION

The objective of planning facility protection is to ensure both the integrity of operations and the security of assets. Planning for security must be an integral part of selecting, constructing, reconfiguring, or moving into a location.

The modification of a facility or addition of security measures after occupying a facility can be costly and impractical. Therefore, the responsible security manager and the facility management personnel need to coordinate closely, from the outset, on any addition, alteration, or new construction. The coordination should begin with the designers and architects and continue through the contracting process and actual construction and installation.

Facility protection may include guards, access control, intrusion detection (alarms), closed circuit television surveillance, and even inspection of packages.

It is imperative that security systems and procedures are considered from the design phase on, so that conduit runs and alarm wiring, heavy-duty materials, reinforcing devices and other necessary construction requirements are put in place in the original plans.

FACILITY AND BUILDING LOCATION

If it is possible to help in planning the location of a building on an initial physical security survey, start by determining the sensitivity of the projected facility, whether it will be open to the public and the time it will take for law enforcement to respond to incidents. Check geographical factors carefully. Avoid locating sensitive facilities near high crime, high traffic, or industrial areas. Take into account approach routes, traffic patterns, and nearby transportation.

Office entrances should be kept to a minimum commensurate with fire safety, to control access or prevent crime. Although convenience of employee access, parking, and deliveries must be considered, one entrance with multiple interior routes is preferable to several outside entrances. Entrances should be planned with guard posts, access control systems, and procedures in mind. Reception desks, barriers, and other controls should be planned from the start.

Plan for locking devices or controls at perimeter and interior doors. Provide for effective key control. Plan for protective, cleaning, and maintenance forces and determine hours, locations, and levels of access for such personnel.

Utility systems should be protected against unauthorized access. Plan for protection of telephone and electrical closets and conduit runs, heating and cooling systems, water supplies, boilers and generators, and valves, regulators, and controls.

Special emphasis should be placed on security systems and safeguards when constructing or modifying special or sensitive activities such as computer facilities, equipment storage or shipping and receiving areas, classified work areas and mail rooms, and special use areas such as warehouses or hazardous materials storage areas.

A contingency plan must be developed for each facility to protect personnel and property in the event of emergencies such as fire, bomb threats, civil disturbances, and natural disasters.

No survey is considered complete until all three of the factors below have been given full consideration and weight.

Criticality is the effect that partial or total loss of the facility or area would have on the facility's mission. The adversity of the effect is directly related to the criticality factor. Examples of adverse effects include the interruption of a vital function, disruption of the continuity of operations, or the compromise of sensitive information. A higher classification level of information handled or stored in a facility or area will increase the criticality.

Vulnerability of the facility or area is the susceptibility of a facility or area to damage or destruction or the possible theft or loss of property. Factors used to determine vulnerability include the size, configuration, and location of the facility or area, the local crime rate, and the proximity of law enforcement and emergency response services.

Probability deals with an assessment of the chances that certain events could or might occur, such as a penetration of the perimeter, compromise of a system, or the occurrence of a variety of unauthorized activities.

TYPES OF SURVEYS

Initial Survey. The initial survey is conducted prior to constructing, leasing, acquiring, modifying, or occupying a facility or area. It describes any modification required to raise the level of security commensurate with the levels of criticality and vulnerability.

Follow-up Survey. When recommendations are made in the initial survey, a follow-up survey is conducted to ensure the completion of modifications. This survey should be conducted before acceptance of the property or occupancy.

Supplemental Survey. The supplemental survey is conducted when changes in organization, mission, or facility alter or affect the security posture of the facility or area.

Special Survey. The special survey is conducted to examine or resolve a specific issue, such as when there is a request to investigate or assess damage resulting from an incident.

AWARENESS AND EDUCATION

A security program is most effective when employees practice security daily. That sort of interest and support can be gained through an effective security awareness and education program, which encompasses all aspects of security. The security manager is responsible for carrying out and administering a comprehensive, ongoing security awareness and education program for all employees in his/her respective activity.

The security manager must plan an effective program of instruction and efficient use of training material provided for specific training purposes. The security manager may also tailor presentations to the organization and solicit other security professionals to speak on their areas of responsibility, training, and experience. For example, a local police representative could address crime prevention.

SUMMARY

- The first step toward an effective security program is a complete, professional assessment of your security needs.

- The risk assessment team identifies the controls in place and additional controls needed to provide adequate security for the system and reduce the level of risk to one that is acceptable to the system owner.

- The system owner performs periodic vulnerability testing of the controls to monitor the continued adequacy of system security.

- A risk assessment is a methodical identification and measurement of threats to a system or information processed or stored by the system, vulnerability of the system to the threats, and the probability, or risk, that a given threat could exploit the vulnerabilities.

- The Security Manager can assist by providing the system owner with a risk assessment methodology, and by providing assistance in interpreting the risk assessment results and suggesting possible cost-effective security countermeasure alternatives.

- In the process of performing a Risk Analysis, attention should be given to business continuity plans and disaster recovery plans. The number one priority of business continuity or disaster recovery is the safety and security of people.

- A very popular type of risk analysis is called a *FRAP* (Facilitated Risk Analysis Procedure).

- System owners must begin an initial risk assessment during the initiation stage of new systems, or in the design of major modifications to existing systems.

- There will be a need for entrance security, visitor control, perimeter security, a need for video and motion detection throughout, and a need for access control, whether it be very sophisticated biometrics or a simple lock and key system. The physical security specialist should analyze the operations of a company around the clock.

- A physical security survey is an in-depth analysis to determine the extent of security measures that will be needed for protecting personnel, property, and information.

- Each type of physical security survey will include a security evaluation (threat assessment) which addresses the criticality of operations, the vulnerability of the facility or area, and the probability of compromise of the personnel or property contained therein.

■ Planning for security should be an integral part of any function or project undertaken. Selecting, constructing, or modifying a facility without considering the security implications to employee safety and assets protection can result in costly modifications and lost time.

■ The objective of planning facility protection is to ensure both the integrity of operations and the security of assets.

KEY TERMS

Physical Security Survey

Secure Rooms

Annualized Rate of Occurrence (ARO)

Single Loss Expectancy (SLE)

Annualized Loss Expectancy or Exposure (ALE)

FRAP

Cold Site

Warm Site

Hot Site

Disaster Recovery

Business Continuity

Risk Assessment

Risk Management

DISCUSSION QUESTIONS

1 What is the first step in an effective security program?

2 Define risk management.

3 What is a risk assessment?

4 What is the number one concern about business continuity or disaster recovery?

5 Define business continuity.

6   How often should risk assessments be performed?

7   Name some interruptions to normal business activity.

8   What is the most common type of risk analysis that is performed?

9   What is a FRAP?

10   How long should a FRAP last?

11   Name some things that should be in a secure room.

12   Define SRE, ALO, and ALE.

13   Put SRE, ALO, and ALE together in a formula.

14   What is the first thing that a security specialist needs to know before performing a security survey for a company?

15   What is a supplemental survey?

RESEARCH QUESTIONS

1   What is the difference between a *business impact analysis* (BIA), and a risk analysis?

2   Define what a CAP Index is, and how it can be used in the risk analysis procedure.

3   There are several different ways to formulate ALE. List another formula for ALE not found in this text

APPENDIX A

Common Lock and Key Control Terms

Access Control	A method of controlling the movement of persons into or within a protected area.
ANSI	American National Standards Institute, the coordinator of the United States voluntary standards system. The system meets national standards needs by marshaling the competence and cooperation of commerce and industry, standards-developing organizations, and public and consumer interests. ANSI specifications listed in this guide have been adopted by the United States Department of Defense.
Anti-Passback	An access control software feature that prevents two individuals from using the same access control card to gain access at the same time (i.e., first individual swipes card to gain access then passes the card to a second individual for the same purpose.)

ASTM — American Society for Testing and Materials, from the work of 133 technical standards-writing committees, ASTM publishes more than 8,000 standards each year in sixty-eight volumes of the Annual Book of ASTM Standards. The ASTM Committee F12 on Security Systems and Equipment develops and standardizes terminology, test methods, specifications, performance specifications, classifications and practices for security systems, components, and equipment referenced in this book.

Barrel Key — A key with a round hollow post and a projecting wing to actuate the tumblers and the bolt of the lock. It is sometimes known as a "pipe key."

Bit Key — A key with one or more wings or bits that project from the round solid post and that operate the tumblers and the bolt of the lock. This key is sometimes referred to as a "wing key" or a "skeleton key." It was once popular in earlier locks used in residential buildings.

Bitting — The cuts in a key that are configured to match the specific tumbler code of a lock or core.

Blade — The part of a key that may contain the cuts and/or milling.

Blank — Any uncut key produced by a manufacturer to fit its own lock keyways or keyways made by other lock manufacturers. It is sometimes referred to as a key blank.

Bow	The portion of a key that serves as a grip or handle.
Building Master Key	A master key that operates all or most master-keyed locks in a specific building.
Change Key	A key that will operate one lock or a group of keyed-alike locks.
Code	The alphanumeric or numerical symbols assigned to a key or lock cylinder that indicate the depth of the cuts and their location on the blade of the key.
Compromise	A security violation resulting in confirmed or suspected exposure of classified information to an unauthorized person.
Construction Key	A key supplied with construction-keyed locks. During construction, a builder gains entry using the construction key. Upon completion of the building, action is taken to render the construction key inoperative.
Control Key	A key issued by the lock manufacturer for disassembly and maintenance only. Never use this key for normal operation of the lock. In the case of interchangeable core locks, the key is specifically cut for removing and replacing the lock core.
Core	The term is sometimes used as a synonym for plug, but core is also used to refer to the figure-eight shaped unit that can be removed and replaced in interchangeable core cylinders.

Covert Threat	A threat that uses stealth or deception to gain entry. For access control, examples include picking and bypassing of locks and the use of duplicated or stolen access cards
Cylinder	A complete operating unit that usually consists of the plug or cylinder, shell, tumblers, springs, plug retainer, a cam/tailpiece or other actuating device, and all other necessary operating parts.
Double-Bit Key	A key bitted on two surfaces.
Emergency Master Key	A key sometimes known as a "lockout key." It is normally used in emergency situations when the door to a hotel or motel room is locked from the inside. When the dead bolt is secured from inside a room, the emergency key is the only key that can unlock the locking device from the outside. It is used in emergency situations only, and if a door is locked with the emergency key, it cannot be unlocked using any other key.
Enclave	A secured area within another secured area.
Hasp	A device that consists of either a hinged plate with a slot in it that fits over a staple, or two pieces designed for the shackle of a padlock to pass through in order to secure the pieces to each other.
High-Security	Locks, hasps, alarms, and security devices that offer a great degree of resistance to certain methods of attack.

Key Change Number	The recorded code number that is stamped on the bow of a key that indicates the key change. For example, in the key change number A-2, "A" might mean that the key is assigned to master system A, and the "2" indicates change 2 under the master.
Keyed-Alike System	A system that allows a number of locks to be operated by the same key. It is often used in perimeter applications. There is no limit to the number of locks that can be keyed alike.
Key Indexing	A method of associating every lock/core to a specific key by referring to a coded index.
Keyway	The opening in the plug of a lock cylinder into which the key that operates the lock is inserted.
Maison-Keyed System	A form of a master-keyed system in which each lock has its own individual key that will not open any other office, but all keys will operate the locks to communal entry doors or service areas.
Master-Keyed System	A method of keying locks that allows a single key to operate multiple locks. Several levels of master keying are possible: a single master key is one that will operate all locks of a group with individual change keys; a grand master key will operate all locks of the master-keyed system.

Padlock	A detachable and portable lock with a shackle that locks into its case. Components performing the same purpose of a shackle but differing in design are sometimes used instead of a shackle.
Paracentric	Of or pertaining to a keyway with one or more wards on each side projecting beyond the vertical center line of the keyway to hinder picking. A term used to distinguish a milled cylinder key from others, such as bit keys and flat keys. The word paracentric is defined as "deviating from the center." The term describes the irregular shape of keyways used in pin tumbler locks. The deviation from the center adds to the security of the cylinder, because it makes inserting lock picks difficult, and the bearing surface of the key will assure longer life.
Plug	The rotating portion of a tumbler or disc type lock or lock cylinder that contains the keyway.
Post	The round part of a bit key to which the wing or bit is attached.
Preauthorization	The previously established right to enter a controlled or restricted area.
Preventative Maintenance	Scheduled periodic inspection, cleaning, repair, and lubrication of equipment to ensure continued performance in a working environment.
Push Key	A key that performs its function of aligning the tumblers with the shear line by inward rather than rotary motion.

Restricted Keyway	A special keyway configuration that is not freely available and that must be specifically requested from the manufacturer.
Rekey	Changing the core or pins in a cylinder to prevent a previously issued key from opening the lock.
Security Container	A container usually equipped with a mounted combination lock specifically designed for protection of classified material or sensitive items.
Service Life	The amount of time that a product meets or exceeds the performance criteria for which it was designed.
Shackle	The part of a padlock that passes through an opening in an object or fits around an object and is ultimately locked into the case.
Shank	The part of a bit key between the bow and the stop; or, if there is no shoulder stop, the part between the bow and the near side of the bit.
Shoulder	The flat portion at the end of the bow on most keys.
Stem	The rounded portion at the end of a shank of a bit key to which the wing or bit is attached. The part forming the axis on which a bit key rotates in the lock is also referred to as the post.
Surreptitious Entry	A method of entry which would not be detectable during normal use or during inspection by a qualified person.

Tailgating	A specific method of gaining entry in which access is achieved by walking or driving immediately behind an authorized individual or automobile with a valid access card to gain entry before the entry point has been allowed to close. Tailgating is also referred to as piggybacking.
Throughput Rate	The maximum number of people that can enter an area in a given time period.
Two-Person Rule	A policy that requires two people to be present when an area or asset is accessed.
UL, Inc.	A national testing laboratory that tests, lists, and labels various categories of equipment for safety and reliability. They also publish standards for a wide range of products, including security products.

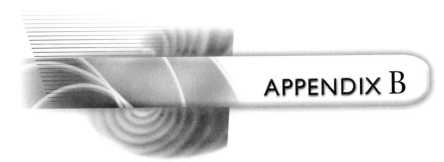

APPENDIX B

Answers to Odd Numbered Questions

CHAPTER I

1-1 We install security systems to protect us from break-ins and theft. Would security planning also be necessary for natural disasters? Explain.

There are many threats to any physical entity whether it is a corporation, a person, a home, or property. The form of the threat could be a natural disaster such as an earthquake, hurricane, flood, fire, or many other tragedies that we see daily on TV. There is the threat from people who want what you have, whether it is in the form of property or information.

1-3 What is a *security survey?*

Security surveys review existing systems and setup, aid in establishing the budget and assess the threat level. Some of the functions provided are feasibility studies, designing security consoles, setting up central stations, installing closed circuit television, establishing computer management of the system, designing physical intrusion detection and access control, establishing fire detection and suppression, ensuring code compliance, inspection and acceptance, and of course, cost estimating. This can take a great deal of time with many people involved including engineers, fire professionals, architects, accountants, and security professionals. These security surveys are usually done in phases. After a walk around and review, establishing guide-lines, and operational characteristics, the design phase begins. After design, construction and inspection phases follow

1-5 Define CCTV

Closed Circuit Television

1-7 What is the purpose of a *man-trap*?

These are entry ways or exits where an individual has to go through one door into a small enclosure, wait for the door to close, and then approach a second door and open it to enter or exit. A security guard could lock both doors when the person is in the enclosure, or this could happen automatically if the person does not have proper access control credentials, thus *trapping* him. These enclosures would be equipped with reinforced walls and bullet resistant glass.

1-9 Who is the person behind *The Uncertainty Principle*?

In 1927, Werner Heisenberg (1901–1976) published a paper on "The Uncertainty Principle."

1-11 Is there a difference between the terms, *layers of security* and *concentric rings of security*?

The terms tend to be used interchangeably, but "layers of security" would probably be more descriptive since coverage is not also necessarily "concentric."

1-13 What do you suppose would be involved in an *Employee Background Check*?

These checks usually include a criminal record check, a credit report, and a driving record check.

1-15 What is meant by *weatherizing* a building?

Sealing cracks around doors and windows. Gaps around windows and doors, and holes in the building shell, allow conditioned air to escape the building, and outside air to enter.

CHAPTER 2

2-1 **What are the various units of measurement for the following: Power, Resistance, Current, Electromotive Force, Inductance, Capacitance, Impedance?**

Power = Watts (W)

Resistance = Ohms (Ω)

Current = Amperes (I)

Electromotive Force = Voltage = Volts (V) sometimes (E)

Inductance = Henries (L)

Capacitance = Farads (C)

Impedance = Ohms (Z)

2-3 **In terms of Ohm's law what are the differences in performing calculations for AC versus DC?**

In AC, phase angle has to be taken into consideration since the current (or voltage) is fluctuating from zero to plus and minus its peak value.

2-5 **Without performing any calculation, what could we say about the total resistance in a circuit consisting of two resistors in parallel, where R1 = 20 k and R2 = 1 M?**

Total resistance will always be less than the smallest resistance in the parallel circuit. If the difference is very great between two resistors, the total will be almost equal to the smaller of the two.

2-7 **If capacitors of value = 50 pF (C1, C2, C3) were put just below each of the parallel resistors, R2, R3, and R4, waht would be the total DC resistance of the circuit?**

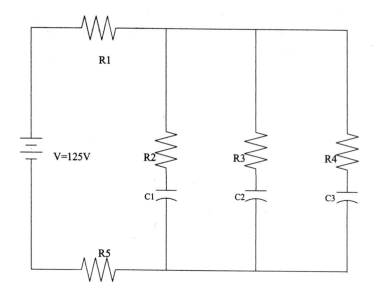

DC resistance would be infinite. The capacitors will not pass a DC current.

2-9 **How is a square wave made?**

By summing the primary and odd number harmonics of a sine wave.

2-11 **Why is it easier to calculate gains and losses using *decibels*?**

Gains and losses are found using simple addition and subtraction.

2-13 **What is a 6 dB gain?**

For power, a 6 dB gain is four times the original signal.

2-15   **Explain dBm. If a spectrum analyzer has a label by the input connector that states, "+15 dBm max", what does that mean?**

A very common unit of measurement is the dBm. This is the logarithmic ratio of some power quantity compared to *one milliwatt*

$$dBm = 10\log\frac{P}{0.001}$$

This is a very convenient unit of measurement that you will see over and over when working with test and measurement instruments. Even when a piece of equipment is labeled as having a safe unit of input power that shouldn't be exceeded, that unit will be expressed in *dBm*.

+15dBm max means that the power P in the above formula should never exceed 31.62 mW.

CHAPTER 3

3-1   **For security communications, why would all of these scenarios belong?**

Joe sends Shirley an email message.

Jack, the security officer, waves his guard tour wand at a sensor on the wall.

John talks to Mike on a 2-way radio.

All belong because security communications deals with systems communicating with each other, and people could be a part of the system as well as machines.

3-3   **What is the lowest grade of cabling that could be used for wiring telephones in your house?**

Category 1

3-5   **Into which category does 150 MHz fall?**

VHF

3-7   What is a Propagation Chart?

Propagation charts consider things such as sunspot activity, weather patterns, time of year, time of day, frequency, and other factors to predict the effectiveness of communications.

3-9   What is the minimum number of frequencies that would be used by a repeater. Why?

Two frequencies. One to receive a signal, and the other to retransmit it.

3-11   If a courier company was using a repeater, what frequency band would they most likely be using?

VHF

3-13   What is a *Cafeteria Card?*

A card that can be "loaded up" monetarily to a certain dollar value, to use in a Cafeteria or other place of business similar to a banking debit card.

3-15   What is the typical bandwidth for an OC3 circuit? To what does OC refer?

155.5 Mb. OC refers to a fiber optic cable.

CHAPTER 4

4-1   Identify some features that would be found on a modern multimeter.

The Digital Multimeter measures resistance (in ohms), voltage (in volts), current (in amperes), and other features depending on model and make. Some digital multimeters have the ability to measure temperature. Some also have automatic features built in such as transistor checks, capacitor tests, continuity tests, or diode checkers.

4-3   **With regard to a digital multimeter, what does the term, "not wanting to load the circuit" mean?**

The multimeter itself would have some resistance, and putting it across a circuit would influence the circuit. This is why high quality instruments have very high resistances—they will have very little influence if they are in parallel with another resistance.

4-5   **What does a four-channel input on an oscilloscope refer to? What is a mixed signal input?**

The number of channels refers to the number of signals that can be measured (and displayed) at the same time. A mixed signal oscilloscope usually has two analog inputs, and 16 (or more) additional digital inputs.

4-7   **A Fast Fourier Transform is used to change the x-axis from one base to another—name these bases.**

Time and Frequency

4-9   **How are pulse widths measured on a TDR? Why would anyone want to use a larger pulse width?**

Most TDRs offer choices of pulse width. The pulse width allows the pulse to travel along a cable at certain energy levels. The wider the width, the more energy transmitted and the farther the signal can travel. Sometimes, it is necessary to decrease this pulse width because the fault is close to the input side, and the width of the "regular" sized pulse would hide it. When testing a cable, it is a good idea to start with the shortest pulse width available. Pulse widths are measured in units of time.

4-11   **What is the advantage of using a Non Linear Junction Detector?**

The NLJD will detect an electronic circuit even if it is turned off.

4-13 **What is a near-field transmission? Which instrument should be used to detect near field transmissions?**

A near-field transmission is the strongest signal that is being detected. It is usually a good indicator of the transmission being generated nearby. A receiver that will lock onto the closest or strongest signal such as the CPM 700 should be used.

4-15 **Can an RF Probe such as the CPM 700 check electric lines?**

Yes. The equipment filters out the 60 Hertz electric signal.

CHAPTER 5

5-1 **How often is BICSI's Telecommunications Distribution Methods Manual (TDMM) updated?**

The manual is updated every three years to provide the latest information on techniques, methodologies, codes, and standards.

5-3 **Name three different methods of connecting components in an access control system to form a network.**

In an electronic circuit of any type, the components must be connected in some manner. This connection can take the form of wire, electromagnetism, light waves, or other types of media.

5-5 **What type of insulation would one find on cabling that is running through duct work?**

Teflon

5-7 **What is the difference between UTP and STP?**

UTP is "Unshielded" Twisted Pair, and STP is "Shielded" Twisted Pair.

5-9   **What is the difference between multi mode and single mode fiber? Which is more expensive, and why?**

There are two types of fiber, single mode and multi mode. The diameter of the fiber determines which type it is. If the diameter is 5 to 10 micrometers, it will support only one mode and is referred to as single mode. Light in single mode fiber tends to follow just one path as it bounces along. Single mode fiber is the most expensive of the two and has a cladding of 125 micrometers. The bandwidth potential of single mode fiber is over 50 MHz. Multi mode fiber is further classified as being step-index or graded-index fiber. Step index is multi mode glass or plastic with a core diameter of about 100 to 970 micrometers, and is the most often used cable. It is called *multi* mode because the core is wide enough to have light reflect at several different angles as it travels through the fiber. This creates light dispersion and there will be multiple paths as the light travels along. Graded-index fiber has a core diameter from 50–85 υm and cladding of 125 micrometers. It is used in the telecommunications field where high bandwidth is needed. A standard of 62.5 micrometers for the core is being considered as an industry standard. When discussing fiber optic cable, the nomenclature is expressed by mode, and then core and cladding diameters, such as Multi mode 62.5/125.

5-11   **Why is it frequently necessary to splice fiber cable?**

Fiber has splices because it is usually purchased in no greater lengths than 1 to 5 kilometers because it becomes difficult to pull after that, but the cable is useful at much greater lengths say 20-30 kilometers.

5-13   **What is the frequency band for HF communications?**

Three (3) to Thirty (30) MHz.

5-15   **What size wire is generally used in the telephone and security industry at a customer location? Why is it twisted?**

The wire pair, twisted at approximately 20 turns per foot, is between 22 and 26 gauge. The reason for the twist is to prevent cross talk or electromagnetic interference from wire to wire.

CHAPTER 6

6-1 **Name three different types of cameras.**

Still (Film), Still (Digital), Video or Still (Viewfinder), Still (SLR), Video

6-3 **Name an application in the security field where a still camera may be used.**

ATM, Bank, Manual Surveillance (operator held)

6-5 **What part of a DVR determines how much recording time it can handle?**

The hard drive, specifically its size.

6-7 **What is the basic difference between color and black and white film types?**

The number of emulsion coatings on the film.

6-9 **If I wanted to control depth of field by making it very broad, what would I make sure to pay attention to?**

The f-stop. For a broad (wide) depth of field, the f-stop should be a high number.

6-11 **On film, silver halide crystals make up the light areas. What makes up these areas in digital photography?**

In digital photography, there is no intermediary stage such as negatives with silver halide. The image is positive and is made up of tri-colored pixels, which vary in color and intensity.

6-13 **What is meant by the "focal length" of a lens?**

The focal length of a fixed focal length lens is indicated by the distance from the center of the lens to the focal point/plain. A lens has two focal points, one on the object side, called the primary focal point, and one on the image side, called the secondary focal point. When the term "focal point" is used alone, it means the secondary focal point.

6-15   What does the term "panchromatic" mean?

One type of black and white film is called *panchromatic*, meaning that it is affected by "all" colors.

CHAPTER 7

7-1   Approximately when did magnetic contacts first appear?

As early as 1850, magnetic contacts were used as window alarm sensors. The entire circuit consisted of a bell, a battery and magnetic contacts. A magnet attached to the window or door would hold together the contacts fastened to the adjoining frame.

7-3   What was an early method of glass break detection? How does the modern glass break sensor work?

Many years ago, glass break detectors consisted of ribbons of metallic tape that would be epoxied to the glass surface, usually around the edges of windows and glass doors. If the glass broke, ideally, a crack would work its way to a taped area, and create an open circuit by separating the tape. The tape had a certain resistance added at the end, and it would simply be set up as a closed path to the control box. This type of sensor was used in the 1800s, and can still be found at some installations.

The modern glass break detector is a small unit encapsulated in a small plastic "box" or ceiling housing similar in appearance to a smoke detector. The detector "listens" for the distinctive sound of glass breaking, and even has different types of glass breaking in its "memory." In addition to the sound sensor, the detector senses a vibration from the surface it is attached to and that vibration corresponds to the sound. If the timing of the glass break sound and vibration are concurrent, an alarm sounds.

7-5 **Besides the possibility of customer preference, why would an installer use a wireless system instead of a wired system?**

The use of wireless sensors could depend on the trade-off of labor and cost of wireless versus wired. the trade-off having to do with whether the building provides an easy path for wiring (less labor cost), or a difficult path for wiring (labor cost exceeds wireless cost).

7-7 **What is polling?**

Polling is sending a signal down the cable, or in the case of wireless, through the airwaves, and then waiting for a response. If no response is received within a specified amount of time, the system is presumed to be compromised, and some type of alarm is initiated. If the system is active, the polling alarm would be from the annunciator, and a signal would be sent to the central station. If the system is inactive, a notification would most likely show up on the face of the keypad, and the system would not allow itself to be armed without an override.

7-9 **If I were to say that a system supports Radionics Low Speed as well as Sescoa, what would I be talking about?**

These are dialer formats found in alarm systems.

7-11 **What is the purpose of little red light in the front of a motion detector?**

Usually, for setup purposes, the units have a small red light in the front, which illuminates when detecting movement from within the coverage area. This is very handy for setup, but many users erroneously leave this light on during operation. The light function should be turned off to conserve battery power, that is, unless you want people to know they are being detected.

7-13 **Name three ways to activate an alarm system.**

Not long ago the only way to activate an alarm system was to use a key activated switch at the control panel. Now, there are numerous models of keypads available, the decision being mainly determined by style preference. A system can also be activated by a key fob device, similar to one used with automobiles to lock and unlock doors. Systems can even be activated remotely, or from inside the premises, using the touchpad of a telephone. Some systems can be voice activated through the telephone.

7-15   What is involved with polling to accomplish "communications security"?

The polling signal itself is usually encrypted or sent via encryption and spread spectrum to ensure communications security.

CHAPTER 8

8-1   Besides having a picture taken for a badge at the *badging station*, where else does the video information go?

The badging station not only makes up an ID card, but it also sends pertinent personnel data, including pictures, to an employee database. This database contains access privileges, perhaps iris, retinal, or thumbprint info, and historical information.

8-3   What is the difference between a DVR and a VTR?

A VTR is a Video *Tape* Recorder and uses magnetic tape to store images. The DVR is a *Digital* Video Recorder, and stores its image on a hard drive.

8-5   What is a guard tour?

A guard tour can be set up in real time to show the location of any guard using not only the traditional guard tour stations, but also radio location devices.

8-7   Discuss how a biometric reader operates.

Quite simply, biometrics is the act of using sensors to measure many different parameters of the human body, and then make comparisons to a database.

8-9   Why would anyone want to hook up an alarm system to a WAN?

An alarm system would be connected to a WAN so that the alarm system can be monitored remotely.

8-11   The chapter stated that an alarm system at a company is set up as a "system of closed loops". What does that mean?

Each "closed loop" represents an area that can be independently turned on and off for monitoring.

8-13   What is a GUI?

A Graphical User Interface.

8-15   What is QUARTUS?

Altera's software is called QUARTUS. This software has a graphical interface and compiler as well as a more traditional programming input with compiler. The user can draw a logic diagram using symbols provided by the GUI such as gates (AND, OR, NAND, NOR), inputs, outputs, and so forth. The finished circuit can be tested by the software, checked for design errors, and then compiled. Once compiled, the operation of the circuit can be simulated, and then finally downloaded to the PLD chip.

CHAPTER 9

9-1   Name splicing activities that would call for different *types* of splices in a security installation.

Very often, it becomes necessary to splice wires together, whether for a telephone wire connection, or for alarm wiring. Red (UR) Connectors provide three openings for 19–26 AWG wire, ideal for pigtail and load coil splice applications. Yellow (UY) Connectors are used for 22–26 gauge. Green (UG) Connectors are for tapping onto 19–26 AWG wires.

9-3 **If an open circuit along a wire was suspected as a problem, and the wire ran in an underground plastic conduit, which two tools would be used to locate the open?**

We can use a time domain reflectometer to determine the distance to a fault on an underground cable, but we need another special purpose tool to determine the routing of underground cable. This tool would be the underground cable locator.

9-5 **What is a good alternative to a DMM for quickly checking whether there is voltage on a wire? Why would a technician want to use this alternative?**

A tester such as the Fluke® Voltalert AC Voltage Detector can be carried in a shirt pocket like a pen. This is a very easy device to use. Just touch the plastic tip to a control wire, conductor, or outlet. When it glows red, there is voltage on the line.

9-7 **If a technician was working with a wire pair at a workstation and wanted to determine where those wires were at the patch panel on the other side of the building, which tool would she use?**

One of the most useful testers in a security engineer's kit is the tone tester. A transmitter injects a tone onto any coax terminated with an F connector, or twisted pair and distribution cables with an adapter. It will send a signal through splitters, traps, and directional couplers, and will indicate continuity and presence of voltage on the line. The receiver can pick up the tone on terminated and unterminated cable via induction.

9-9 **What would be a good way to pull wire through a jumble of wires atop a false ceiling? What is an alternative method if there were not as much wire scattered everywhere?**

Telescoping fiberglass poles such as the Gopher Pole® will stretch out to 22 feet long from a collapsed length of 52 inches. This push-pull installation tool is used for fishing wires over long spans or hard to reach areas such as suspended ceilings, sub floors, crawl spaces, and attics.

Another handy instrument is the Cablecaster®, which is a plastic gun similar to the type kids use with suction cup darts.

CHAPTER 10

10-1 **How does the U.S. Department of Defense define access control?**

Access control is for ensuring that only authorized personnel enter a designated area.

10-3 **When was the principle of pin tumblers first used with locks?**

The first wooden locks were most likely created by several civilizations at the same time. Records show them in use over 4,000 years ago in Egypt. Secured vertically on a door post, the wooden lock contained movable pins or "pin tumblers," that gravity forced to drop into openings in the crosspiece or "bolt," and lock the door.

10-5 **How should blank access control cards and materials be stored? Why?**

Blank access control cards and materials should be stored in a security container with access limited to the security manager and one alternate. Treat blank access control cards in the same manner as sensitive documents.

10-7 **What does the term, "automated key control" refer to?**

Paper-based key control systems are time-consuming. Reports other than those contained on the single record sheet require a significant amount of time to produce.

Computer-based programs track keys and users and produce reports, such as the number of keys in the system, users, locations, and check-out/check-in data. Other programs are available to aid in core/lock rotation and maintenance, pinning/key cutting codes, and cylinder/core locations. Still others can interface with electronic locking systems to activate and deactivate locks remotely and provide specific access control for spaces and key storage.

10-9 **When controlled areas are compartmentalized, how are badges coded for access?**

When a controlled area is compartmentalized, the badge should identify specific areas of access. This is usually done using code numbers or colored stripes.

10-11   What is the principle of "badge exchange"?

In this method of access control, an individual receives a primary security identification badge. A second badge, different from the first or with different access coding, is kept inside the controlled area at all times. When access is required, security personnel exchange the second badge for the individual's primary badge. The individual wears the second badge while in the controlled area.

10-13   Explain fail-safe/fail-secure operations.

One of two operations can take place with electric door locks during a power failure. These two operations are termed fail safe and fail secure. If the power fails, the lock becomes either safe for entry and exit or secure for locked.

10-15   Refer to question 13. How does a fail-safe/fail-soft system differ from a fail-safe/fail-secure system?

If communication between the controller and the central processor is lost, the default parameters within the system are exercised. Two schemes are available to address this problem. The first, fail-safe, bans all access, even if the criterion of correct facility code is met. The fail-soft scheme, also referred to as degraded mode, normally grants access on correct facility code entry. A caution must be observed: few systems in the degraded mode record access information for later transmission to the computer when the communication line is restored.

CHAPTER 11

11-1   What is the purpose of Technical Surveillance Countermeasures?

The purpose of Technical Surveillance Countermeasures is to determine existence and location of eavesdropping or surreptitious surveillance equipment.

11-3 Why would a coach on the sidelines of a football game want to cover his mouth when he discusses strategy with another coach?

In combination with a good pair of binoculars, a lip reader can be a very effective eavesdropper.

11-5 Explain "snuggling".

Snuggling is something that many eavesdroppers do. The eavesdropper will *snuggle* or try to hide the transmission of his bug next to a stronger signal. At his listening post, the eavesdropper will use a very sensitive receiver with a narrow filter to retrieve the snuggled signal.

11-7 What is the use of an acoustic leakage detector?

Some microphones pick up sound via airwaves striking an internal disk, which then vibrates at the same rate as the airwaves. An acoustic leakage detector uses a small peg attached to a disk to measure sound vibrations. The peg is touched to the duct work and carries vibrations through the peg to the disk. The disk then vibrates against material that will change in resistance from being compressed to expanded (very minutely, of course), and then produce varying electrical signals. These electrical signals are then taken to an amplifier where they are amplified enough to hear or be recorded from a "line output."

11-9 What type of device would show division of frequencies in a wavelength division multiplexed fiber optic?

An Optical Spectrum Analyzer.

11-11 Of what use is a protector block?

This block is not only used as a patch panel, but also has fusing to protect the residential wiring from any current spikes from the outside, such as a lightening strike.

11-13 Why would a spy use a "sniffer"?

A LAN analyzer set to so-called *promiscuous mode* can literally read every piece of email that travels through the line that the analyzer is connected to. This equipment, in this configuration, is sometimes referred to as a *sniffer*, and it can be software or hardware.

11-15 What do you think the most important part of a TSCM procedure is, and why?

The physical search part of a TSCM inspection is the most time consuming, and probably the most important part of the whole process. Surprisingly, the least amount of technology in the process is used during this phase. Because of this part of the TSCM procedure, the technicians should be experienced, well trained, and very diverse in their knowledge of construction, electronics, engineering, acoustics, communications, antenna theory, and just plain common sense.

CHAPTER 12

12-1 What is the first step in an effective security program?

A complete, professional assessment of security needs is the first step toward an effective security program.

12-3 What is a risk assessment?

A risk assessment is a methodical identification and measurement of threats to a system or information processed or stored by the system, vulnerability of the system to the threats, and the probability, or risk, that a given threat could exploit the vulnerabilities.

12-5 Define business continuity.

Business continuity refers to the prevention of interruptions to normal business activity from natural or man-made disasters

12-7   Name some interruptions to normal business activity.

Fire, explosion, or environmental disaster

Blackouts or brownouts

Communications or long-term network failure

Sabotage, bombings, attacks from outside or inside

12-9   What is a FRAP?

Facilitated Risk Analysis Procedure

12-11   Name some things that should be in a "secure room".

Steel doors and protected ventilation system

First aid equipment

Phone and backup communication equipment

Fire extinguishers

Bomb blankets and hardened walls

Sand bags

Emergency tool kit

Extra food and clothing

Large flashlight and batteries

Firearms (if permitted under established policy)

12-13   Put SLE, ARO, and ALE together in a formula.

$SLE \times ARO = ALE$

12-15   What is a "supplemental survey"?

The supplemental survey is conducted when changes in organization, mission, or facility alter or affect the security posture of the facility or area.

APPENDIX C

Companies and Addresses

Alphone Corporation
1700 130th Avenue NE
Bellevue, WA 98005
425-455-0510/800-692-0200
Fax: 425-455-0071
www.aiphone.com
marketing@aiphone.com

  Access Control Communication Equipment

Alarm Lock Systems, Inc.
345 Bayview Avenue
Amityville, NY 11701
800-ALA-LOCK
Fax: 631-789-3383
www.alarmlock.com

  Door Control Hardware Locks

Allied Tube & Conduit
16100 S. Lathrop Avenue
Harvey, IL 60426
708-339-5081
Fax: 708-331-2301

Allsafe Technologies, Inc.
290 Creekside Drive
Amherst, NY 14228
716-691-0400
Fax: 716-691-0404
www.allsafe.com

Access Control Identification Products Parking

AlphaPoint, LLC
227 N. Sierra Vista
Santa Barbara, CA 93108
805-969-1263
Fax: 805-456-0165
www.alphapoint.com

Closed-Circuit Television
Digital Video Recorders
Homeland Security
IP Networking Products
Integrated Security Systems/Building Management Systems
Object Detection
Software
Surveillance
Video Encryption
Video Transmissions

ALTRONIX CORP.
140 58th Street, Building A-3W
Brooklyn, NY 11220
718-567-8181
Fax: 718-567-9056
www.altronix.com

Access Control Alarms
Closed-Circuit Television
Door Control Hardware
Integrated Security Systems/Building Management Systems
Power Sources

ALVARADO MANUFACTURING COMPANY, INC.
12660 Colony Street
Chino, CA 91710
800-423-4143
Fax: 909-628-1403
www.alvaradomfg.com
information@alvarodomfg.com

> Access Control
> Integrated Security Systems/Building Management Systems
> Perimeter Protection
> Protective Barriers

AMAG Technology
20701 Manhattan Place
Torrance, CA 90501
310-518-2380
Fax: 310-834-0685
www.amagaccess.com

> Access Control
> Biometrics
> Identification Products
> Integrated Security Systems/Building Management Systems
> Software

American Auto-Matrix
1 Technology Lane
Export, PA 15632
724-733-2000
Fax: 724-327-6124
www.aamatrix.com

> Access Control
> Asset Tracking
> Biometrics
> Identification Products
> Integrated Security Systems/Building Management Systems
> Software

American Fibertek, Inc.
120 Belmont Drive
Somerset, NJ 08873
732-302-0660
Fax: 732-302-0667

Alarms
Closed-Circuit Television
Communication Equipment
Perimeter Protection

American Security Products Company
11925 Pacific Avenue
Fontana, CA 92337
800-421-6142
Fax: 909-685-8544
www.amsecusa.com

Biometrics Locks
Safes and Security Containers

Ameristar Fence Products
P.O. Box 581000
Tulsa, OK 74158
918-835-0898
Fax: 918-877-4454
www.ameristarfence.com

Homeland Security
Integrated Security Systems/Building Management Systems
Perimeter Protection
Protective Barriers

AMICO
3245 Fayette Avenue
Birmingham, AL 35208-0928
800-366-2642/205-787-2611
Fax: 205-786-6527
www.amico-securityproducts.com

Homeland Security
Perimeter Protection
Protective Barriers

AMSECO
228 E. Star of India Lane
Carson, CA 90746
310-538-4670
Fax: 310-538-9932
www.amseco-kai.com

> Alarms
> Closed-Circuit Television
> Fire Safety
> Intrusion Detection Equipment
> Perimeter Protection

Analogic
8 Centennial Drive
Peabody, MA 01960
978-977-3000
Fax: 978-977-6809
www.analogic.com

> X-ray, Metal, Weapons, and Bomb Detection Equipment

Andover Controls
300 Brickstone Square
Andover, MA 01810
978-470-0555
Fax: 978-470-0946
www.andovercontrols.com

> Access Control
> Biometrics
> Door Control Hardware
> Identification Products
> Integrated Security Systems/Building Management Systems

Anixter, Inc.
2301 Patriot Boulevard
Glenview, IL 60025
800-323-8166
Fax: 224-521-8555
www.anixter.com

Access Control
Asset Tracking
Closed-Circuit Television
Communication Equipment
Digital Video Recorders
IP Networking Products
Signal Transmission Systems
Still Cameras/Surveillance and Evidentiary Surveillance
Video Transmissions

APOLLO
3610 Birch Street
Newport Beach, CA 92660
949-852-8178
Fax: 949-852-8172
www.apollo-security.com

Access Control
Alarms
Digital Video Recorders
Door Control Hardware
Identification Products
Integrated Security Systems/Building Management Systems
Intrusion Detection Equipment
Power Sources
Software Training

Apollo Video Technology
1331 118th Avenue SE, Suite 300
Bellevue, WA 98005
425-453-0430/800-641-1401
Fax: 425-453-0959
www.apollovideotechnology.com
sales@apollovideotechnology.com

    Closed-Circuit Television
    Covert Video
    Digital Video Recorders
    Global Positioning Systems
    Patrol Accessories
    Still Cameras/Surveillance and Evidentiary Surveillance
    Video Transmissions

APPRO TECHNOLOGY, INC.
982 Yorktown Drive
Sunnyvale, CA 94087
408-245-5708
Fax: 408-245-5105
www.approtech.com

    Closed-Circuit Television
    Covert Video
    Digital Video Recorders
    Night Vision Devices
    Surveillance
    Video Transmissions

APW Enclosure Solutions
N22-W23685 Ridgeview Parkway
Waukesha, WI 53188
262-523-7719
Fax: 262-523-7588
www.apw.com

> Bullet Resistant Systems
> Closed-Circuit Television
> Computer Security
> Crisis and Emergency Management Fire Safety
> Guard Shelters
> Homeland Security
> IP Networking Products
> Safes and Security Containers
> Technical Furniture—Consoles and Racks

The Armored Group, LLC
5221 N. Saddlerock Drive
Phoenix, AZ 85018 602-840-2271
Fax: 602-840-6162
www.armored-trucks.com

Arrow Lock Manufacturing Company
325 Duffy Avenue
Hicksville, NY 11801
516-704-2700
Fax: 516-704-2792
www.arrowlock.com

> Key Controls, Locks

ASIS International
1625 Prince Street
Alexandria, VA 22314-2818
703-519-6200
Fax: 703-519-6299
www.asisonline.org

> Certification Education
> Publications Training

ASI Technologies, Inc.
5848 N. 95th Court
Milwaukee, WI 53225
414-464-6200
Fax: 414-464-9863
www.asidoors.com

> Door Control Hardware
> Doors and Door Frames
> Homeland Security
> Perimeter Protection
> Protective Bafflers

ASSA, Inc.
110 Sargent Drive
New Haven, CT 06511
800-235-7482
Fax: 800-892-3256
www.assalock.com

> Key Controls
> Access Control
> Identification Products

Automatic Control Systems
8 Hayden Avenue
Port Washington, NY 11050
516-944-9498
Fax: 516-767-3446
www.automaticsystems.com

> Access Control
> Intrusion Detection Equipment Parking
> Perimeter Protection
> Protective Barriers

Automation Displays, Inc.
3533 N. White Avenue
Eau Claire, WI 54703
715-834-9595
Fax: 715-834-9596
www.adipanel.com

Access Control Alarms

B & B ARMR Corporation
14113 Main Street, P.O. Box 99
Norwood, LA 70761
800-367-0387
Fax: 225-629-5407
www.bb-armr.com

Access Control
Bullet Resistant Systems
Consulting Services
Guard Shelters
Homeland Security
Integrated Security Systems/Building Management Systems
Parking
Perimeter Protection
Protective Barriers

BAE SYSTEMS
6500 Tracor Lane
Austin, TX 78725-2070
512-929-2484
Fax: 512-929-2381
www.na.baesystems.com

Computer Security
Object Detection
Perimeter Protection

Bandit America, Inc.
1901 E. Lambert Road, Suite 209
La Habra, CA 90631
562-266-3100
Fax: 562-266-3103
www.banditamerica.com

> Access Control
> Alarms
> Executive Protection
> Integrated Security Systems/Building Management Systems
> Intrusion Detection Equipment
> Perimeter Protection
> Personal Protection Devices
> Protective Barriers
> Still Cameras/Surveillance and Evidentiary Surveillance

Barantec, Inc.
777 Passaic Avenue, 4th Floor
Clifton, NJ 07012
973-779-8774
Fax: 973-779-8768
www.barantec.com

> Access Control

BARCO Visual Solutions
3240 Town Point Drive
Kennesaw, GA 30144
770-218-3200
Fax: 678-460-2211
www.barco.com

> Central Station Monitoring
> Closed-Circuit Television
> Homeland Security
> IP Networking Products
> Integrated Security Systems/Building Management Systems
> Surveillance

BARTIZAN DATA SYSTEMS
217 Riverdale Avenue
Yonkers, NY 10705
800-899-BART
Fax: 914-965-7746
www.bartizan.com

Access Control Identification Products

Battery Zone, Inc.
P.O. Box 6435
Bridgewater, NJ 08807
800-824-0558
Fax: 800-664-0274
www.batteryzone.com

Power Sources

BCM Advanced Research
1 Hughes
Irvine, CA 92618
949-470-1888
Fax: 949-470-0971
www.bcmcom.com

IP Networking Products

BearCom
4009 Distribution Drive, Suite 200
Garland, TX 75041
800-252-1691
Fax: 214-765-7405
www.bearcom.com

Closed-Circuit Television
Communication Equipment
Homeland Security
IP Networking Products
Travel Safety and Security

BEI Security
12502 Exchange Drive, #408
Stafford, TX 77477
281-340-2100
Fax: 281-340-2104
www.beisecurity.com

> Access Control
> Alarms
> Closed-Circuit Television
> Homeland Security
> Intrusion Detection Equipment
> Perimeter Protection

Bekaert Specialty Films, LLC
13770 Automobile Boulevard
Clearwater, FL 33762-3818
800-282-9031
Fax: 727-540-0132
www.solargard.com

> Safety and Security Window Film

Belden Electronics Division
2200 U.S. Highway 27 South
Richmond, IN 47374
765-983-5200
Fax: 765-983-5294
www.belden.com

> Access Control
> Alarms
> Closed-Circuit Television
> Communication Equipment
> Electronic Article Surveillance
> Intrusion Detection Equipment
> Signal Transmission Systems

Bosch Security Systems
130 Perinton Parkway
Fairport, NY 14450
800-289-0096
Fax: 585-223-9180
www.boschsecurity.us

> Access Control
> Alarms
> Closed-Circuit Television
> Communication Equipment
> Digital Video Recorders
> IP Networking Products
> Integrated Security Systems/Building Management Systems
> Intrusion Detection Equipment
> Personal Protection Devices
> Surveillance

Bristol ID Technologies
1370 Rochester Street
Lima, NY 14485
585-582-5120
Fax: 585-582-5110
www.bristolid.com

> Access Control
> Forgery/Fraud Identification Products

CamLite Corporation
10221 N. 32nd Street, Suite A
Phoenix, AZ 85028
602-494-6311
Fax: 602-494-6314
www.camlite.com

> Covert Video Surveillance
> Video Transmissions

CECO Door Products, an ASSA ABLOY Group Company
9159 Telecom Drive
Milan, TN 38358
888-232-6366
Fax: 731-686-4211
www.cecodoor.com

Doors and Door Frames

Chance-i USA Corp.
43 Corporate Park, Suite 200
Irvine, CA 92606
949-833-1010
Fax: 949-833-1015
www.divisdvr.com

Central Station Monitoring
Closed-Circuit Television
Digital Video Recorders
Security Personnel
Software
Still Cameras/Surveillance and Evidentiary Surveillance
Video Transmissions

Checkpoint Systems, Inc.
101 Wolf Drive
Thorofare, NJ 08086
800-257-5540
Fax: 856-845-8355
www.checkpointsystems.com

Access Control
Asset Tracking
Closed-Circuit Television
Electronic Article Surveillance Identification Products
Software

CIM USA
10813 N.W. 30th Street, Suite 108
Miami, FL 33172
305-639-3040
Fax: 305-639-3060
www.cim-usa.com

Access Control Identification Products

CISCOR
2411 S. Classen Boulevard
Norman, OK 73071
405-447-4955
Fax: 405-447-0254
www.ciscorcom

Access Control Alarms
Asset Tracking
Closed-Circuit Television
Communication Equipment
Covert Video Executive Protection
Intrusion Detection Equipment

CitySafe, Inc.
312 Squankum Yellowbrook Road
Farmingdale, NJ 07727
732-751-0100
Fax: 732-751-1800
www.citysafe.com

Safes and Security Containers

Clark Security Products
7520 Mission Valli Road
San Diego, CA 92108
800-542-5625
Fax: 619-718-9755
www.clarksecurity.com

    Access Control
    Biometrics
    Closed-Circuit Television
    Door Control Hardware
    Doors and Door Frames
    Key Controls
    Locks
    Safes and Security Containers

Clinton Electronics Corporation
6701 Clinton Road
Loves Park, IL 61111
815-633-1444
Fax: 815-633-8712
www.clintonelectronics.com

    Access Control
    Closed-Circuit Television
    Digital Video Recorders
    Intrusion Detection Equipment
    Still Cameras/Surveillance and Evidentiary Surveillance

Cogent Systems, Inc.
209 Fair Oaks Avenue
South Pasadena, CA 91030
626-799-8090
Fax: 626-799-8996
www.cogentsystems.com

    Access Control
    Biometrics
    Computer Security
    Employee Screening
    Homeland Security
    Identification Products

ColorID
20480-F Chartwell Center Drive
Cornelius, NC 28031
704-987-2238
Fax: 704-987-2240
www.colorid.com

Identification Products

Compu-Lock
29 Harwich Circle
Westwood, MA 02090
781-440-9900
Fax: 781-440-9903
www.compu-lock.com
sales@compu-lock.com

Computer Security Locks

CORBIN RUSSWIN Architectural Hardware, an ASSA ABLOY Group Company
425 Episcopal Road
Berlin, CT 06037
800-543-3658
Fax: 800-447-6714
www.corbin-russwin.com

Access Control
Door Control Hardware Key Controls
Locks

Corrugated Metals, Inc.
4800 South Hoyne Avenue
Chicago, IL 60609
773-254-1611
Fax:773-254-1106
www.corrugated-metals.com

Blast Mitigation
Fixed Shades
Bullet Resistant Systems
Homeland Security
Perimeter Protection

CPFilms, Inc.
4210 The Great Road
Fieldale, VA 24089
800-255-8627
Fax: 276-627-3032

Safety and Security Window Film

CPI Card Group
10368 W. Centennial Road
Littleton, CO 80127
303-973-9311
Fax: 303-973-8420
www.cpicardgroup.com
info@cpicardgroup.com

Access Control Identification Products

Custom Vault Corporation
162 Danbury Road
Ridgefield, CT 06877
203-431-7646
Fax: 203-431-7656
www.customvault.com

Safes and Security Containers

DAC Industries, Inc.
615 11th Street, NW
Grand Rapids, MI 49504
616-235-0140
Fax: 616-235-2901
www.dacindustries.com

Access Control
Homeland Security
Perimeter Protection
Protective Barriers

Dallas Semiconductor/ MAXIM
4401 S. Beltwood Parkway
Dallas, TX 75244
972-371-4000
Fax: 972-371-3715
www.ibutton.com

  Access Control
  Asset Tracking
  Biometrics
  Computer Security Identification Products Key Controls
  Locks
  Patrol Accessories

Deggy Corp.
600 Bricked Avenue, Suite 604
Miami, FL 33131
305-377-2233
Fax: 305-377-8711
www.deggy.com

  Identification Products
  Patrol Accessories

Deister Electronics
9303 Grant Avenue
Manassas, VA 20110
703-368-2739
Fax: 703-368-9791
www.deister.com

  Access Control
  Biometrics
  Key Controls
  Patrol Accessories

Detex Corporation
302 Detex Drive
New Braunfels, TX 78130
830-629-2900
Fax: 830-620-6711
www.detex.com

> Access Control
> Alarms
> Door Control Hardware
> Integrated Security Systems/Building Management Systems
> Key Controls
> Locks
> Patrol Accessories
> Perimeter Protection

Diebold, Inc.
5995 Mayfair Road, NW
North Canton, OH 44720
330-489-4129
Fax: 330-489-4272
www.diebold.com

> Access Control
> Alarms
> Biometrics
> Central Station Monitoring
> Closed-Circuit Television
> Homeland Security
> Integrated Security Systems/Building Management Systems
> Intrusion Detection Equipment
> Still Cameras/Surveillance and Evidentiary Surveillance

Digital Infrared Imaging
174 Semoran Commerce Place, Suite 111
Apopka, FL 32703
407-884-0202
Fax: 407-884-8282
www.dii-llc.com

Closed-Circuit Television
Digital Video Recorders
Intrusion Detection Equipment
Night Vision Devices Object Detection
Perimeter Protection
Still Cameras/Surveillance and Evidentiary Surveillance

Direct Low Voltage Supply
P.O. Box 7429
St. Matthews, KY 40257
800-471-3562
Fax: 800-471-3566
www.directlvs.com
info@directlvs.com

Access Control
Closed-Circuit Television
Covert Video
Digital Video Recorders
Homeland Security
Mirrors
Pilferage
Still Cameras/Surveillance and Evidentiary Surveillance
Video Transmissions

Diversified Optical Products
282 Main Street
Salem, NH 03079
603-898-1880
Fax: 603-893-4359
www.diop.com

Perimeter Protection
Still Cameras/Surveillance and Evidentiary Surveillance

DMP
2500 N. Partnership Boulevard
Springfield, MO 65803-8877
417-831-9362/800-641-4282
Fax: 417-831-1325/800-743-5724
www.dmp.com

> Access Control
> Alarms
> Central Station Monitoring
> Fire Safety
> IP Networking Products
> Integrated Security Systems/Building Management Systems
> Intrusion Detection Equipment

DoorKing, Inc.
120 Glasgow Avenue
Inglewood, CA 90301
800-826-7493
Fax: 310-641-1586
www.doorking.com
info@doorking.com

> Access Control
> Homeland Security
> Identification Products
> Integrated Security Systems/Building Management Systems
> Locks
> Parking
> Perimeter Protection

Dortronics Systems, Inc.
1668 Sag Harbor Turnpike
Sag Harbor, NY 11963
631-725-0505
Fax: 631-725-8148
www.dortronics.com
sales@dortronics.com

> Access Control
> Door Control Hardware Locks

DSI (Designed Security, Inc.)
1402 Hawthorne Street
Bastrop, TX 78602-9820
512-321-4426
Fax: 512-321-9181
www.dsigo.com

  Access Control
  Alarms
  Door Control Hardware
  Homeland Security
  Integrated Security Systems/Building Management Systems
  Intrusion Detection Equipment
  Key Controls
  Object Detection
  Perimeter Protection
  Still Cameras/Surveillance and Evidentiary Surveillance

DSX Access Systems, Inc.
10731 Rockwall Road
Dallas, TX 75238-1219
888-419-8353
Fax: 214-553-6147
www.dsxinc.com
sales@dsxinc.com

  Access Control
  Alarms
  Central Station Monitoring
  Homeland Security
  Integrated Security Systems/Building Management Systems

DVTel, Inc.
52 Forest Avenue
Paramus, NJ 07652
201-368-9700
Fax: 201-368-2615
www.dvtel.com
info@dvtel.com

Closed-Circuit Television
Communication Equipment
Digital Video Recorders
IP Networking Products
Integrated Security Systems/Building Management Systems
Video Transmissions

DynaLock Corp.
P.O. Box 2728
Bristol, CT 06011-2728
860-582-4761
Fax: 860-585-0338
www.dynalock.com

Access Control
Door Control Hardware
Locks
Power Sources

Eastman Security, division of Eastman Telebell International
15436 Valley Boulevard
City of Industry, CA 91746
800-526-7777
Fax: 626-336-1939
www.eastmansecurity.com

Closed-Circuit Television Covert Video
Digital Recorders
Video Transmissions Weapons

ECSI International, Inc.
P.O. Box 677
790 Bloomfield Avenue, C-1
Clifton, NJ 07012
973-574-8555
Fax: 973-574-8562
www.ecsiintemational.com

> Homeland Security
> Integrated Security Systems/Building Management Systems
> Intrusion Detection Equipment
> Perimeter Protection
> Personal Protection Devices

ELMO
1478 Old Country Road
Plainview, NY 11803
800-947-3566
Fax: 516-501-0429
www.elmousa.com

> Closed-Circuit Television
> Digital Video Recorders
> IP Networking Products
> Night Vision Devices

EMC Corporation
42 South Street
Hopkinton, MA 01748
508-435-1000
Fax: 508-249-6213
www.emc.com

> Covert Video
> Digital Video Recorders
> Homeland Security
> Pilferage
> Still Cameras/Surveillance and Evidentiary Surveillance
> Threat Assessments
> Travel Safety and Security
> Video Encryption
> Video Transmissions

EMCOR Enclosures
1600 4th Avenue, NW
Rochester, MN 55901
507-287-3535
Fax: 507-287-3405

 Access Control
 Central Station Monitoring
 Closed-Circuit Television
 Communication Equipment
 Homeland Security
 IP Networking Products
 Integrated Security Systems/Building Management Systems
 Surveillance
 Technical Furniture—Consoles and Racks

EMIT Technologies, LLC
2206 Queen Anne Avenue North, #301
Seattle, WA 98109
206-378-5518
Fax: 206-378-5516
www.emittech.com

 Access Control
 Biometrics
 Employee Screening Homeland Security
 Object Detection
 Perimeter Protection
 Substance Abuse
 Threat Assessments
 Travel Safety and Security
 X-ray, Metal, Weapons, and Bomb Detection Equipment

Emsec Systems, LLC
P.O. Box 1679
Wake Forest, NC 27588-1679
919-562-4900
Fax: 919-562-4901
www.emsecsystems.com

Computer Security
Countereavesdropping
Executive Protection
Homeland Security
Integrated Security Systems/Building Management Systems
Personal Protection Devices

EPS, Inc.
78 Apple Street
Tinton Falls, NJ 07724
732-747-8277
Fax: 732-530-4726
www.epscorp.com

Access Control
Closed-Circuit Television
Communication Equipment
Covert Video
Identification Products
Integrated Security Systems/Building Management Systems
Perimeter Protection
Software
Surveillance

ESSEX Industries, an ASSA ABLOY Group Company
110 Sargent Drive
New Haven, CT 06511
203-624-5225
Fax: 203-777-9042
www.essexopenings.com

Access Control
Door Control Hardware Key Controls

Fargo Electronics, Inc.
6533 Flying Cloud Drive
Eden Prairie, MN 55344
800-459-5636
Fax: 952-941-7836
www.fargo.com

> Access Control
> Biometrics
> Homeland Security
> Identification Products

Farpointe Data, Inc.
2177 Leghorn Street
Mountain View, CA 94043
650-964-2615
Fax: 650-988-6687
www.pyramidseries.com

> Access Control
> Biometrics
> Door Control Hardware
> IP Networking Products
> Identification Products Parking

FLIR Systems, Inc.
16505 S.W. 72nd Avenue
Portland, OR 97224
503-684-3731
Fax: 503-684-3207
www.flir.com

> Closed-Circuit Television
> Night Vision Devices
> Perimeter Protection

FORECAST CONSOLES, INC.
367C Bay Shore Road
Deer Park, NY 11729
800-735-2070
Fax: 631-253-0277
www.forecast-consoles.com
info@forecast-consoles.com

    Technical Furniture—Consoles and Racks

Fujinon, Inc.
10 High Point Drive
Wayne, NJ 07470-7431
973-633-5600
Fax: 973-633-5216
www.fujinoncctv.com

    Closed-Circuit Television

Fuji Photo Film USA
1100 King Georges Post Road
Edison, NJ 08818
800-659-3854
www.fujifilm.com

    Identification Products
    Still Cameras/Surveillance and Evidentiary

Garrett Metal Detectors
1881 W. State Street
Garland, TX 75042-6797
800-234-6151
Fax: 972-494-1881
www.garrett.com

    X-ray, Metal, Weapons, and Bomb Detection Equipment

General Lock Service
4775 Viewridge Avenue
San Diego, CA 92123
877-819-6039
Fax: 858-974-5269
www.generallockservice.com

> Access Control
> Alarms
> Biometrics
> Closed-Circuit Television
> Door Control Hardware
> Doors and Door Frames
> Key Controls
> Locks
> Safes and Security Containers

Genwac, Inc./Watec Company, Ltd.
60 Dutch Hill Road, Suite 6
Orangeburg, NY 10962
845-359-1490
Fax: 845-359-1391
www.wateccameras.com

> Closed-Circuit Television

GE Security
300 W. 6th Street, Suite 1850
Austin, TX 78701
800-469-1676
Fax: 714-427-2098
www.gesecurity.com

> Access Control
> Central Station Monitoring
> Chemical Trace Detection
> Closed-Circuit Television
> Covert Video
> Digital Video Recorders
> Fire Safety
> Homeland Security
> Intrusion Detection Equipment
> Video Transmissions

GlassLock, Inc.
461 Perrymont Avenue
San Jose, CA 95125
408-999-0979
Fax: 408-999-0993
www.glasslock.com

> Blast Mitigation
> Fixed Shades
> Bullet Resistant Systems
> Homeland Security

Globe Amerada Architectural Glass
616 Selfield Road
Selma, AL 36703
800-633-2513
Fax: 334-875-2704
www.security-glazing.com

> Blast Mitigation
> Fixed Shades
> Bullet Resistant Systems
> Doors and Door Frames
> Fire Safety
> Perimeter Protection
> Safety and Security Window

Govsupply—a Division of Intellimar, Inc.
7566 Main Street, Suite 113
Sykesville, MD 21784
410-552-9950
Fax: 410-552-9939
www.govsupply.com

> Blast Mitigation
> Fixed Shades
> Chemical Trace Detection
> Door Control Hardware
> Guard Shelters
> Perimeter Protection
> Safety and Security Window Film

Harrington Signal
2519 4th Avenue
Moline, IL 61265
309-762-0731/800-577-5758
Fax: 309-757-8579
www.harringtonfire.com

> Alarms
> Communication Equipment
> Fire Safety
> Homeland Security
> Integrated Security Systems/Building Management Systems
> Signal Transmission Systems

HID Corporation—an ASSA ABLOY Group Company
9292 Jeronimo Road
Irvine, CA 92618-1905
949-598-1600
Fax: 949-598-1690
www.htdcorp.com

> Access Control
> Biometrics
> Computer Security
> Homeland Security

Hirsch Electronics
1900 Carnegie Avenue, Building B
Santa Ana, CA 92705-5520
949-250-8888
Fax: 949-250-7372
www.HirschElectronics.com

> Access Control
> Alarms
> Biometrics
> Closed-Circuit Television
> Homeland Security
> Identification Products
> Integrated Security Systems/Building Management Systems
> Intrusion Detection Equipment
> Software

Honeywell
172 Michael Drive
Syosset, NY 11791
516-921-6704
Fax: 516-921-1661
www.security.honeywell.com

> Access Control
> Alarms
> Closed-Circuit Television
> Digital Video Recorders
> Integrated Security Systems/Building Management Systems
> Intrusion Detection Equipment
> Perimeter Protection
> Personal Protection Devices
> Still Cameras/Surveillance and Evidentiary Surveillance

Hunt Electronic USA, Inc.
978 W. 10th Street
Azusa, CA 91702
626-812-8868
Fax: 626-812-8828
www.huntcctv.com

> Closed-Circuit Television
> Covert Video
> Digital Video Recorders
> Homeland Security
> IP Networking Products
> Signal Transmission Systems
> Video Transmissions

Hy-Security Gate Operators
1200 W. Nickerson Street
Seattle, WA 98119
800-321-9947
Fax: 206-286-0614/888-321-9946
www.hy-security.com

> Access Control
> Homeland Security
> Perimeter Protection

ICONICS, INC.
100 Foxborough Boulevard
Foxborough, MA 02035
508-543-8600
Fax: 508-543-1503
www.iconics.com

> Access Control
> Biometrics
> Computer Security
> Database
> IP Networking Products
> Integrated Security Systems/Building Management Systems
> Intrusion Detection Equipment
> Project Management
> Signal Transmission Systems
> Software

IDenticard
40 Citation Lane, P.O. Box 5349
Lancaster, PA 17606-5349
800-233-0298
Fax: 717-569-2390
www.identicard.com

> Access Control
> Biometrics
> Identification Products
> Integrated Security Systems/Building Management Systems

Ikegami Electronics
37 Brook Avenue
Maywood, NJ 07607
201-368-9171
Fax: 201-569-1626
www.ikegami.com

> Closed-Circuit Television
> Covert Video
> Electronic Article Surveillance

INDALA
6850 B Santa Teresa Boulevard
San Jose, CA 95119
408-361-4700
Fax: 408-361-4701
www.indala.com

Access Control Identification Products

INDIGO SYSTEMS, A DIVISION OF FLIR SYSTEMS
70 Castilian Drive
Goleta, CA 93117
805-964-9797
Fax: 805-685-2711
www.indigosystems.com

Covert Video
Digital Video Recorders Forgery/Fraud
Integrated Security Systems/Building Management Systems
Night Vision Devices Object Detection
Perimeter Protection Surveillance

IndigoVision, Ltd.
1 Merrimack Street, Suite 200
Haverhill, MA 01830
978-556-9955/866-556-9955
Fax: 978-556-0842
www.indigovision.com

Closed-Circuit Television
IP Networking Products
Software
Surveillance
Video Transmissions

InstaKey Security System
1498 S. Lipan Street
Denver, CO 80223
800-316-5397/303-761-9999
Fax: 303-761-6359
www.instakey.com

Access Control Locks

INTELLIKEY Corporation
4325 Woodland Park Drive, Suite 102
Melbourne, FL 32904
321-724-5595
Fax: 321-724-5695
www.intellikey.com

> Access Control
> Biometrics
> Door Control Hardware
> Key Controls
> Locks
> Safes and Security Containers

International Fiber Systems/GE
16 Commerce Road
Newtown, CT 06470
203-426-1180
Fax: 203-426-3326
www.ifs.com

> Access Control
> Closed-Circuit Television
> Communication Equipment
> Consulting Services
> Integrated Security Systems/Building Management Systems
> Signal Transmission Systems
> Surveillance
> Video Transmissions

IR Security & Safety
111 Congressional Boulevard, Suite 200
Carmel, IN 46032
317-805-5679
Fax:317-805-5777
www.securityandsafety.com

> Access Control
> Biometrics
> Door Control Hardware
> Doors and Door Frames
> Key Controls
> Locks

Jamieson Manufacturing Company
12300-A Amelia Drive
Houston, TX 77045
713-434-7907/888-286-3362
Fax: 713-434-7924
www.jamiesonfence.com

> Access Control
> Alarms
> Closed-Circuit Television
> Identification Products
> Key Controls
> Perimeter Protection
> Protective Barriers
> Surge Protectors

JVC Professional Products Company
1700 Valley Road
Wayne, NJ 07470
973-317-5000
Fax: 973-317-5030
www.jvc.com

> Closed-Circuit Television
> Digital Video Recorders
> IP Networking Products
> Surveillance
> Video Encryption
> Video Transmissions

Kouba & Associates, Inc.
P.O. Box 1036
Bastrop, TX 78602
512-303-5033
Fax: 512-321-4692
www.koubasystems.com

> Access Control
> Alarms
> Door Control Hardware
> Perimeter Protection

LG Electronics, IRIS Tech Division
1095 Cranbury S. River Road, Suite 1
Jamesburg, NJ 08831
609-860-8456
Fax: 609-860-0666

Access Control

Lenel Systems International
1212 Pittsford-Victor Road
Pittsford, NY 14534-3816
585-248-9720
Fax: 585-248-9185
www.lenel.com

Access Control
Identification Products
Integrated Security Systems/Building Management Systems

March Networks
555 Legget Drive, Tower B, Suite 140
Ottawa, ON K2K 2X3
CANADA
613-591-8181/800-563-5564
Fax: 613-591-7337
www.marchnetworks.com

Closed-Circuit Television
Digital Video Recorders
Global Positioning System
Homeland Security
1P Networking Products
Software
Surveillance
Travel Safety and Security Video Transmissions

Marks USA
5300 New Horizons Boulevard
Amityville, NY 11701
631-225-5400
Fax: 631-225-6136
www.marksusa.com

> Access Control
> Door Control Hardware Locks

Marshall Electronics, Inc.
1910 E. Maple Avenue
El Segundo, CA 90245
310-333-0606
Fax: 310-333-0688
www.inars-cam.com

> Closed-Circuit Television

Master-Halco
4000 W. Metropolitan Drive, Suite 400
Orange, CA 92868
714-385-0091
Fax: 714-385-0107
www.FenceOnline.com

> Access Control
> Consulting Services
> Integrated Security Systems/Building Management Systems
> Intrusion Detection Equipment
> Perimeter Protection

Matrix Systems, Inc.
7550 Paragon Road
Dayton, OH 45459
800-562-8749
Fax: 937-438-0900
www.matrixsys.com

> Access Control
> Alarms
> Integrated Security Systems/Building Management Systems

Medeco High Security Locks
3625 Allegheny Drive
Salem, VA 24153
800-839-3157
Fax: 800-421-6615
www.medeco.com
comments@medeco.com

    Key Controls Locks

Mitsubishi Digital Electronics America, Inc.
9351 Jeronimo Road
Irvine, CA 92618
949-465-6000
Fax: 949-465-6338
www.mitsubishi-imaging.com

    Digital Video Recorders

Morse Watchman, Inc.
2 Morse Road
Oxford, CT 06478
203-264-4949
Fax: 203-264-8367
www.morsewatchman.com

    Access Control
    Guard Services
    Key Controls
    Patrol Accessories

NAPCO Security Group
333 Bayview Avenue
Amityville, NY 11701
631-842-9400
Fax: 631-789-3363
www.napcosecurity.com

Access Control
Alarms
Fire Safety
Identification Products
Integrated Security Systems/Building Management Systems
Locks

NAVCO Security Systems
1300 Kellogg Drive
Anaheim, CA 92807
800-776-2623
Fax: 714-779-2619
www.navco.com

Access Control
Alarms
Closed-Circuit Television
Digital Video Recorders

ObjectVideo
11600 Sunrise Valley Drive
Reston, VA 20191
703-654-9300
Fax: 703-654-9399
www.objectvideo.com

Homeland Security
Object Detection
Perimeter Protection
Software
Surveillance

Optex
1845 W. 205th Street
Torrance, CA 90501
800-966-7839
Fax: 310-533-5910
www.optexamerica.com

Panasonic Security Systems
Three Panasonic Way, Panazip 2H-2
Secaucus, NJ 07094
866-726-2288
Fax: 866-808-9115
www.panasonic.com

> Biometrics
> Closed-Circuit Television
> Digital Video Recorders
> Homeland Security
> IP Networking Products
> Identification Products
> Still Cameras/Surveillance and Evidentiary Surveillance
> Travel Safety and Security
> Video Transmissions

PCSC
3541 Challenger Street
Torrance, CA 90503
310-638-0400
Fax: 310-638-6204
www.1pcsc.com

> Asset Tracking
> Closed-Circuit Television
> Door Control Hardware
> Integrated Security Systems/Building Management Systems

Pelco
3500 Pelco Way
Clovis, CA 93612
800-289-9100/559-292-1981
Fax: 559-294-3782
www.pelco.com

> Closed-Circuit Television
> Digital Video Recorders

Pentax Imaging Company
600 12th Street, Suite 300
Golden, CO 80401
800-877-0155
Fax: 303-728-0393
www.pentax.com

> Closed-Circuit Television
> Covert Video
> Digital Video Recorders
> IP Networking Products
> Still Cameras/Surveillance and Evidentiary Surveillance

Perimeter Defense Technologies
4315 S. County Road 1290
Odessa, TX 79765-9506
432-561-8006
Fax: 432-561-8031
www.perimeterdefensetech.com

> Perimeter Protection
> Protective Barriers

Porta-King Building Systems
4133 Shoreline Drive
Earth City, MO 63045
800-284-5346
Fax: 314-291-2857
www.portaking.com

> Access Control
> Guard Shelters
> Parking
> Smoking Shelters

ProxID
97-77 Queens Boulevard, Suite 630
Rego Park, NY 11374
718-830-0755
Fax: 718-830-0529
www.proxid.com

> Access Control
> Computer Security
> Digital Video Recorders
> Patrol Accessories Software

Research Electronics International, LLC
455 Security Place
Algood, TN 38506
931-537-6032
Fax: 931-537-6089
www.reiusa.net

> Countereavesdropping
> Training

Richardson Electronics, Security Systems Division
13105 NW Freeway, Suite 900
Houston, TX 77040
800-772-CCTV
Fax: 713-996-3850

> Closed-Circuit Television
> Video Transmissions

SARGENT & GREENLEAF, INC.
1 Security Drive
Nicholasville, KY 40356
859-885-9411
Fax: 859-885-3063
www.sargentandgreenleaf.com

    Access Control
    Biometrics

Schlage—see IR Security & Safety
111 Congressional Boulevard, Suite 200
Carmel, IN 46032
317-805-5679
Fax: 317-805-5777

    Access Control
    Door Control Hardware
    Key Controls
    Locks

Securitron Magnalock Corp.
550 Vista Boulevard
Sparks, NV 89434-6632
775-355-5625/800-624-5625
Fax: 775-355-5636
www.securitron.com

    Access Control
    Door Control Hardware
    Homeland Security
    Locks
    Power Sources

Simplex Grinnell
100 Simplex Drive
Westminster, MA 01441-0001
978-731-2500
Fax: 978-731-7899
www.simplexgrinnell.com

> Access Control
> Alarms
> Central Station Monitoring
> Closed-Circuit Television
> Communication Equipment
> Identification Products
> Integrated Security Systems/Building Management Systems
> Intrusion Detection Equipment
> Perimeter Protection

SONITROL CORPORATION
1000 Westlakes Drive, Suite 150
Berwyn, PA 19312
610-725-9706
Fax: 610-725-9707

> Access Control
> Central Station Monitoring
> Closed-Circuit Television
> Integrated Security Systems/Building Management Systems
> Intrusion Detection Equipment
> Still Cameras/Surveillance and Evidentiary Video Transmissions

Sony Security Products
Sony Drive
Park Ridge, NJ 07656
201-358-4954
Fax: 201-358-4927
www.sony.com

> Access Control
> Closed-Circuit Television
> Digital Video Recorders
> Homeland Security
> IP Networking Products
> Integrated Security Systems/Building Management Systems
> Surveillance
> Video Transmissions

Southwest Microwave, Inc.
Security Systems Division
9055 S. McKerny Street
Tempe, AZ 85284-2946
480-783-0201
Fax: 480-783-0401
www.southwestmicrowave.com

> Alarms
> Homeland Security
> Intrusion Detection Equipment
> Perimeter Protection
> Signal Transmission Systems
> Video Transmissions

Toshiba Security Products
9740 Irvine Boulevard
Irvine, CA 92618-1697
800-550-8674
Fax: 949-470-9390
www.cctv.toshiba.com

> Central Station Monitoring
> Closed-Circuit Television
> Digital Video Recorders
> Homeland Security
> IP Networking Products
> Perimeter Protection
> Still Cameras/Surveillance and Evidentiary Surveillance
> Travel Safety and Security

Triplett Test and Measurement
1 Triplett Drive
Bluffton, OH 45817
800-874-7538/800-TRIPLETT
Fax: 419-358-7956
www.triplett.com

Tyco Fire & Security
6600 Congress Avenue, B40
Boca Raton, FL. 33431
561-912-6108
Fax: 561-912-6625
www.tycosecuritybusinesspartners.com

> Asset Tracking
> Central Station Monitoring
> Closed-Circuit Television
> Identification Products
> Integrated Security Systems/Building Management Systems

VistaScape Security Systems
5901-B Peachtree-Dunwoody Road, Suite 550
Atlanta, GA 30328
678-919-1130
Fax: 678-919-1142
www.vistascape.com

Closed-Circuit Television
Homeland Security
Intrusion Detection Equipment
Object Detection
Perimeter Protection
Still Cameras/Surveillance and Evidentiary Surveillance

Watec America Corp.
3155 E. Patrick Lane
Las Vegas, NV 89120
702-434-6111
Fax: 702-434-3222

Closed-Circuit Television
Covert Video

Yale Commercial Locks & Hardware, an ASSA ABLOY Group Company
100 Yale Avenue
Lenoir City, TN 37771
800-438-1951
Fax: 800-338-0965
www.yalecommercial.com

Access Control
Door Control Hardware Key Controls
Locks

INDEX

Numerics

620K Security/Alarm kit 234
802.11(a) standard 137–138
802.11(b) standard 137
802.11(g) standard 138–139

A

aberrations 147, 151
access authorization 270
    anti-passback 272
    occupant listing 271
    time zoning 271
access control 248
    centers 253
    credential disposal 254
    defined 325
    devices 207
    electronic 253–254
    levels of protection 248–249
    lockout procedures 254
    personnel termination 254
    records management 254
access control cards 259–262
    high resistance 261–262
    low resistance 259–260
    moderate resistance 260–261
    protection of 254
access control systems 256
    accessories 269–270
    anti-passback 272
    automated 259

badge readers 262
badges 257–258
    cards 259–262
    central controllers 266–269
    components of 255–256
    electric door locks 265–266
    equipment-based 258
    fail-safe 265
    fail-safe/fail-soft 271
    fail-secure 265
    general applications 272–273
    multiple authorization 270–271
    occupant listing 271
    personnel-based 256–257
    secondary verification 262–264
active electronic cards 261
alarm switch monitors 269
alarm systems 175
    activation 192
    brief history 174–175
    components 206
    control units 175–190
    false alarms 194–198
    fire detectors 192
    gas detectors 192
    glass break detectors 191
    installer training and licensing
        199–201
    integrity of 193–194
    motion detectors 190–191
    photoelectric beams 191–192
    smoke detectors 192
    switches 46–47, 192

alternating current (AC) 36–39
American National Standards Institute (ANSI) 325
American Society for Testing and Materials (ASTM) 326
ammeters 88
amplitude modulation 39
analytic system and software for evaluating safeguards and security (ASSESS) 221
annualized loss expectancy (ALE) 310–311
anti-passback 249, 272, 325
aperture 151
Ares III watchman system 213–214
assessment 317
astigmatism 151
AutoCAD (software) 220
auto-iris lenses 148

B

badges 257–258
badging stations 206
bandwidth 75, 151
bar code cards 260
barrel key 326
baseband 75
Bayonet Neill-Concelman (BNC) connector 127
beepers 112–113
binary phase shift keying (BPSK) 138
binary system 75–77
biological attacks 11–13
biometric systems 70, 257
bit key 326
bitting 326
black and white films 153
blade 326
block check character 78
Bluetooth 73, 139
Boolean identities 51–52
bow 327
branch currents 32

broadband 75
bugs 301
building master key 327
bumper beepers 112–113
business continuity 307–309
butt sets 239

C

cable analyzers 102
cable checkers 238
cable testers 232
Cablecaster® 241
cables 61
    categories 128
    coaxial 127
    fiber optics 131–132
    running 242–243
    telephone lines 293–294
    topologies 130
CableTracker® 233
CAD software 219–221
CAD X11 (software) 220
CADKEY (software) 220
CADopia IntelliCAD (software) 220
CADVANCE (software) 220
cameras 146
    charge coupled devices (CCDs) 156
    film 153–154
    lenses 146–153
    pan, tilt, and zoom (PTZ) 159
    signals 158
    sizes 157–158
    still 146
    surveillance system 166–168
    video processing and storage 159–168
    video tube technology video cameras 154–156
capacitance access control cards 261
capacitor microphones 281
carbon microphones 281
carpet tape 241
carrier frequency 39
cathode ray tube (CRT) 154
central control unit 266–269

central processor 268
change key 327
charge coupled devices (CCDs) 156
chemical attacks 11–13
chromatic aberration 147
closed circuit television (CCTV) 5–6, 116, 207
coaxial cable 127
coded orthogonal frequency division multiplexing (COFDM) 138
codes 327
cold sites 309
color cameras 154
color films 153
coma 151
commercial phone lines 299–300
communications systems 59
    bandwidth 75
    binary 75–77
    data 68–72
    error checking 78
    open systems interface (OSI) platform 79
    radio frequency (RF) 62–68
    speech 60
    spread spectrum 73–74
    wireline 60–62
complementary code keying (CCK) 138
complex lens 151
complex programmable logic devices (CPLDs) 217
compound lens 151
compromise 327
computers 206
concentric rings theory 17–18
condenser lens 151
condenser microphones 281
conjugates 151
connectors 127
construction key 327
contact memory buttons 261
contingency plan 319
control key 327
control units 175

Vista-10P 176–180
Vista-250P 180–190
core 327
counterfactual historical analysis 16
covert threats 248, 328
CPM-700 radio frequency (RF) probe 109
    auxiliary input amplifier 114
    body transmitters 112
    cable and closed circuit TV 116–117
    computers and related equipment 116
    frequencies 109–110
    infrared link radio frequency (RF) probes 117
    outside flooding 116
    phone line audio test 114
    power 110
    room monitoring 112
    sweep 110–111
    telephone sweep 112
    Tempest approved equipment 115
    tracking devices 112–113
    uses of 290
    very low frequency (VLF) 113–114
    video transmitters 111
    video/audio valuation 114–115
crime prevention assessment 306–307
crimpers 240
critical paths 14–16
criticality 319
cross talk 126
customer service office 314
cyclic redundancy check (CRC) 78
cylinder 328

D

data communications 68–72
DataCAD (software) 220
decibels 43–45
Deggy controls 214
delay 317
dense wavelength division multiplexing (DWDM) 133
design software 217

DesignCAD 3-D MAX (software) 220
detection 317
dielectric materials 127
digital electronics 50
digital multimeter (DMM). See multimeters
digital video recorder (DVR) 163–165
direct current (DC) 31
direct sequence spread spectrum (DSSS) 73, 137, 289
disaster recovery plans 307–309
distortion 151
double-bit key 328
doublet 151
DSP-4300 cable tester 232
dual tone multi frequency (DTMF) 299

E

eavesdropping 279–283
    inside walls 285–286
    listening 279–281
    microphones and wires 281–283
    radio frequency (RF) phase 286–291
    telephone lines 291–300
    See also technical surveillance countermeasures (TSCM)
effective focal length (EFL) 151
electret microphones 281–283
electric bolt 266
electric circuit cards 260
electric door locks 265–266
electric lockset 266
electric strike 265–266
electrical wiring 126
electromagnetic locks 266
electromechanical locks 258
emergency master key 328
enclave 328
enrollment console 267–268
equal level FEXT (ELFEXT) 130
erbium doped fiber amplifiers (EDFA) 133
error checking 78
espionage 278–279

estimate of adversary sequence interruption (EASI) 222
executive information file 312–313
expert systems 206
eye scanning systems 264

F

facilitated risk analysis procedure (FRAP) 309–310
facility protection 318
fail-safe operation 265, 271
fail-secure operation 265
fail-soft operation 271
fall time 70
false alarms 194–198
far end cross talk (FEXT) 129
fast Fourier transforms (FFT) 94
FastCAD (software) 220
fences 7
fiber optics 131–132
    cable terminations 133
    vs. copper cables 70–72
    multiplexing 133
    wavelengths 132
field of view 152
film 153–154
fingerprint identification systems 264
fire detectors 192
fish tape 241
flooding 288–289
Fluke® Voltalert AC Voltage Detector 231
follow-up survey 320
forcible entry safeguards effectiveness model (FESEM) 221
freeCAD (software) 220
frequencies 37–38
frequency division multiplexing (FDM) 137
frequency hopping spread spectrum (FHSS) 73, 289
frequency modulation 39
front-line office 313–314

G

gas detectors 192
Generic CADD (software) 220
glass break detectors 191
Gopher Pole® 240
Graphite (software) 220
ground wave 136
GTWorks (software) 220
guard tour systems 208
    Ares III watchman 213–214
    Deggy controls 214
    iButton® 212–213
    security management system (SMS)
        214–215
guidelines 23–24

H

hand geometry 263
harmonic distortion 97
harmonic frequencies 38–39
hasp 328
Heisenberg, Werner 16
high band communications 66
high-level access control 249
high-level security 8
    examples of 8
Hollerith card 259
Home RF standard 72
hot sites 308
HVAC systems 12–13

I

iButton® 212–213
IDRAW 2000 (software) 220
IGEStoolbox (software) 221
impedance 40–42
infrared link 117
initial survey 320
insider safeguards effectiveness model
        (ISEM) 221
insulation 125
interface modules 269–270
intermediate frequency (IF) filter 95

intermodulation distortion 97
iris 152

J

Jensen Tools® JTK-45 toolkit 228–230
Jensen Tools® security screwdriver kit
        242

K

key blank 326
key change number 329
key control systems 252–253
key controllers 251–252
key indexing 329
keyed locks 258
keyed-alike system 329
keys 251
keyway 329
Kirchoff's current law 32–33
Kirchoff's voltage law 34

L

lamp cords 126
lateral color 152
Lawrence Berkeley National Laboratory
        11–13
lenses 146–153
levels of protection 248–249
light 152
limited spectrum 66
line casters 240–241
load coils 294
local area network (LAN) 69, 300–301
local loop 291–292
lock-out key 328
lockout procedures 254
locks 251
    in Colonial America 250–251
    electric 265–266
    electromechanical 258
    history of 249–250
    key control systems 252–253
    key controllers 251–252

locks (continued)
    mechanical 258
    padlocks 250
low band communications 66
low-level access control 248
low-level security 5–6
    examples of 5

M

M4000 recorder 213–214
magnetic probes 231
magnetic spot cards 260
magnetic stripe cards 260
magnification 152
Mag-Probe® 231
maison-keyed system 329
mantraps 9
master-keyed system 329
maximum-level security 8–10
    examples of 9
mechanical locks 258
medium-level access control 248–249
medium-level security 7–8
    examples of 7
metallic strip cards 260
microphones 281–283
    capacitor 281
    carbon 281
    electret 281–283
Microscanner Pro® 232
MicroStation (software) 221
microwave 136
minimum-level security 4–5
mixed technology cards 262
Modular CAD (software) 221
modulation 39
motion detectors 6, 190–191
multimeters 85–90
    ammeters 88
    digital 85
    ohmmeters 88
    specifications 89–90
    uses of 231
    voltmeters 87

multimode fiber 131
multiplexers 269
multiplexing 133
multipoint networks 130
museum security 4

N

nanometer 152
National Television System Committee
    (NTSC) 154
near end cross talk (NEXT) 129
network testers 232
networks 124, 130
non-alerting physical search 283–284
non-linear junction detector (NLJD)
    102–108
    audio demodulation 108
    breakup of nonlinear junctions 107
    frequency interference 108
    long-rate detection 107–108
    power output 104–106
    quieting effect 106–107
non-linear junctions 45–46, 102

O

objective lens 152
ObjectVideo 215–216
occupant listing 271
office security. See workplace security
Ohm's law 31–32
ohmmeters 88
open systems interface (OSI) 79
optical cards 260–261
orthogonal frequency division
    multiplexing (OFDM) 139
oscilloscopes 90–94
    analog vs. digital 90–91
    autoscale 93
    bandwidth 93
    cursors 94
    functions 38, 94
    input 93
    intensity 92
    measurements 91, 97

probes 94
sample rate 93
switches 92
timebase 92
triggering 92
voltage base 92

P

packet binary convolutional coding (PBCC-22) 139
padlocks 250, 330
Paladin Tools All-in-One Telephone Tool® 240
Paladin Tools Wire Ferrule Crimp Tool® 240
palm print recognition 264
panchromatic film 153
parity check 78
passback 257
personal identification number (PIN) 248, 263
personnel termination 254
phase modulation 39
photoelectric beams 191–192
physical search 283–285
physical security 2–3
    awareness and education 320
    customer service office 314
    elements of 317
    facility and building location 318–320
    facility protection 318
    front-line office 313–314
    planning and administration 317–320
    surveys 314–317
piggybacking 272
pinhole camera 146
pixels 154
plastic insulated conductor (PIC) 293
plug 330
point-to-point networks 130
polling 193–194
polyethylene 125
post 330
power (optics) 152

Power Investigator® 232
power line carriers (PLCs) 73
power monitors 232
power sum ELFEXT (PSELFEXT) 130
power sum NEXT (PSNEXT) 129
PowerCAD Professional (software) 221
preauthorization 330
pressure sensors 9
preventative maintenance 330
principal point 147
printers 268–269
probability 320
programmable logic devices (PLDs) 217
Progressive Electronics 234
proximity access control cards 261
pulse width 99
push button locks 258
push key 330

Q

quadrature amplitude modulation (QAM) 138
quadrature phase shift keying (QPSK) 138
QUARTUS (software) 217
QuickCAD (software) 221

R

radio frequency (RF) communications 62–68
    eavesdropping 286–291
    flooding 288–289
    repeaters 66–67
    spread spectrum 289–290
    ultra high frequency (UHF) 68
    very high frequency (VHF) 66
    See also communications systems
radio frequency (RF) probes 108–109
    body transmitters 112
    cable and closed circuit TV 116–117
    computers and related equipment 116
    frequencies 109–110
    outside flooding 116
    phone line audio test 114

radio frequency probes (continued)
    power 110
    room monitoring 112
    sweep 110–111
    telephone sweep 112
    Tempest approved equipment 115
    tracking devices 112–113
    very low frequency (VLF) 113–114
    video transmitters 111
    video/audio valuation 114–115
    waterfall display 291
RC time constant 42–43
reactance 40
records management 254
regulations 22–23
rekey 331
remote control units 267
repeaters 66–67
residential phone lines 296–297
resistance 32
resistors 32
resolution 152
resonant circuits 48–49
resonant frequency 48–49
response 317
restricted keyway 331
RG58 cable 127
RG8 cable 127
rise time 70
risk assessments 307
    frequency of 311–312
    prioritizing 310–311
risk management 307
    business continuity 307–309
    disaster recovery 307–309
    team 309–310
RJ-31X phone jack 69

S

safeguards automated facility
        evaluation (SAFE) 221
safeguards network analysis procedure
        (SNAP) 222
screwdriver kit 242

secondary verifications 262–264
secure areas 313
security container 331
security data management system
        (SDMS) 210–211
security layers 10
security levels 3–10
    high 8
    low 5–6
    maximum 8–10
    medium 7–8
    minimum 4–5
    See also physical security
security management system (SMS)
        214–215
security manager 307
security screwdriver kit 242
security surveys 316
    areas of importance 315–316
    initial stages of 315–317
    overview 314–315
    services 3
    types of 320
    See also physical security
security systems 130–131
service life 331
shackle 331
shank 331
shielded twisted pair (STP) 127
shoulder 331
shutter speed 149–150
signature verification 263–264
single mode fiber 131
sky wave 136
smart cards 69, 262
smoke detectors 192
snuggling 96, 288–289
software 209–211
    computer-aided drawing (CAD)
            219–221
    design 217
    system design 219–222
    system modeling 221–222
special survey 320

spectrum analyzers 94–97
    dynamic range 96
    inputs 97
    limitations 96
speech 60
speech verification 264
speed (optics) 152
splices 230
spread spectrum 73–74, 289–290
stem 331
still cameras 146
stop (optics) 152
stray light 152
supplemental survey 320
surreptitious entry 331
surveillance system 166–168
sweep 110–111
sweep rate 96
switches 46–47, 192
system analysis of vulnerability to
    intrusion (SAVI) 222
system design software 219–222
system modeling software 221–222

T

tailgating 272, 332
tapes 241
taps 301
technical surveillance countermeasures
    (TSCM) 278
    bugs 301
    eavesdropping methods 279–283
    espionage 278–279
    inside walls 285–286
    local area network (LAN) 300–301
    physical search 283–285
    radio frequency (RF) phase 286–291
    telephone lines 291–300
    wide area network (WAN) 300–301
Teflon 125
Telecommunications Distribution Methods
    Manual 124
telephone lines 291–300

    analyzing 297–299
    cables 293–294
    color coding 294–296
    commercial circuits 299–300
    local loop 291–292
    parameters 293
    residential circuits 296–297
telephone sweep 112
telephoto lenses 148
telescoping poles 240–241
Tempest guidelines 10, 223
termination of personnel 254
terrorism threats, planning for 11
test equipment 85–117
    cable analyzers 102
    multimeters 85–90
    non linear junction detector (NLJD)
        102–108
    oscilloscopes 90–94
    radio frequency (RF) probes 108–117
    spectrum analyzers 94–97
    time domain reflectometers (TDRs)
        97–101
Texas Instruments 155
Thevenin's theorem 35–36
throughput rate 332
time constant 42–43
time domain reflectometers (TDRs)
        97–101
    digital 99
    graphical 98, 101
    pulse width 99
    uses of 19
    velocity of propagation (VOP) 100
time zoning 271
Tivicon tube 155–156
tone testers 234
tracking devices 112–113
transmission wire 126
    coaxial cable 127
    twisted pair cabling 126–127
triggering 92
trunked repeaters 67
truth tables 50
TurboCAD (software) 221

twisted pair cabling 126–127
two-person rule 332

U

UL, Inc. 332
ultra high frequency (UHF)
       communications 68, 136
uncertainty principle 16
underground cable locators 233
ushielded twisted pair (UTP) 127

V

vacuum tube volt-ohm-meter (VTVOM)
     86
Vdraft (software) 221
VectorWorks (software) 221
velocity of propagation (VOP) 70, 100
VersaCAD (software) 221
very high frequency (VHF)
       communications 66, 136
very high-level access control 249
very low frequency (VLF) probes
     113–114
video recorders 159–162
video transmitters 111
vidicon tube 154
viewfinder cameras 150
vinyl 125
Vista-10P (control unit) 176–180
Vista-250P (control unit) 180–190
VistaScape 210
voice communications 60

voltage 34
voltmeters 87
vulnerability 319–320

W

warm sites 308
wave division multiplexing (WDM) 133
weak link theory 18–20
wide area network (WAN) 69, 300–301
wide-angle lenses 148
Wiegand access control cards 261
Wi-Fi 72–73, 137
wire 124–125
    insulation 125
    types of 126
wireless communications 135–136
    802.11 standards and frequencies
       137–139
    advances in 243
    Bluetooth 139
    frequency bands 136–137
wireless local area networks (WLANs)
    72–73
wireless personal area networks
    (WPANs) 73
wireline communications 60–62
workplace security 306
    crime prevention assessment 306–307
    customer service office 314
    front-line office 313–314
    secure areas 313
    surveys 314–317
    See also physical security